# MARY GILLIATT'S
# FABULOUS FOOD AND FRIENDS

*In memory of Roger, a much-loved host;
for our elder daughter, Sophia, who
presciently saved the dinner books on which
this book is based and for Francis Finlay who
generously encouraged me in the project
from the first.*

# MARY GILLIATT'S FABULOUS FOOD AND FRIENDS

## Entertaining Princess Margaret, Spike Milligan and Other Friends

by

MARY GILLIATT

First published in Great Britain in 2008 by
Remember When
an imprint of
Pen & Sword Books Ltd
47 Church Street
Barnsley
South Yorkshire
S70 2AS

Copyright © Mary Gilliatt, 2008

ISBN 978-1-84468-044-3

Printed and bound in England
by Biddles Ltd

Typeset in 10/12 Palatino by
Concept, Huddersfield, West Yorkshire

Pen & Sword Books Ltd incorporates the Imprints of Pen & Sword Aviation, Pen & Sword Maritime, Pen & Sword Military, Wharncliffe Local History, Pen & Sword Select, Pen & Sword Military Classics, Leo Cooper, Remember When, Seaforth Publishing and Frontline Publishing.

For a complete list of Pen & Sword titles please contact
**PEN & SWORD BOOKS LIMITED**
47 Church Street, Barnsley, South Yorkshire, S70 2AS, England
E-mail: enquiries@pen-and-sword.co.uk
Website: www.pen-and-sword.co.uk

# Contents

# ACKNOWLEDGEMENTS

I am most grateful to the team at Remember When for all the really hard work they have put into this book. So I give my special thanks to my editor, Fiona Shoop, always generously available with her limited time and warmly, gracefully and helpfully at the answering end of the e-mail or telephone; Tamsin Johnson and Jessica Mitchell for all their hard work co-ordinating and copy editing, Ian Helliwell for his designing and typesetting ability, Sylvia Menzies-Earl for making such good plates out of old pictures and the talented Marie Parkinson for her very cleverly designed jacket around my very much younger self. I cannot say, alas, that I have not changed ...

I am also very grateful to my agents, Fiona Lindsey and Mary Bekhait of Limelight Management, not to forget Alison Lindsey (for always keeping the accounts so well) and to my goddaughter, Jane Milligan and to Roxanna Tynan for all their help and efficiency in routing out family photographs. And although I have acknowledged my daughter, Sophia Gilliatt elsewhere in the book for her family archival efficiency there is no doubt that without her thoughtfulness and care this text could not have been written. Lastly, I should acknowledge the major role played by Smythsons, that most elegant of English stationers for so many decades, for producing such useful and well-made books in which to record one's entertaining.

# DRAMATIS PERSONAE

**Abu Simbel:** The great Egyptian temple of Rameses the Second and of Nefertari in Egypt discovered in 1813. In 1968 it was dismantled and relocated to a desert plateau 200 feet above and 600 feet west of its original location, south of Aswan on the west bank of the Nile, to make sure it was conserved during the building of the Aswan Dam.

**Adler, Larry:** Well-known 'mouth organist' as he liked to be called, who was exiled in the UK to escape testifying in the witch hunts – instigated by Senator Joe McCarthy in the 1950s – to hunt down so-called Communist sympathisers. Oscar-winning Larry Adler never returned to the US.

**Albee, Edward:** Twentieth Century American playwright, author of *Who's Afraid of Virginia Woolf* amongst many other fine plays.

**Algonquin Hotel:** New York City Hotel particularly associated with *The New Yorker* magazine and its 'round table' frequented by many of the American literati of the early Twentieth Century, including Dorothy Parker.

**Alexander, Czar Alexander II of Russia:** Late Nineteenth Century Russian Czar, assassinated in 1885.

**All Souls' College:** Distinguished postgraduate college at Oxford University.

**Allen & Unwin:** Old-established UK publishers, now operating from Australia.

**Amis, Kingsley:** Well-known mid-Twentieth Century UK novelist and writer of *Lucky Jim* amongst many other titles. Father of writer Martin Amis.

**Ampleforth College:** Roman Catholic public school in Yorkshire, UK.

**Anderson, Lindsay:** Another writer and playwright of the time and author of *The Loneliness of the Long Distance Runner*, amongst others.

**Andrade, James (Jimmy):** Antiquarian with a shop in the King's Road, Chelsea, London in the 1950s and 1960s.

**Annan, Noel:** Well-known English academic, one time Master of King's College, Cambridge.

**Anstee, Paul:** London Interior designer of the mid-Twentieth Century and for many years the partner of actor, Sir John Gielgud.

**Anstruther, the late Sir Ian, Bart:** Author, English eccentric, our landlord in Thurloe Square and, with his wife Susan and family, former next door neighbours and friends of the Gilliatts. Died 2007.

**Anstruther, Lady Susan:** Also working as the London architect, Susan Walker, and widow of the later Sir Ian Anstruther, Bart.

**Anstruther, Sir Toby, Bart:** Property Developer, landowner, the younger son of Ian and Susan Anstruther and one of my godsons.

**Archigram:** Much admired avant-garde Architectural Group of the mid-Twentieth Century.

**Armstrong-Jones, Tony, The Earl of Snowdon, GCVO:** Brilliant photographer and designer, and former Provost of the Royal College of Art. Married to the late HRH, Princess Margaret, Countess of Snowdon.

**Arnaud, Etienne:** French student and my neighbour in France.

**Arnaud, Gilles:** French aid to disadvantaged youth, and neighbour.

**Artists' Market:** London Gallery set up in the 1960s by Vera Russell to showcase work of new young painters and sculptors.

**Astor, Colonel John Jacob:** Well-known New Yorker and hotel developer of the early-Twentieth Century who went down with the Titanic.

**Bacon, Francis, 1561–1626:** Sixteenth Century English philosopher and religious writer.

# DRAMATIS PERSONAE

**Bacon, Francis, 1909–1992:** Distinguished Twentieth Century painter. Died April 9th, 1992.

**Baker:** Gardener of Thurloe Square garden during the 1960s.

**Baker, Stanley:** UK actor and film star, mid-Twentieth Century. Died June 28th, 1976.

**Bannister, Sir Roger:** Neurologist, runner, holder of the record for the first four-minute mile, Master of Pembroke College, Oxford.

**Bannister, Lady, Moira:** Wife of Sir Roger Bannister.

**Baring, Mark:** Chairman of Thurloe Square Garden Committee in the 1960s and our next-door neighbour, along with his wife, Vita, of the Gilliatts.

**Baring, Peter:** Ex-chairman of the former Barings Bank before its demise.

**Baring, Tessa:** Sociologist and wife of Peter Baring.

**Barnes, Susan:** Writer, journalist and widow of Anthony Crosland, Labour Foreign Secretary in the Callaghan government, 1976–1977.

**Barrie, J.M.:** Nineteenth Century writer and author of *Peter Pan*.

**Barrington-Ward, Lady:** Widow of Sir Launcelot Barrington-Ward, a surgeon.

**Barrington-Ward, Sir Robert:** Editor of *The Times* in the UK.

**Barron, Sir David:** Chairman of Shell Oil in the late 1960s and later of The Midland Bank.

**Barron, Lady Jane:** Charity worker and wife of Sir David Barron.

**Baynham, David:** Son of Claudie Worsthorne by a previous marriage.

**Beattie, Warren:** US film star.

**Belloc, Hilaire:** Late Nineteenth Century, early-Twentieth Century writer of mainly comic verse.

**Benchley, Robert:** Twentieth Century US humourist and writer for *The New Yorker*.

**Bennet, Jill:** Actress and third wife of John Osborne, playwright.

**Bennett, Alan:** UK writer, playwright, humourist, satirist and one of the original *Beyond the Fringe* members.

**Benson, Lonsdale:** Former UK Merchant Bank which segued into Kleinwort, Benson.

**Bentley, Barbara:** Writer and wife of Nicholas Bentley, daughter of Sir Patrick Hastings, a well-known British litigator.

**Bentley, Edmund Clerihew:** Writer, poet and inventor of a particular form of comic verse, named 'Clerihew' after him.

**Bentley, Nicholas:** Writer and cartoonist, son of Edmund Clerihew Bentley and godson of G.K. Chesterton, the writer.

**Bergman, Ingrid:** Actress and Film Star of the mid-Twentieth Century.

**Betjeman, John:** Twentieth Century English poet, writer and satirist.

**Bevan, Aneurin ('Nye'):** Post World War Two Labour politician in the Atlee and Wilson governments and founder and master-mind of the UK National Health Service.

**Beyfuss, Drusilla:** Writer, journalist, editor, lecturer and widow of the film and theatre critic Milton Shulman.

**Bilsby, Leslie:** Housing developer in the mid-Twentieth Century, principally known for his comparatively avant-garde Span developments.

**Blair, Tony:** Labour Prime Minister of the UK 1997 to 2007.

**Blanch, Lesley:** Twentieth Century, UK traveller and writer (*The Wilder Shores of Love* etc.) married to French writer Gary Romain.

**Bodley, Sir Thomas:** Eighteenth Century academic. Founder of the Bodleian Library, Oxford University.

# Dramatis Personae

**Bodley Head:** Old-established UK publishers, now owned by Random House.

**Bond, James:** Character invented by UK writer Ian Fleming, star of many eponymous movies and reputed to be based on Anthony Nutting (p. 31) – amongst others.

**Bosch, Hieronymus, c.1460–1516:** Dutch painter of the Fifteenth and Sixteenth Century who specialised in the bizarre, sin and mortal failings.

**Box, E.** Name used by Eden Fleming, the Twentieth Century UK naïve painter.

**Boxer, Lady Arabella:** Journalist and cookery writer during the second half of the Twentieth Century; married to the late Mark Boxer, journalist, cartoonist and magazine publisher.

**Braine, John:** Twentieth Century UK writer and one of the so-called 'Angry Young Men' of the 1960s.

**Brando, Marlon:** Twentieth Century US actor and film star. Died 2004.

**Bratby, John:** Twentieth Century, UK painter. Died 1992.

**Brogan, Colm:** Twentieth Century, UK Roman Catholic writer and columnist.

**Brogan, Mary:** UK journalist, daughter of Colm Brogan and colleague on *The Sunday Telegraph* in the early 1960s.

**Brown, Lancelot, 'Capability', c.1716–1763:** Famous English Eighteenth Century landscape gardener and architect.

**Brown, Gordon:** Long-serving Chancellor of the Exchequer in the Labour Government 1997 to 2007 and current Prime Minister of the UK, 2007.

**Byron, Lord, c.1788–1824:** Nineteenth Century English poet.

**Buckner, Robert:** US scriptwriter living in Paris in the 1950s.

**Buckner, Sharon:** Daughter of Robert Buckner and my fellow student at the Sorbonne, the University of Paris.

**Bull, Edith:** Local Politician in London in the 1960s and 1970s, charity worker and wife of James Bull.

**Bull, James:** Neurologist and Dean of the Department of Clinical Neurology, Queen Square, London in the 1960s.

**Burnand, Sir Francis, c.1836–1917:** Editor of *Punch* magazine, 1880–1906.

**Burnand, Winnie:** British woman cartoonist and daughter of Sir Francis Burnand. Mother of Jeanne Wilkins.

**Butler, Rab:** Leading Conservative politician, one of the few to have served as Chancellor of the Exchequer, Home Secretary and Foreign Secretary and rival to Harold Macmillan as party leader in the mid-Twentieth Century.

**Butterfield, Jill:** UK journalist and Editor of the *Daily Express* woman's pages in the 1960s. Died in the 1980s.

**Burt: Ivor and Jan:** Very good and supportive friends. Jan died in 1999.

**Burt, James:** Lloyds of London broker and another of my godsons.

**Caccia, Angela (née Reed):** Writer, journalist, my colleague on *The Sunday Telegraph* in the early 1960s; widow of David Caccia, now married to South African academic, Philip (Taffy) Lloyd.

**Caccia, The Hon. David:** Ex-Foreign Office, writer, son of Lord Caccia and husband of Angela Caccia.

**Caccia, Lord, formerly Sir Harold:** Ex-British Ambassador in Washington. He was appointed Head of the UK Foreign Office in 1961 and, after his retirement, became Provost of Eton College.

**Callaghan, James:** Labour Politician and UK Prime Minister.

**Campbell, Sir Jock:** Ex-Chairman of Booker Brothers and co-founder of the Man Booker literary prize.

**Canby, Vincent:** Former US writer and film critic for *The New York Times*. Died, 2000.

**Caron, Leslie:** Twentieth Century French film star.

# Dramatis Personae

**Carrier, Robert:** Twentieth Century US restaurateur and food writer, resident in the UK till the 1980s.

**Casson, Sir Hugh:** Twentieth Century architect, writer, artist, architectural apologist. Director of Architecture at the 1951 Festival of Britain and President of the Royal Academy (1976–1984) and Provost of the Royal College of Art. Died 1999.

**Casson, Lady Margaret, 'Rita':** Architect and wife of Sir Hugh Casson.

**Carr, Winifred:** Editor of *The Daily Telegraph* Women's Pages in the 1960s and 1970s.

**Carter, Ernestine:** Editor of *The Sunday Times* Women's Pages in the 1960s and 1970s.

**Carter, Jake:** Antiquarian book expert at Sotheby's in the 1960s and 1970s.

**Cavendish, Hugh, Baron Cavendish of Furness:** Conservative politician and son in law of Mary Cookson.

**Cavendish, Lady, Grania, née Caulfield:** Wife of Hugh Cavendish and daughter of Mary Cookson.

**Caulfield, Grania:** See above.

**Chaplin, Charlie:** One of the best-loved early Twentieth Century comedians and film stars.

**Chaplin, Oonagh:** US actress, daughter of Eugene O'Neill, great American playwright and wife of Charlie Chaplin.

**Charles, Prince of Wales:** The eldest son of HM Queen Elizabeth II and HRH The Duke of Edinburgh, and heir to the Throne.

**Cheshire, Leonard, VC:** World War Two hero and founder of the Cheshire Homes for displaced people. Married to Sue Ryder, founder of the Sue Ryder Homes.

**Chesterton, G.K.:** Early Twentieth Century writer and poet.

**Chichester, Sir Francis:** First man to sail around the world single-handed. Died 1972.

**Chichester, Lady Sheila:** Wife of Francis Chichester.

**Child, Julia:** Well-known Twentieth Century US food writer and TV personality.

**Christie, Julie:** Academy Award-winning British film star.

**Churchill, Sir Winston, KG.:** UK Boer War correspondent, writer, historian, painter, iconic Conservative Prime Minister (1939–1945 and 1951–1956) and World War Two leader. Died 1965.

**Churchill, Lady, Clementine:** Wife of Sir Winston Churchill. Died 1977.

**Clendinning, Max:** Twentieth Century avant-garde designer and architect.

**Cocteau, Jean:** Much admired early-Twentieth Century French designer, artist and director.

**Cole, Lester:** Twentieth Century film writer, lecturer and member of 'The Hollywood Ten' exiled to the UK in the 1950s and 1960s because of the so-called 'Un-American activities' witch hunts instigated by Senator Joe McCarthy. See also Larry Adler and Donald Ogden Stewart.

**Coleman, Ronald:** Twentieth Century Hollywood film star.

**Compton Verney:** Stately English home designed by Robert Adam and a former proposed site for another English music and opera Centre.

**Connaught Hotel:** Well-known old-established London hotel.

**Conran, Lady, Caroline:** UK journalist, food writer, third wife of Sir Terence Conran and, with Terence, a good friend of ours.

**Conran, Jasper:** UK fashion and product designer, son of Sir Terence and Shirley Conran.

**Conran Octopus:** UK publishers founded by Sir Terence Conran and Lord Hamlyn with the distinguished publisher, Alison Cathie, as its first managing director.

# DRAMATIS PERSONAE

**Conran, Sebastian:** Designer and son of Sir Terence and Shirley Conran.

**Conran, Shirley:** Designer, journalist, novelist and second wife of Sir Terence Conran.

**Conran, Sir Terence:** Hugely successful UK entrepreneur, design and restaurant guru.

**Constable, John:** Late English romantic painter from Suffolk who coined the phrase: 'Painting is but another word for feeling'. Died 1837.

**Constantine, Annie:** Interior designer and Mary Gilliatt's younger daughter.

**Constantine, David:** Business coach and Mary Gilliatt's son-in-law.

**Constantine, Georgia:** Mary Gilliatt's second oldest granddaughter.

**Constantine, Iona:** Mary Gilliatt's youngest English grandaughter.

**Constantine, Olivia:** Mary Gilliatt's eldest granddaughter.

**Connolly, Cyril:** Twentieth Century literati, critic and Editor of the Literary magazine, *Horizon* from 1939-1950. From 1952–1974 he was joint chief book reviewer of *The Sunday Times* with Raymond Mortimer.

**Cook, Sir Peter:** Distinguished British architect and founder of the Archigram, avant garde architectural group of the 1960s.

**Cookson, Gerald:** Scientist, inventor, benefactor and very good friend of the Gilliatts.

**Cookson, Mary:** Painter, hostess, widow of Gerry Cookson, mother of Grania Cavendish and a dear friend of the Gilliatts.

**Cooper, Douglas:** Twentieth Century Australian art critic and collector, resident in France, who adopted Billy McCarty the American designer, as his heir.

**Cooper, Lady Diana, Viscountess Norwich:** Famous early-Twentieth Century beauty and hostess, widow of the writer and diplomat, Duff Cooper, Viscount Norwich and mother of the writer and historian John Julius Norwich.

**Cooper, Colonel Robert:** A Suffolk friend of M.G.'s parents.

**Corke, Martin:** Ex-Chairman of Greene King Brewery, philanthropist and good friend of the Gilliatts.

**Corke, Jean:** Married to Martin Corke and good friend.

**Courtoux, Pierre:** French second husband of Sharon Grangier de la Marinière, née Buckner, a very good friend from M.G.'s Sorbonne student days.

**Coward, Noel:** Twentieth Century UK playwright, song writer and wit.

**Cowles, Fleur:** Well-known naïve painter, writer, hostess and Editor during the 1950s of the remarkable, famous, but short-lived, *Flair* magazine. Married first, Mike Cowles, Publisher of *Life* and *Look* magazines, and second, Tom Montagu Meyer, an ex-army friend of Roger Gilliatt.

**Crosland, Sir Anthony:** Intellectual Labour politician, policy maker, founder of 'New Labour' and Foreign Secretary in the Callaghan Government (1976–1977). Died while in office in 1977.

**Crosland, Lady, Susan, nee Barnes:** Writer and novelist under her maiden name of Susan Barnes and widow of Anthony Crosland.

**Dada Movement:** Early-Twentieth Century avant garde art movement. Its members were known as 'Dadaists'.

**Dali, Salvadore:** Famous Spanish Dadaist and Surrealist painter and eccentric.

**Darwin, Sir Robin:** Painter, writer and a former Rector of the Royal College of Art. Died 1974.

**Darwin, Lady, Ginette:** AKA Ginette Spanier, fashionista and former Directrice of Christian Dior.

**David, Elizabeth:** Distinguished food writer and historian who pretty well single-handedly re-awakened the art of cooking for the British after the World War Two privations.

**Davidson, Andrew, Viscount:** Politician, landowner and Suffolk friend.

# DRAMATIS PERSONAE

**Davidson, Margaret, Viscountess:** Good Suffolk friend, now married to Lord (Mark) Colville, Conservative politician.

**Dawson, Frank:** American lawyer, legal historian, academic and good friend. Died 2007.

**Dawson, Hélène:** AKA the painter and sculptor, Hélène Fesenmaier, good friend.

**Dawson, Helen:** Writer, critic and fifth wife of the writer and dramatist, John Osborne.

**Dawson Neville, Bill:** Lawyer, antiquarian book and art collector and eccentric. A Suffolk friend of both my parents and ourselves and godfather to my elder daughter, Sophia.

**Dawson, Jane Neville:** Suffolk eccentric, friend of my parents and ourselves and wife of Bill Neville Dawson.

**Dean, Patrick:** Farmer, a director of Hutchinson's, the publishers and a good ex-army friend of Roger Gilliatt.

**Dean, Susan:** First wife of Patrick Dean and a good friend.

**De Beauvoir, Simone:** Acclaimed Twentieth Century French writer: lover, for a time, of equally acclaimed writer and philosopher, Jean-Paul Sartre.

**Delany, Mary:** Pen name of Muriel Forbes, a former Women's Page Editor of *The Times,* when she held the same post on *The Sunday Times.*

**Denney, Anthony:** Esoteric interior designer, taste-maker and Condé Nast photographer for *House & Garden* in the 1950s.

**Denney, Celia:** Wife of Anthony Denney.

**Denny Brown, 'Denny':** Influential Twentieth Century Professor of Clinical Neurology at Harvard Medical School and a mentor to Roger Gilliatt.

**Denny Brown, Sylvia:** Wife of 'Denny' Denny Brown.

**Dietrich, Marlene:** Famous Twentieth Century German/US film star and friend of Ken and Kathleen Tynan and Penelope Gilliatt.

**Digby, Sir Kenelm:** Distinguished Seventeenth Century scientist, religious thinker and writer.

**Dobbs, Dickie and Phil:** Good friends and neighbours of Don and Ella Ogden-Stewart.

**Drabble, Margaret:** UK novelist and biographer of Angus Wilson.

**Dumond, Miraille:** A French neighbour, and daughter of courageous parents who hid French Resistance fighters in their house throughout World War Two.

**Eden, Anthony, Viscount Eden, 1st Earl of Avon:** Leading Conservative politician and diplomat: British Foreign Secretary in three periods from 1935–1955 and throughout World War Two and Prime Minister after Churchill retired from 1955–57. The Eden government caused great controversy over their invasion of Egypt. Died, 1977.

**Eerie Canal:** US canal in Ohio, engineered and built in the Nineteenth Century.

**Ekland, Britt:** Swedish film star and a second wife of Peter Sellers.

**Eliot, T.S.:** Acclaimed Twentieth Century US poet living in the UK in the first part of the Twentieth Century.

**Elliott, Denholm:** UK actor and film star.

**Ernst, Max:** Surrealist German painter, painting in Paris in the 1920s and 1930s.

**Errington: Reginald and Cecilia:** Old Suffolk friends.

**Fainlight, Ruth:** US writer and poet married to the UK writer, Alan Sillitoe.

**Feddon, Mary:** An English painter.

**Fenton, Colin:** On the staff of Harveys of Bristol in the 1950s and 1960s and a poet.

# Dramatis Personae

**Fields, W.G.** An early-Twentieth Century comedian and film star.

**Fesenmaier, Hélène:** American painter and sculptor resident in the UK since the late 1960s and a good friend. Formerly married to Frank Dawson.

**Fiorati, Helen:** Owner of a shop in Manhattan for Russian antiquities.

**Fischer, Gordon:** An American investment banker who bought our house in Thurloe Square.

**Fitzgerald, F. Scott:** An American writer of the 1920s who wrote *The Great Gatsby* and *Tender is the Night* amongst other works. He had a well-known tumultuous relationship with his wife, Zelda.

**Fitzwilliam, Juliet, Countess of:** A former wife of the 6th Marquess of Bristol, later married to Somerset de Chair.

**Flemati, Yannick and Audrey:** Neighbours in France.

**Fleming, Eden:** Twentieth Century naïve painter who used the name of E. Box. She was married to Professor Marston Fleming, both good friends.

**Fleming, Ian:** Twentieth Century writer who created the James Bond character, partly based on our friend Anthony Nutting.

**Fleming, Professor Marston:** A Canadian academic and good friend who had the Chair of Mineral Engineering at Imperial College, London in the 1960s and was also the Dean and later Pro-Rector of the College.

**Fletcher, Sandy and Nicky:** Old friends of Roger Gilliatt.

**Flory, Frederique:** Neighbour and friend in France.

**Flory, Charlotte:** Daughter of Frederique.

**Fonda, Jane:** US film star.

**Fonteyn, Dame Margot:** Acclaimed Twentieth Century British prima ballerina. Died 1991.

**Forster, Peter:** Twentieth Century British novelist and film critic.

**Frink, Elizabeth:** Twentieth Century British sculptor.

**Gainsborough, Thomas, c.1727–1788:** British, early Eighteenth Century painter. One of the best British portraitists and landscape painters.

**Gaitskill, Hugh:** Leader of the British Labour party in the 1950s.

**Garrett Anderson, Dr Elizabeth:** The first woman doctor to be allowed to practice in the UK.

**Garland, Ailsa:** Ex-Editor of British *Vogue* living in Suffolk in the 1960s.

**Garrett, Tony:** Partner of Angus Wilson, the novelist.

**Gary, Romain:** A French novelist and writer, married to the British writer, Lesley Blanch.

**Gielguid, Sir John:** Well-known British actor.

**Gilliatt, Alice:** Roger Gilliatt's aunt, a suffragette, first woman Mayor of Fulham and first Labour Mayor of Fulham.

**Gilliatt, Lady Anne:** My mother-in-law, an early anaesthetist.

**Gilliatt, Annie:** My younger daughter, now Constantine, an interior designer.

**Gilliatt, Eliza:** A former Private Secretary to Sir Winston Churchill, and then to subsequent Lord Mayors of London. My sister-in-law.

**Gilliatt, Freddie:** My elder grandson.

**Gilliatt, Joe:** My younger grandson.

**Gilliatt, Penelope:** Writer, librettist, novelist, film writer (*Sunday, Bloody Sunday*) film critic for both the UK *Observer* and the US *New Yorker* (alternating with Pauline Kael) and first wife of Roger Gilliatt.

**Gilliatt, Professor Roger M.C.:** First Clinical Professor of Neurology at The National Hospital for Nervous Diseases, Queen Square, London and my late husband. Died 1991. He was the Best Man at the wedding of Tony Armstrong-Jones and Princess Margaret.

# DRAMATIS PERSONAE

**Gilliatt, Rosie:** My Australian grandaughter.

**Gilliatt, Sophia:** My elder daughter, a wine consultant and marketer.

**Gilliatt, Sophie:** My Australian daughter-in-law married to my son, Tom Gilliatt and youngest daughter of my great friends, Jim and Judy Lance.

**Gilliatt, Tom:** My son, a publisher and Director of Non-Fiction at Pan Macmillan, Australia.

**Gingold, Hermione:** Twentieth Century British actress.

**Glazer, Professor Gil:** Professor of Clinical Neurology at Yale Medical School and a friend of Roger Gilliatt.

**Gloucester, Prince Richard of:** Good friend of Paul William White, the architect, who brought him to dinner on occasion.

**Glyn, Prue:** A Former Fashion Editor of *The Times*, formerly married to Viscount Windlesham, a Conservative politician.

**Goguel, Anna de:** A painter and friend from the 1960s.

**Gordon, Lydia:** An American fashion historian with a fabulous collection of clothes from the Nineteenth Century to the present.

**Green, Anthony:** Ex-farmer, consultant and magistrate and my brother.

**Green, Arthur:** My father, ex-Chairman of Braby of Britain, one of Britain's oldest engineering companies.

**Green, Carmel:** My sister, married to John Jones, a barrister, and herself an Immigration Judge.

**Green, Dr Cecil:** Former head of Texas Instruments and President of Geophysical Services Inc.; a philanthropist and founder of Green College, Oxford, now called Green Templeton College.

**Green, Constance:** My mother.

**Greene, Graham:** An acclaimed Twentieth Century British novelist.

**Greene, King:** A Suffolk Brewery.

**Griggs, Barbara:** A British journalist and writer specialising in herbal remedies and health care, formerly on *The Daily Express* and, for many years, Editor of the Women's Pages on *The Evening Standard*.

**Grigson, Jane:** A Twentieth Century British cookery writer. Died 1990.

**Graves, Diana:** An ex-girl friend of Roger Gilliatt and niece of the poet, Robert Graves.

**Gooddy, Dr William:** A Neurologist friend and colleague of Roger Gilliatt.

**Grangier de la Marinière, Jacques:** A Frenchman originally married to my American Sorbonne friend, Sharon Buckner.

**Guggenheim, Peggy:** A famous art collector, and collector of artists, whose collection can be seen at her old Palazzo in Venice. Died 1979.

**Guinzberg, Tom:** Then Editorial Director of the American Viking Press, now *Viking Penguin*.

**Guinzberg, Rusty:** Wife of Tom Guinzberg.

**Gunary, George:** A former boyfriend of Mary Gilliatt.

**Gunning, Annie:** A famously beautiful model in the 1950s, subsequently married to Sir Anthony Nutting, 'Bart'. Related to the beautiful Eighteenth Century Gunning sisters.

**Habitat:** Chain of furnishing stores originally opened by Sir Terence Conran in 1964.

**Hall, Sir Peter:** Twentieth Century British Producer and former Director of The Royal Shakespeare Company.

**Haley, Sir William:** Editor of *The Times* during the 1960s.

**Halton, Kathleen:** Half-Canadian journalist and writer, daughter of CBC correspondent, Mathew Halton. She married the theatre critic, Ken Tynan.

**Hamlyn, Lord (Paul):** Founder of Octopus publishing company and co-founder with Sir Terence Conran of publishers, *Conran Octopus*.

# DRAMATIS PERSONAE

**Hammarskjöld, Dag:** Second Secretary General of the UN (1953–1961) killed under mysterious circumstances in a plane crash while still in office. He was the only person to win the Nobel Prize for Peace posthumously. He was a great friend of Roger Gilliatt's stepfather-in-law, George Ivan-Smith.

**Hanbury-Tennyson, Marika:** A Twentieth Century British cookery writer who died very young and was formerly married to explorer Robin Hanbury-Tennyson.

**Hardy-Roberts, Brigadier Geoffrey:** Former Secretary Administrator of the Middlesex Hospital, London and later Master of the Queen's Household.

**Hare, Robert:** A Twentieth Century British playwright.

**Harewood, Marion, Lady:** Pianist and first wife of Lord Harewood, a cousin of the Queen.

**Harrow School:** Old-established British public school.

**Harveys of Bristol:** An old-established sherry and wine importing British company, headed, for some important years, by George McWatters whose mother was a Harvey.

**Hawkins, Jack:** A Twentieth Century British actor and film star.

**Hay, Dr David:** Our family doctor in the 1960s.

**Hay, Susan:** David Hay's wife.

**Heath, Edward:** Former Conservative Prime Minister (1970–1974; leader of Conservative Party 1965–1975).

**Heidseick, Charles:** Former Head of Heidseick Champagne.

**Heinz, Dru:** A friend of Princess Margaret and well-known American hostess.

**Henson, Bill:** A diplomat and head of the UN Information Services.

**Henson, Maria:** A Russian photographer, married to Bill Henson.

**Herbert, Caroline:** British journalist, cookery writer and third wife of Sir Terence Conran.

**Heron, Patrick:** A well-known Twentieth Century British painter.

**Hervey:** Family name of the Marquesses of Bristol.

**Hervey, Lady Isabella:** Daughter of the 6th Marquess of Bristol.

**Hervey, Victor:** The 6th Marquess of Bristol.

**Hervey, Lady Victoria:** Another daughter of the 6th Marquess of Bristol.

**Heveningham Hall:** Family house of the Vanneck family in Suffolk, famously built, furnished and decorated by the Regency British architect, James Wyatt.

**Hicks, David:** An influential Twentieth Century British interior designer and landscape gardener married to the former Lady Pamela Mountbatten.

**Hicks, Lady Pamela:** The younger daughter of Lord Mountbatten of Burma, married to David Hicks.

**Hitchcock, Manfred:** A Suffolk Miller and good friend of my parents.

**Hitchcock, Margaret:** A feminist mentor and good friend of my mother.

**Hitchcock, Witgar:** The Hitchcocks' son.

**Hjorth, Dr Bob:** US Neurologist, friend and colleague of Roger Gilliatt.

**Hollywood Ten:** A group of American scriptwriters, producers and directors forced to leave Hollywood, California in the 1950s when Senator Joe McCarthy instigated his ill-begotten communist witch hunts.

**Hope, Alice:** A journalist on the Women's pages of *The Daily Telegraph* in the 1960s.

**Hope, Francis:** A British journalist and writer killed in the Turkish Airlines crash between Paris and London in 1974. Son of Michael Hope.

**Hope, Michael:** Married Helen Cohen after Andrew died, and father of Francis Robin Hope.

# Dramatis Personae

**Hopkins, Professor Tony:** Another neurological colleague of Roger Gilliatt.

**Hornsey, Irene:** One of my maternal aunts.

**Horlock, Joyce:** A friend of my mother's and fellow charity worker.

**Horowitz, Vladimir:** Famous Twentieth Century Russian pianist. Died 1989.

**Horrocks, Lt. General, Sir Brian:** Well-respected British World War Two General. Died 1985.

**Horrocks, Lady:** Sir Brian's wife.

**Howell, Billie:** One of the beautiful Hume sisters and mother of John Howell.

**Howell, D'Arcy, née McGeorge:** Old friend and colleague on UK *House & Garden* and later Chairman of East Sussex County Council.

**Howell, John:** British engineer, inventor and collector of vintage cars, antique clocks and flintlocks (guns); married to D'Arcy McGeorge and an old friend.

**Howell, Miles:** Well-known Twentieth Century British cricketer and father of good friend, John Howell.

**Hume, Benita:** Early-Twentieth Century British film star married to first, Ronald Colman, second George Saunders. Aunt of John Howell.

**Huntingfield, Lord (Gerald):** Brother of the Hon. Peter Vanneck, who was a Lord Mayor of London.

**Huntingfield, Lady Ginty:** Writer, married to Gerald Huntingfield and a daughter of Reggie and Cecilia Errington, good Suffolk friends.

**Huston, John:** Well-known Twentieth Century American film director. Died 1987.

**Huston, Erica 'Ricki':** A former wife of John Huston, mother of Angelica Huston and a good friend.

19

**Ivan-Smith, George, OA:** Australian former broadcaster, diplomat, poet and painter. Established the UN's first Information Centre and was closely associated with the development of the UN in general, a close friend of Dag Hammerskjöld, the second Secretary General of the UN whom he accompanied on many missions including the Suez Crisis in 1956 and Personal Representative of Secretary-General U. Thant in East Africa (1962–66). Stepfather of Penelope Gilliatt.

**Ickworth Park:** Former country estate of the Marquess of Bristol near Bury St. Edmunds, Suffolk. It is now jointly owned by the UK National Trust and a hotel.

**Institute of Neurology:** The University department at the National Hospital for Nervous Diseases, Queen Square, London, WC1. Roger Gilliatt had the first Chair of Clinical Neurology there.

**Jabavu, Noni:** Gifted African writer of *The Ochre People* amongst other books, later married to Michael Crosfield. Shared a flat with Mary Gilliatt in the early 1960s.

**Jackson, Winefride:** Former Editor of *The Sunday Telegraph* Women's Pages in the 1960s.

**Jacobsen, Per:** Head of the International Monetary Fund (1956–1963) and father of Moira Bannister, wife of Roger Bannister.

**Janson-Smith, Peter:** Mary Gilliant's then literary agent.

**Janson-Smith, Celia:** Wife of Peter Janson-Smith.

**Jardine Matheson:** Famed UK Far East Trading Company founded in the Nineteenth Century.

**Jeffries, Arthur:** Owner of the Jeffries Gallery in London in the 1960s.

**Johnson, Dr Samuel:** Eighteenth Century writer and scholar who produced the first English Dictionary and a vast number of adages.

**Joll, James:** Distinguished economist and Fellow of All Souls, Oxford. Former colleague of Mary Gilliatt and Angela Caccia on *The Sunday Telegraph* in the 1960s.

**Joll, Thalia** Married to James Joll.

# DRAMATIS PERSONAE

**Jones, Carmel:** My younger sister, an Immigration Judge.

**Jones, John:** A barrister and recorder specialising in Criminal Law and my brother-in-law.

**Kanawa Te, Dame Kiri:** Famous New Zealand opera singer.

**Kaufman, George, S.:** A former member of the famed *New Yorker* 'round table' in New York in the 1920s and 1930s.

**Keaton, Buster:** Early American comedian and film star of the silent movies.

**Keeble, Harold:** Editor of *The Daily Express* in the 1950s.

**Kelly, Dr Reginald:** Dean of The Institute of Neurology, Queen Square in the 1960s and a colleague of Roger Gilliatt.

**Kennedy, John F.:** President of the United States, assassinated in November, 1963.

**Kennet, Wayland (Young), Lord Kennet of the Dene:** A Labour politician and writer and good friend of Roger Gilliatt.

**Kennet, (Liz Young) Lady:** Writer, general do-gooder and friend of Roger Gilliatt.

**Keswick, Henry:** A member of one of the families who owned Jardine Matheson, the huge Far Eastern trading company.

**Khan, Louis:** Iconic US architect of the 1950s and 1960s.

**Klee, Poul, c.1879–1940:** Well-known Swiss painter of the early Twentieth Century.

**Kleinwort Benson:** Merchant Bankers.

**Klöcke, Sophia:** Roger Gilliatt's aunt who married a German just after World War One.

**Klöcke, Ursula:** Roger Gilliatt's first cousin who is also a good friend of the Gilliatts.

**Koch de Gooreynd, Alexander:** Father of Sir Peregrine Worsthorne and Sir Simon Peter Towneley who changed the family name to Worsthorne in the early 1920s and changed his own name back again in 1937.

**Koestler, Arthur:** Ex-Communist Hungarian polymath writer who could write fluently in several languages and on many subjects. His books include *Darkness at Noon, Thieves in the Night* and *The Midwife Toad.* He and his wife, Cynthia, performed a double suicide in the 1970s.

**Kruschev, Nikita:** Premier of the Soviet Union (1958–1964).

**Lambert, Liz:** American journalist and writer living in the UK, and London correspondent for many years of the US magazine, *Architectural Digest.* Old friend.

**Lambert, Jack:** American architect, long term resident in the UK and married to Liz Lambert. Old friend.

**Lance, Professor James, OA, CBE:** Australian distinguished internationally-known Neurologist at the University of New South Wales; an expert on headache, a writer (*Migraines and Other Headaches* and *The Mechanics and Management of Headache* and a children's book *The Golden Trout*), Fellow of the Australian Academy of Science, father-in-law of Tom Gilliatt and very dear friend of Roger and Mary Gilliatt.

**Lance, Judy:** Wife of James Lance, Australian mother-in-law of Tom Gilliatt and very dear friend of Roger and Mary Gilliatt.

**Lance, Sophie:** Australian journalist, writer, purveyor of special food, married to Tom Gilliatt and my daughter-in-law.

**Lane, Pamela:** First wife of the writer and playwright, John Osborne.

**L'Antiquaire:** Esoteric Russian Antiques store in Manhattan owned by Helen Fiorati in the 1960s.

**Lawrence, D.H.:** Well-known writer of the 1920s and 1930s and writer, amongst other books, of *Lady Chatterley's Lover*, the subject of a controversial obscenity trial in the UK in the 1960s.

# Dramatis Personae

**Lawrence, Christopher:** Designer friend of Billy McCarty and erstwhile colleague of Mary Gilliatt who later lived and worked in Rome and Milan.

**Lawson, Nigel, Baron Lawson of Blaby:** Former Chancellor of the Exchequer (1983–1989) in the Margaret Thatcher government and former City Editor of *The Sunday Telegraph* in the 1960s.

**Lawson, Nigella:** Famed cookery writer (*How to Eat)* and TV presenter, former deputy Literary Editor of the UK *Sunday Times;* daughter of Nigel Lawson.

**Ledward, William:** Economic historian and banker; shares French house with Mary Gilliatt and is good friend of Sophia Gilliatt with whom he is opening a new restaurant (Le Restaurant du Lac) in the Luberon, France.

**Lee, Sarah Tomerlin:** Former right hand to Helena Rubinstein, Director of *Lord & Taylor*, Managing Editor of American *Vogue,* Editor of *House Beautiful*. Became a distinguished US hotel designer when she took over her husband's design business after his death. Good friend of Mary and Roger Gilliatt. Died, aged 90, in 2001.

**Lee, Tom:** Well-known window and hotel designer in the 1940s to the early 1970s. Husband of Sarah Tomerlin Lee, he was killed in a motor car accident in California. Good friend of Mary and Roger Gilliatt. Died 1971.

**Leeds, Harold:** US designer and former President of Pratt Design School in New York City in the 1960s.

**Leeson, Nick:** The UK trader employed by Barings Bank in Hong Kong who single-handedly brought the bank down in the 1980s after some 200 years of existence.

**Legislative Council of Uganda:** The Ugandan Parliament.

**Lehmann, Rosamund:** Well-known novelist of the first half of the Twentieth Century, former wife of Baron Phillips (the 'Red' Peer) and mother of Hugo Phillips, who was formerly married to Mollie Makins, now Lady Norwich and sister of Virginia Makins, a colleague of Mary Gilliatt's on *The Sunday Telegraph*.

MARY GILLIATT'S FABULOUS FOOD AND FRIENDS

**Lehrer, Tom:** Harvard professor of Mathmatics and satirical songwriter in the 1950s and 1960s.

**Leighton, Margaret:** British actress in the 1950s who died prematurely. First wife of Max Reinhardt, the publisher and former Chairman of Bodley Head.

**Lewis, Charles:** Publisher, a representative of Oxford University Press in India and Pakistan later a director of the company. Formerly engaged to Mary Gilliatt.

**Lewis, Primula:** The Indian writer and political activist imprisoned by Mrs Ghandi in the 1960s and married to Charles Lewis.

**Limerick, Sylvia, Countess of:** Head of the UK Red Cross for many years and widow of Lord Limerick; near neighbours and good friends of Mary Gilliatt in Victoria Road, London, just round the corner from Douro Place.

**Limerick, Patrick, Earl:** Former Conservative politician and banker whose family gave its name to the light verse form. Neighbour, friend and husband of Sylvia, Lady Limerick. Died 2003.

**Lloyd, Roger:** A US banker in London for a period in the 1960s and a Director of the NY Opera House.

**Lloyd, Svetlana:** Eclectic hostess, married to Roger Lloyd.

**Lloyd, Angela:** Formerly Angela Caccia (née Reed), journalist, writer and broadcaster in South Africa, married to the late David Caccia (then to Taffy Lloyd). Old friend and former colleague of Mary Gilliatt's on *The Sunday Telegraph* (they also shared flat in the early 1960s).

**Lloyd, Professor Philip, 'Taffy':** Chair of Mining Engineering, University of Capetown, pianist and second husband of Angela Caccia.

**Long, Stephen:** Long-time owner of eponymous antique store in the New King's Road, London where Mary Gilliatt always seemed to find splendidly appropriate presents.

**Louisiana Purchase:** Purchase from France of the State of Louisiana in the US by President Jefferson in 1802. John and Francis Baring Company (later Barings Bank) helped fund the purchase.

24

# Dramatis Personae

**Lyle, Gavin:** Late acclaimed crime and thriller writer, married to Katherine Whitehorn, the equally acclaimed columnist.

**MacDonald, Ramsay:** Labour Prime Minister, 1929–1931 and 1931-1935, whose house in Frognal, Hampstead was bought by Don and Ella Ogden Stewart.

**Macmillan, Sir Harold, later first Earl of Stockton, OM, PC:** Known by his admirers as 'Super Mac' and by his detractors as 'Mac the Knife', Conservative Prime Minister after Sir Anthony Eden resigned (1957–1963). When asked by a reporter what were the most powerful forces in politics, he replied, 'Events my dear boy, events'.

**Magistretti, Vico:** Well-known Italian furniture designer of the 1950s to the 1990s.

**Makins, The Hon. Virginia:** Former Editor of *The Times Educational Supplement* and a former colleague and friend of Mary Gilliatt on *The Sunday Telegraph*.

**Mailer, Norman:** Well-known Twentieth Century American writer and friend of Ken Tynan.

**Man Booker:** The distinguished annual literary prize started by Booker Brothers in the late 1960s.

**Margaret, HRH the Princess, Countess of Snowdon:** Queen Elizabeth the Second's younger sister, married to the Earl of Snowdon.

**Martin, Maria:** The victim in the famous Nineteenth Century 'Murder in the Red Barn' in Polstead, Suffolk.

**Marion-Smith, Dr:** A neurological colleague of Roger Gilliatt.

**Maschler, Tom:** Publisher and Chairman of Jonathan Cape.

**Mason, Ailsa (Garland):** Former Women's Editor of the *Daily Mirror* who succeeded Audrey Withers as Editor of *Vogue* Magazine in the late 1950s.

**Mason, John:** Husband of Ailsa Garland.

**Matthews, Joy:** Journalist, Women's Editor of *The Daily Express* in the 1950s followed by Editor of the *Femail* section of *The Daily Mail*. She married George McWatters, her third husband in the late 1950s and became a noted hostess and tireless charity worker and patron of the Arts. She was Mary Gilliatt's first newpaper boss and although she fired her she remained a dear life long friend. Died 2006.

**Maudling, Reginald:** Leading Conservative Politician, Chancellor of the Exchequer (1962–64) in the Macmillan Government, rival to Edward Heath for the leadership of the party in 1968 and Home Secretary (1970) during the time of a deeply troubled Northern Ireland.

**Maudling, Beryl:** The former actress, Beryl Laverick, who married Reginald Maudling.

**Mattli, Jo:** Couturier in London during the 1950s and 1960s.

**Mboya, Tom:** Kenyan Politician in the Jomo Kenyatta government from the 1950s until his assassination in 1969.

**McCarthy, Senator Joe:** Over-assertive router out of so-called Communists and other perpetrators of so-called 'Un-American Activities' in the early-1950s.

**McCarty, William (Billy):** Talented American designer who worked first with the architect, Louis Khan, in Philadelphia and then with David Hicks in London. He started his own company in the 1960s. Mary Gilliatt learnt much from working with him and he became a great friend of all the Gilliatts and Godfather to Tom. The Australian Collector and critic Douglas Cooper adopted him as his son and heir in the 1970s.

**McCullers, Carson:** Well-known American novelist of the 1940s, 1950s and early 1960s (*Ballad of the Sad Café* etc.) from Columbus, Georgia. Used to stay with Mary Gilliatt in London). Died 1967.

**McDonald, Professor Ian:** A New Zealand neurologist and Rhodes Scholar who worked at The Institute of Neurology with Roger Gilliatt, was his great friend and eventually succeeded him. Editor of *Brain*.

# DRAMATIS PERSONAE

**McLeod, Iain:** Admired leading Conservative Politician and potential leader of the Party who was appointed Chancellor of the Exchequer by Prime Minister Edward Heath in June 1970. He died exactly a month later.

**McLeod, Professor James 'Jim' A.O.:** Australian Neurologist, Emeritus Professor of Neurology, the University of Sydney, and a friend and colleague of Roger Gilliatt.

**McLeod, Robin:** Wife of Jim McLeod.

**McNulty, Bettina:** American ex-Condé Nast journalist living in UK who had the same profile as representations of the ancient Egyptian Queen Nefertiti. She was a close friend of photographer Lee Miller and Roland Penrose.

**McNulty, Henry:** American publicist living and working in the UK.

**McWatters, George:** Former Chairman Harveys of Bristol (1956–1966) Chairman of Ward White (1966–1980) Vice-Chairman of Harlech TV; Chairman when it became HTV (1986–1990); High Sheriff of Cambridgeshire 1979. Married to Joy Matthews and old friend of the Gilliatts.

**McWatters, Christopher:** Barrister son of George and Joy McWatters and a godson of Mary Gilliatt.

**McWilliam, 'Mac':** Twentieth Century British sculptor.

**McWilliam, Beth:** Wife of Mac McWilliam.

**Mendès France, Pierre:** President du Conseil in France 1954–1955. Died 1982.

**Metcalfe, John:** Well-known advertising executive and literary critic in the 1960s and 1970s.

**Metcalfe, Sheila:** London hostess married to John Metcalfe.

**Melly, George:** Well-known Twentieth Century British Jazz musician, Blues player and writer. Died 2007.

**Melly, Victoria:** Married to George Melly.

**Meyer, Fleur Cowles:** Well-known US hostess, writer, painter, editor living in London and married to Tom Montagu Meyer. (See Fleur Cowles.)

**Meyer, Tom Montagu:** Second husband of Fleur Cowles and ex-army friend of Roger Gilliatt.

**Middleton, Michael:** Editor of British *House & Garden* during the 1950s.

**Miller, Beatrix:** Editor of British *Vogue* for over three decades.

**Miller, Johnny:** An early President of the World Bank and one of the early investors along with the Aga Khan in Sardinia as a tourist resort.

**Miller, Dr Jonathan:** Polymath-neurologist, writer, scientist, broadcaster, play, film, TV and opera director.

**Miller, Lee:** Iconic beauty of the 1920s and 1930s, photographer, Surrealist, lived with Man Ray in Paris, only woman World War Two photographer (for *Vogue*), married to Roland Penrose. Died 1977.

**Miller, Tim:** Wine expert and art collector who worked with George McWatters at Harveys. Son of Johnny Miller.

**Miller-Jones, Keith:** Former Chairman of the National Hospital for Nervous Diseases, Queen Square, London.

**Milligan, Jane:** Musician, singer, TV presenter, daughter of Spike and Paddy Milligan and a goddaughter of Mary Gilliatt.

**Milligan, Paddy:** Singer and dear friend of the Gilliatts, second wife of Spike Milligan.

**Milligan Spike, Sir:** Iconic Irish comedian, member of the famous BBC Radio *Goon Show,* writer and musician. Married to Paddy Milligan, dear friend of the Gilliatts and Godfather to the Gilliatt's younger daughter, Annie Constantine. Died 2002.

**Miró, Joan:** Well-known Twentieth Century Spanish abstract painter.

**Mitchell Beazley:** UK publishing company co-started by James Mitchell.

# Dramatis Personae

**Mitchell, James:** A Twentieth Century British publisher.

**Mondadori:** Italian publishers.

**Monserratt, Nicholas:** Twentieth Century British writer particularly known for his World War Two Navy novel, *The Cruel Sea.*

**Moore, Henry:** Famed Twentieth Century British sculptor.

**Morrell, Lady Ottoline:** Well-known Bloomsbury Group hostess and literati in both her London home and Garsington House, near Oxford. Died 1938.

**Morris, Jan:** Distinguished Travel Writer, and as James Morris, an old army acquaintance of Roger Gilliatt.

**Mosley, Nick:** Twentieth Century British writer, old army friend of Roger Gilliatt and son of Oswald Mosley, whose Fascist politics he in no way shared.

**Mountbatten, Admiral Lord Louis:** Former Viceroy of India who presided over Indian Independence. Uncle of the Duke of Edinburgh and father of Lady Pamela Hicks.

**Murphy, Betty, Lady:** Mother of Mary Cookson – a great friend of the Gilliatts.

**Narbonne de, Jean-Louis:** A French friend of Angus Wilson and Tony Garrett.

**Nasser, Colonel:** The president of Egypt during the Suez Crisis, 1956.

**Nefertiti:** Ancient Egyptian Queen.

**Newsome-Davies, Professor John:** A neurologist colleague of Roger Gilliatt.

**Nichols, Mike:** Acclaimed American film director who lived with Penelope Gilliatt when she left John Osborne in the late 1960s.

**Nicolson, Harold:** Well-known Twentieth Century writer and diplomat married to the Bloomsbury Group writer Vita Sackville West, and great gardener friend of Virginia Woolf.

**Norman, Sir Montagu:** Former Governor of the Bank of England who married Peregrine Worsthorne's mother.

**Normande, Pierre:** Frenchman working in London during the 1960s who Mary Gilliatt knew from her Sorbonne days.

**Norwich John Julius, Viscount:** Writer and historian son of the former beauty and hostess, Lady Diana Cooper, Viscountess Norwich. He is married to the former Molly Phillips, née Makins.

**Norwich, Molly, Viscountess:** Married to John Julius Norwich and sister of Virginia Makins.

**Ntiro, Sam:** Twentieth Century African painter from Tanzania, Professor and first African High Commissioner in London (1961–64), Professor of Fine Arts at Makerere University of Uganda. Married to Sarah Ntiro the East African politician.

**Ntiro, Sarah:** The first woman university graduate (St. Anne's College, Oxford) in East and Central Africa and one of first two women members of the Legislative Council of Uganda (parliament). Exiled to Nairobi, Kenya from 1978–86. Founded the Forum for African Women Educationalists.

**Nureyev, Rudolf:** Russian ballet dancer famed for both his extraordinary dancing and his beauty. Died 1992.

**Nutting, Sir, Anthony 'Bart':** One of the youngest ever Secretaries of State and one of Fleming's inspirations for James Bond.

**Nutting, Annie (née Gunning):** Former model, married to Anthony Nutting.

**Obolensky, Colonel Serge:** Russian World War One hero, originally married to a daughter of Czar Alexander the Second, Serge moved to New York, helped open a couple of the leading Manhattan hotels and managed to be equally heroic in World War Two.

**Obolensky, Teddy:** Film producer, cousin of Serge Obolensky and a neighbour in Thurloe Square.

# Dramatis Personae

**O'Casey, Eileen:** Former actress (she understudied Lady Diana Cooper in *The Miracle*) writer, widow of the Irish playwright, Sean O'Casey. She was also much loved by both George Bernard Shaw and Harold Macmillan and a dear friend of the Gilliatts. Died 1995.

**O'Casey, Sean:** A towering early Twentieth Century Irish playwright (*Juno and the Paycock, The Plough and the Stars* etc). Died 1964.

**O'Casey, Shivaun:** Writer, actress and daughter of Sean and Eileen O'Casey.

**O'Neil, Eugene:** An equally towering American early Twentieth Century playwright (*Morning Becomes Electra* etc) and father of Oonagh Chaplin, married to Charlie Chaplin. Died 1953.

**Ogden Stewart, Donald:** Writer, scriptwriter (*Philadelphia Story* etc.), one of McCarthy's victims exiled to London and a member of the famous Algonquin Hotel Round Table Group in the 1930s and 1940s.

**Ogden Stewart, Don ('Duck') Junior:** Writer/editor and son of Donald Ogden Stewart, originally partnered with Mai Zetterling, the Twentieth Century Swedish actress and film star. Died 1980.

**Ogden Stewart, Ella (Wheeler Winter):** Australian writer, journalist, war correspondent, art collector, people collector, hostess and former Communist. Formerly married to the American political activist, Lincoln Steffens, then to Donald Ogden Stewart. Died 1980.

**Olivier, Sir Laurence:** Acclaimed Twentieth Century British actor and one of the founders of The National Theatre, married first to Vivien Leigh and secondly to Dame Joan Plowright.

**Olivia, Lady:** At that time *Gone with the Wind* star, Vivien Leigh.

**Onassis, Aristotle:** Powerful Greek shipping magnate later married to Jacqueline Kennedy.

**Oppenheim, Sir Duncan:** Then Chairman of the British Amercian Tobacco Company, also a painter and friend of the Gilliatts.

**Oppenheim, George S.:** One of the two founders of the American Viking Press (the other was Alfred Guinzberg) now Viking Penguin.

**Orwell, Sonia:** Writer and widow and literary executor of the writer George Orwell (*1984* etc). Died 1980. (Since George Orwell's name was actually Blair, she was legally Sonia Blair.)

**Osborne, John:** Twentieth Century playwright (*Look Back in Anger*; *A Patriot for me* etc) the original 'angry young man' of the late 1950s and early 1960s. Penelope Gilliatt was his third wife.

**Osborne, Nolan:** Daughter of John Osborne and Penelope Gilliatt named after Captain Nolan, a leading character in the Tony Richardson directed movie, *The Charge of the Light Brigade,* scripted by John Osborne.

**OUDS:** The Oxford Union Debating Society/Dramatic Society.

**Pan Macmillan (Australia):** Tom Gilliatt is Director of Non-Fiction there.

**Papworth, Veronica:** Former Women's Page Editor and fashion illustrator for *The Sunday Express* in the 1950s.

**Parker, Dorothy:** Famous wit and writer and contributor to the early *New Yorker* magazine in the 1920s and 1930s, and a member of the Algonquin Hotel Round Table. Died 1967.

**Parker, Peter:** Old Oxford friend of Roger Gilliatt and Ken Tynan, one of the founders of the Man Booker annual literary prize and a former very proactive head of British Rail.

**Parker, Jill:** Another old Oxford friend of Roger Gilliatt and Ken Tynan, married to Peter Parker.

**Parker Bowles, Brigadier Andrew:** Distinguished ex-army officer, polo player, former husband of Camilla Parker Bowles and a neighbour of Mary Gilliatt's in Wiltshire.

**Parker Bowles, Camilla:** Now the Duchess of Cornwall.

**Parkinson, Norman:** Well-known Twentieth Century photographer who did a great deal of work for Condé Nast on both sides of the Atlantic.

# Dramatis Personae

**Patel, Bhaichand:** Former UN official and representative in New York and Delhi and an old friend of the Jones and Gilliatt families.

**Pearson-Rogers, Bill and Cesca:** Old Suffolk friends.

**Pearson-Rogers, Merlin:** Writer son of the senior Pearson-Rogers.

**Peguy, Charles:** French late-Nineteenth/early-Twentieth Century writer who set up the French *'Pélerinage Péguy'* as an annual pilgrimage to Chartres from universities all over France in thanksgiving for the life of his son, stricken with diptheria.

**Pen and Sword:** Privately owned UK publishers.

**Penrose, Sir Roland:** Co-Founder of the Institute of Contemporary Arts with Sir Herbert Read, writer, critic, collector, British Surrealist painter and good friend of Picasso. Married to Lee Miller. Died 1984.

**Phillips, Hugo:** Son of Rosamund Lehmann, the early-Twentieth Century novelist and Lord Phillips (the 'Red Peer'), formerly married to Molly Makins, now Lady Norwich.

**Piaf, Edith:** Popular French singer with a memorably husky voice in the first half of the Twentieth Century. Died 1963.

**Picasso, Pablo:** One of the great Twentieth Century Abstract painters and sculptors. Died 1973.

**Playfair, Giles:** Twentieth Century writer and penal reformer son of Sir Nigel Playfair, the theatrical impresario and playwright.

**Playfair, Anne:** Married to Giles Playfair.

**Plumb, Barbara:** American writer and journalist and a great friend of Mary Gilliatt.

**Plumb, Christian:** The journalist son of Barbara and Bill Plumb.

**Plumb, William Lansing:** American industrial designer and a winner of *The Prix de Rome.* Former husband of Barbara Plumb.

**Poliakoff, Serge:** Early-Twentieth Century Russian painter living in France.

**Poliakoff, Vera:** Painter, patron of the arts and artists, daughter of Serge Poliakoff and former wife of John Russell, the art critic.

**Ponti, Gio:** Great early-Twentieth Century Italian architect and painter working from Milan.

**Poole, Mary Jane:** Former Editor of US *House & Garden* and a close friend of Lee Miller and Bettina McNulty.

**Popovic, Annabel:** Wife of Michael Popovic.

**Popovic, Michael:** Former Head of the UN Information Office in London in the 1960s and former husband of Annabel Popovic.

**Porter, Basil:** My brother's father-in-law.

**Porter, Bridget:** My brother's mother-in-law.

**Porter, Jane:** The twin sister of my sister-in-law.

**Porter, Sarah:** Married to my brother, Anthony Green.

**Powell, Enoch:** Brigadier Professor. Very right wing Conservative politician academic who was Minister of Health in the Macmillan Government. Died 1998.

**Pratt Institute:** Old-established School of Design in New York City.

**Random House:** Very large US publishing group.

**Ray, Man:** Important Surrealist painter and photographer of the early Twentieth Century and a lover of the well-known beauty and photographer, Lee Miller. Died 1976.

**Read, Sir Herbert:** Twentieth Century painter, critic and co-founder, with Sir Roland Penrose, of the Institute of Contemporary Arts.

**Reilly, Lady, Annette:** Wife of the late Lord Reilly and a dear friend and former neighbour.

**Reilly, Lord, Paul:** Chairman of the Council of Industrial Design and The London Design Centre, writer and critic in the 1960s and 1970s: a dear friend and former neighbour of the Gilliatts.

# Dramatis Personae

**Reinhardt, Joan:** American wife of Max Reinhardt, Chairman of Bodley Head Publishers in the 1960s and 1970s and a friend and neighbour.

**Reinhart, Max:** Chairman of Bodley Head Publishers in the 1960s and 1970s.

**Reinhold, Dr Margaret:** Neurologist and former colleague of Roger Gilliatt.

**Reith Lectures:** Series of lectures on many subjects first instigated by Lord Reith, a former Chairman of the BBC.

**Rense, Paige:** American veteran Editor of US Architectural Digest.

**Richardson, Tony:** Respected film and theatre Director in the 1950s, 1960s and 1970s. The late husband of Vanessa Redgrave and father of the actresses Natasha and Joely Richardson.

**Robertson, Dr Graeme:** Australian neurologist, writer and specialist in decorative cast iron.

**Robertson, Jean:** Cookery writer, she wrote the old Leslie Adrian column on *The Spectator* in the 1950s and early 1960s, and friend and colleague of Mary Gilliatt on *The Sunday Telegraph*.

**Robertson, Joan:** Specialist in cast iron, writer and companion helper and co-author with her father, Dr Graeme Robertson.

**Robinson, Helen (Preston):** Former *Vogue* Magazine Editor, first woman Director of Debenhams Store, former Managing Director of Thomas Goodes and on the board of The Royal College of Art as well as a former marketing director of Aspreys and a director of British Airport Authority, London Transport, The London Electricity Board, The Commonwealth Institute, The World Wild Life Fund and a dear friend of the Gilliatts.

**Rochefoucauld, Duc de la:** A member of an old-established French aristocratic and literary family.

**Romaine, Mason Sr. and Margaret:** American friends of Mary Gilliatt's parents, from Petersburg, Virginia.

**Romaine, Mason Jr. and Anne:** Mason Romaine Sr's nephew and his wife. Friends of the Gilliatts.

**Roosevelt, Eleanor:** Wife of Franklin D. Roosevelt, President of the United States for four terms from the 1930s to 1945.

**Rothermere, Lord Vere (Harmsworth)** Former proprietor of *The Daily Mail*.

**Rothschild, Lord:** Leading member of the Rothschild family and an escort of HRH, Princess Margaret.

**Royal Albert Hall:** Well known lecture and concert hall in Kensington, London.

**Ruggles, Samuel B:** Original developer of Gramercy Park, New York City.

**Russell, John:** Well known British art critic now living in New York City.

**Russell, Vera:** Painter and encourager of painters and sculptors who started the old Artist's Market in London. Daughter of the painter Serge Poliakoff and former wife of John Russell.

**Sackville-West, Vita:** Writer, great gardener, friend of Virginia Woolf and wife of writer and diplomat, Harold Nicolson.

**Sacks, Dr Oliver:** British neurologist and writer living and working in New York (*The Man who Mistook his Wife for a Hat* etc), former colleague of Roger Gilliatt.

**Salazar, President:** President of Portugal in the 1960s.

**Sandoe, John:** Founder of the eponymous bookshop just off Sloane Square, London.

**Sartre, Jean-Paul:** Existentialist French writer and playwright, very well-known in the 1940s and 1950s along with Simone de Beauvoir his sometime mistress. Died 1980.

**Saunders, George:** Early to mid-Twentieth Century film star, married to Benita Hume, aunt of John Howell.

# Dramatis Personae

**Sayre, Norah:** American left wing political writer, film critic, for many years the American correspondent of the UK *New Statesman*, daughter of *New Yorker* writer Joel Sayre and a good friend of the Gilliatts. Died 2001.

**Schlesinger, John:** Twentieth Century film director (*Sunday, Bloody Sunday* etc) and friend of Penelope Gilliatt and Ken Tynan. Died 2003.

**Scott, Elizabeth:** Assistant and speech writer to Sir Anthony Eden during his time as Foreign Secretary during the war and then as Prime Minister. A friend from Suffolk.

**Scott, Guy:** A stockbroker, husband of Elizabeth Scott and, like his wife, a good friend from Suffolk.

**Scott-James, Anne:** A leading woman journalist of the 1950s and 1960s, Women's Editor of the now defunct *Sunday Dispatch*, mother of journalist and editor Max Hastings, and married to cartoonist, Osbert Lancaster.

**Sears, Professor Tom:** A neurological colleague and good friend of Roger Gilliatt.

**Seifert, Max:** Twentieth Century actor.

**Sellars, Sir Peter:** Leading British comedian, actor and film star in the 1950s, 1960s and early 1970s.

**Settle, Alison:** A doyenne among woman journalists in the 1940s and 1950s.

**Shaw, George Bernard:** Famously curmudgeonly playwright and writer (*St. Joan, Man and Superman, Major Barbara* etc). Died 1950.

**Sheekey's:** A long-running fish restaurant in Soho, London.

**Shelley, David:** A friend of Mary Gilliatt's brother.

**Sherfield, Lord:** A former UK diplomat and ambassador, as Sir Roger Makins, to the US and friend of President John F. Kennedy during the Cuban missile crisis. Father of Molly Norwich and Virginia Makins.

**Showerings:** The company (makers of Babycham) who first took over Harveys of Bristol.

**Shulman, Alexandra:** Current Editor of British *Vogue* and daughter of Milton and Drusilla (Beyfuss) Shulman.

**Shulman, Drusilla (Beyfuss):** Journalist, writer, broadcaster, lecturer and a former Editor of *Brides* magazine, married to Milton Shulman.

**Shulman, Milton:** Canadian long-time theatre critic of *The Evening Standard* and writer.

**Sillitoe, Alan:** Twentieth Century novelist and one of the original late 1950s and 1960s 'Angry Young Men'.

**Simple, Peter:** Name of regular humourous column in *The Daily Telegraph* on which Claudie Worsthorne, former wife of Sir Peregrine Worsthorne, worked.

**Slater, Nigel:** Influential writer on food and other subjects.

**Smythson:** Distinguished London stationery shop from which Mary Gilliatt's dinner books came.

**Snowdon, The Earl of, Anthony Armstrong-Jones:** Brilliant photographer and designer formerly married to HRH The Princess Margaret, Countess of Snowdon. (See Armstrong Jones.)

**Solzhenitsyn, Alesander:** Highly regarded Russian writer and poet of the 1950s and 1960s.

**Spanier, Ginette:** Former Director of Dior, married to Sir Robin Darwin, painter and former Rector of the Royal College of Art.

**Spender, Stephen:** Twentieth Century poet, writer and Editor of the literary magazine, *Encounter*.

**Spock, Dr Benjamin:** American writer of classic child-rearing books and ardent anti-war protester during the 1960s war with Vietnam.

**Schwitters, Kurt, c.1887–1948:** Well-known German Dadaist of the early Twentieth Century.

# Dramatis Personae

**Spurling, Hilary:** Well-known biographer including a sympathetic life of Sonia Orwell.

**Steffens, Lincoln:** Radical American political and philosophical writer and lecturer of the early Twentieth Century, formerly married to the Australian political journalist, Ella Wheeler Winter who later married Donald Ogden Stewart. Died 1936.

**Stein, Gertrude, c.1874–1946:** One of the literary and art-collecting American coterie in Paris during the early part of the Twentieth Century.

**Stevenson, John:** A former managing director of the Habitat Stores and Conran who briefly married writer Shirley Conran, second wife of Sir Terence Conran.

**St. John Stevas, Norman, Baron St. John of Fawsley:** Conservative politican, twice Minister for the Arts in the Margaret Thatcher Government (1973–1974, and 1979–1981) and a great party giver.

**Storey, The Hon. Sir Richard, Bart:** Former Chairman of The Portsmouth and Sunderland Group of papers, TV production, Conservative politician and opposite neighbour of the Gilliatts in Douro Place.

**Storey, The Hon. Virginia, Lady Storey:** Friend and opposite neighbour of the Gilliatts in Douro Place.

**Stubbings, Tony:** A painter and guitarist in the 1970s.

**Taittinger Champagne:** An excellent champagne from Reims, France and, one would have thought, a rival to Charles Heidseick who nevertheless served it at his own house.

**Talbot, Suzanne J.:** Couturier and hat milliner in Paris in the 1950s.

**Tapiès, Anton:** Well-known Twentieth Century Spanish painter.

**Tarnowski, Count Jules:** A member of one of the many aristocratic Polish families forced to leave their Polish estates during World War Two. After time spent in Dachau concentration camp, Count Tarnowski ended up with his family in Paris and became a secretary to the Duke of Windsor and Secretary of the Paris Jockey Club.

**Tarnowski, Countess Rosa:** Wife of Count Jules Tarnowski and mentor to Mary Gilliatt in Paris.

**Tarnowski, Count Ladislas:** Polish former investment banker living in Paris, son of Count and Countess Jules Tarnowski and an old friend of Mary Gilliatt.

**Thompson, Kaye:** American composer, actress and singer, and author of the much-loved *Eloise* children's books. Died 1998.

**Toklas, Alice B., c.1877–1967:** Close friend and companion of Gertrude Stein, cookery writer.

**Trevor, William:** Acclaimed Twentieth Century writer.

**Tuckwell, Patricia:** Australian musician, sister of Barry Tuckwell, who became the second wife of Lord Harewood, the Queen's cousin.

**Tynan, Kathleen, née Halton:** Journalist, writer, scriptwriter and second wife of Kenneth Tynan. Next door neighbour and friend of the Gilliatts in Thurloe Square. Died 1995.

**Tynan, Kenneth:** Audacious Twentieth Century theatre critic, writer and literary director of the English National Theatre. Neighbour and good friend of Roger, Penelope and Mary Gilliatt. Died 1980.

**Tynan, Roxana:** Daughter of Ken and Kathleen Tynan.

**United Nations:** Global association of governments meant to facilitate cooperation, International law, security etc.

**Tynan, Tracy:** Daughter of Ken and his first wife, Elaine Dundy.

**Ure, Mary:** 1950s actress and second wife of playwright, John Osborne.

**Van Dyke:** Renowned Dutch painter of the late-Seventeenth Century.

**Vanneck, Cordelia, The Hon. Lady Vanneck:** Writer wife of The Hon. Sir Peter Vanneck, a former Lord Mayor of London.

**Vanneck, The Hon. Gerald, later Lord Huntingfield:** The late older brother of Peter Vanneck.

**Vanneck, The Hon. Ginty Vanneck, later Lady Huntingfield:** Wife of Gerald Vanneck.

**Vanneck, Air Vice Marshall, The Hon. Sir Peter Vanneck:** Former aide de camp to HM the Queen, Deputy Lord Lieutenant of London and former Lord Mayor of London.

**Viking Penguin:** The amalgamation of the old US Viking Books with Penguin Books.

**Vaughan, Keith:** Good Twentieth Century British painter.

**Vaughan-Williams, Ralph:** A Twentieth Century composer.

**Waddington Gallery:** Distinguished London Gallery owned by Leslie Waddington.

**Waddington, Leslie:** An equally distinguished art dealer in Paris at the same time as Mary Gilliatt in the 1950s.

**Waddington, Victor:** An Irish art dealer who represented the Irish painter Jack Yeats among others and father of Leslie.

**Wain, John:** Twentieth Century British novelist.

**Walmsley, Margot:** Former managing editor of the UK literary magazine *Encounter* and a much-loved hostess and friend to the Gilliatts. She died in the 1990s.

**Walmsley, Alaric:** Son of Margot Walmsley, a student at King's College, Cambridge in the 1960s.

**Ward White:** Shoe Company of which George McWatters became chairman when Harveys of Bristol was taken over by Showerings (Harveys is now owned by Allied Domcq).

**Walton, Professor Sir John, now Lord Walton of Detchant:** Distinguished neurologist and academic who became the second Warden of Green College, Oxford, now called Green Templeton College.

**Waugh, Auberon:** British writer and columnist for *Private Eye* and *The Spectator* among other publications and a son of Evelyn Waugh.

**Waugh, Evelyn:** Well-known Twentieth Century British novelist (*Brideshead Revisited*; *A Handful of Dust*; *Decline and Fall, Vile Bodies*).

**Webb, Michael:** Writer and movie expert formerly of *Country Life* and the UK National Film Institute before he moved to California to a similar job.

**Wedgwood-Benn, Anthony:** Senior and vocal Labour politician and one of Labour's longest serving MPs. The term 'Bennite' is used to describe a radical democratic left wing position.

**Wesker, Sir, Arnold:** Twentieth Century British sometime-'kitchen-sink' playwright and writer. (Plays include *Chicken Soup with Barley, Chips with Everthing* etc.)

**Wharton, Michael:** The journalist on the British *Daily Telegraph* who edited the Peter Simple Column.

**Wheldon, Claire:** The daughter of some friends of my parents.

**White, Michael:** Successful UK theatre impresario, with Mary Gilliatt and Leslie Waddington in Paris in the 1950s.

**White, Paul William:** Tazmanian architect and friend of the Gilliatts, now living back in Australia.

**Whitehorn, Katherine:** Brilliant writer and columnist for *The Observer* for several decades and equally popular in *The Spectator*, and now SAGA magazine. Married to the crime writer, the late Gavin Lyall.

**Wilde, Oscar, c.1854–1900:** Great wit, writer, poet and playwright of the turn of the Nineteenth/Twentieth Century who was prosecuted and imprisoned for being a homosexual.

**Wilkins, Jeanne:** Mentor, friend and sometime tennis partner of Mary Gilliatt. The daughter of Winnie Burnand Parsons, one of the first women cartoonists and granddaughter of Sir Francis Burnand, an early Editor of *Punch* magazine.

**Williams, Tennessee:** Great Twentieth Century American playwright and writer.

# Dramatis Personae

**Windlesham, Lord:** Conservative academic and politician in The House of Lords, formerly married to the late Prue Glyn.

**Windlesham, Lady (Prue Glyn):** Journalist and a former Fashion Editor of the London *Times,* formerly married to Lord Windlesham.

**Winter, Ella Wheeler:** Australian political writer, war correspondent, journalist, ex-Communist, art collector, collector of people, regular Sunday hostess who married the US 1920s political activist, Lincoln Steffens when she was still in her teens and, when widowed, married Donald Ogden Stewart who was driven to live in London rather than testifying in the Senator Joe McCarthy witch hunts. See Ogden Stewart.

**Wilson, Sir, Angus:** Distinguished Twentieth Century novelist (*Hemlock and After, The Middle Age of Mrs Elliott, Anglo Saxon Attitudes* etc) and Public Orator for the University of East Anglia. Died 1991.

**Wilson, Harold:** Twice Labour Prime Minister in 1964–1970 and 1974–1976. Died 1995.

**Wilson, Peter:** An old friend of my brother, Anthony Green.

**Windsor, the Duke of:** The title the uncrowned King Edward VIII took when he abdicated the throne of England in favour of marrying the American Wallis Simpson and living in exile in France.

**Windsor, the Duchess of:** See above. Died 1986.

**Woi Woi:** Coastal town in New South Wales (up the coast from Sydney, Australia) where Spike Milligan's parents lived and which he quite often visited.

**Wolfers, David:** Another well-known London gallery owner, formerly married to the journalist and columnist, Joy McWatters (née Matthews) who later married George McWatters. Died 2001.

**Woolf, Virginia:** Well-known early Twentieth Century writer and a leader of the Bloomsbury Group, married to publisher and writer, Leonard Woolf.

**Worsthorne, Claudie:** French former wife of Sir Peregrine Worsthorne who worked with the Free French and General de Gaulle in London and then with Michael Wharton on the Peter Simple column in *The Daily Telegraph*. She married Peregrine Worsthorne and both she and Perry were good friends of the Gilliatts. Claudie died in 1990.

**Worsthorne, Sir Peregrine:** Distinguished Conservative political writer, journalist and a former Editor of *The Sunday Telegraph.*

**Wray, Professor Shirley:** Well-known neuro-opthalmologist with a Chair at Harvard Medical School. An old friend and colleague of Roger Gilliatt and a friend to all the Gilliatts.

**Wyatt, James, c.1864–1813:** Famous Georgian British architect who was commissioned by the Vanneck family to design their family seat, Heveningham Hall in Suffolk. This he did, literally from top to bottom including the furniture.

**Wynn-Parry, Dr Kit:** Neurologist and friend of Roger Gilliatt.

**Yeats, Jack:** A well-known early Twentieth Century Irish painter and brother of W.B. Yeats, the poet. Jack died in 1957 and W.B. Yeats in 1939.

**Young, Liz, Lady Kennet:** Political activist, charity worker, writer and wife of Wayland Young, Lord Kennet and old friend of Roger Gilliatt.

**Young, Wayland, Lord Kennet of the Dene:** Political writer and politician and old friend, along with his wife, of Roger Gilliatt.

**Zuluetta, Father Alphonse de:** Former Catholic Chaplain at Oxford University, later Parish Priest of the Church of the Holy Redeemer, Chelsea, London.

# CHAPTER ONE

# ENTERTAINING BEGINNINGS

F OR A couple of decades or so from the early 1960s, when I was first married, my late husband, Roger Gilliatt, and I entertained a very great deal. Taught the basics by my mother who provided excellent English food and by my father who was an imaginative weekend chef, I much enjoyed cooking and we had had the luck to be given a hundred dozen bottles of carefully chosen wines by my father as a wedding present (to which we added from time to time). We were also fortunate to possess a cellar in the basement of our first house in which to store them properly. Roger, who was rather older than me, had the then newly formed Chair of Clinical Neurology at London University working from the National Hospital for Nervous Diseases, Queen Square. I was a journalist, mainly, by then, specialising in design and architecture and just beginning to work as an interior decorator myself.

In 1960 – although it seems odd now that there had been such a fuss – Roger had had a great deal of unexpected notoriety when he was asked to be Best Man at the wedding of Princess Margaret and Tony Armstrong-Jones, subsequently the Earl of Snowdon. The medical establishment was bemused and embarrassed if not set downright askance by the excess of publicity. But Roger had not been Tony Armstrong-Jones' first choice. Instead, this had been their mutual friend Jeremy Fry, who, for various reasons, had had to bow out and Roger, as a medical academic, was considered a safer choice.

Roger's medical mystique was again somewhat dented by the fact that he had formerly been married to Penelope Gilliatt (then the London *Observer* film critic, later the novelist, short story writer and film critic [jointly with Pauline Kael] for *The New Yorker*). She had subsequently left him and married John Osborne, the original 'angry young man' and pre-eminent 1960s playwright (though never particularly modest about his talents). I remember visiting the Osbornes for the first time in their house in Chester Square and noticing a handsome pile of leather bound books which, in ascending order read: *The Works of Aeschylus, Sophocles, Pliny, Chaucer, Shakespeare, Ibsen, Osborne.*

Through Penelope, Roger had met and remained friends with many people from the media, writing and entertainment fields who joined his own Oxford and medical friends. As well as friends from the 60th Rifle Brigade, aka 'The Green Jackets', his old World War Two army regiment. Also, through his fierce anti-nuclear bomb stance (post the famous Aldermarston Protest March), Roger was acquainted with various politicians and members of the then shadow Labour Cabinet, which came into power in 1964. All of these I was lucky enough to inherit.

As it happened, I had known and respected Penelope for her agile brain and her interestingly arcane way with words when she was Features Editor of British *Vogue* and I was a young, aspiring feature writer on the staff of *House & Garden, Vogue's* sister magazine. For some reason, Penelope, whom I had never met before, had been particularly helpful to me and took my part during the finals of the *Vogue* Talent Contest (then, as now, a kind of annual recruitment vehicle for the Condé Nast magazine group). When, as a runner-up, I had taken up a £5 a week job offer as a feature writer on *House & Garden*, she often passed over invitations and bits of information that she thought would be more appropriate for me to use on *H&G* than for her on *Vogue*. Although I had not actually met Roger until some time after his divorce from Penelope, I had occasionally seen him waiting for her in the evenings outside Vogue House, then in Golden Square, Soho, and had been much taken with his dark good looks, his Mephistophelesian eyebrows and the fact that he came to meet her at all.

After Roger's initial post-divorce hurt and the first few months of our marriage, he and Penelope became at least friends again (she told our future children that she was their 'sort of aunt'). He had always formerly liked John Osborne, so they too became part of our eclectic circle of friends while Penelope and I formed a curious kind of 'Gilliatt wives' association', both in London and New York, which was to last till her death, quite soon after Roger's, in the early 1990s. In fact, I had been so annoyed at the snide and unfair obituaries written about her in both *The New York Times* and *The Times* in England that I had written an indignant letter to both papers which only the former published. It was considered extraordinary that the second wife should be so defensive for the first. Following this, I had some kind letters from various members of the *New Yorker* staff and her great friend Vincent Canby, then film critic of *The New York Times*, who took me to dinner to thank me personally.

Landing on the staff of *House & Garden* aged 20, I had, willy-nilly, to cultivate an interest in design and decoration which, I must own, I had not particularly thought of as a career (although I had been extremely interested in antique furniture since my early teens). What I *had* always wanted was to join a newspaper, most particularly, *The Times.* However that newspaper told me during an interview – about 18 months after joining *House & Garden* – that it was hard to switch from magazines straight to newspapers because the pace was so much more leisurely on the former. I therefore left the magazine and, following the advice of *The Times*, became, for a short period, a copywriter for Everett's Advertising which they said should make one quicker. I was also paid £5 more a week which certainly helped. Whilst there, I was offered a job for £15 a week to copywrite for Harrods (where I was fired for being too flippant) before I joined the staffs in rather quick succession of *The Daily Express*, the now defunct *Daily Sketch* (or *Daily Wretch* as it was often known with good reason, just as the *Express* was *The Daily Excess*), and, eventually, *The Times* (who to my astonishment actually wrote to me out of the blue three years after I had met with them to offer me a job). I was certainly the first and last person to switch from *The Daily Sketch* to the then 'grand old lady of Fleet Street'.

As a matter of fact, I think the best journalistic training I had was on the *Daily Sketch*, at least as far as speedy writing was concerned. We were allotted a subject to write about for the next day at about 4pm, and had to have it written before the first edition went to bed which was around 9 or 10pm. I remember, after some divorce news story or other, being asked to write a piece about whether I would marry a man if I knew he was impotent. Being very young, idealistic, and in those pre-pill days, wholly innocent, I came down on the assertive side and was inundated with mail and proposals of marriage which my hard-bitten male colleagues found very amusing. On the down side, I was made to wait too long and too often in the cold outside people's doors to get a story and ended up with a patch on my lung. At *The Times* everything was a lot more sober. I wrote general features and profiles for the Women's Pages as well as writing about design and architecture, to which, I had become quite wedded.

When *The Sunday Telegraph* was first mooted, I was also offered an irresistibly much better paid job by them (double the money, to be precise) where, although considerably more junior, I was one of the first members of the staff along with Peregrine Worsthorne (later Editor) the late Winefride Jackson (Woman's Editor) and the young

Nigel Lawson (City Editor and later Chancellor of the Exchequer under Margaret Thatcher).

By that time, I had made a good many friends among fellow journalists, architects and designers, and had also subsequently become friends with many of the people I had had the luck to interview, such as the American writer, Carson McCullers who thereafter stayed with me when she visited London (to the detriment of my slender whisky supply); Noni Jabavu, the exotic-looking South African writer, who shared my studio flat for a few months and finally married Michael Crosfield of the Cadbury chocolate family: Geoffrey Clarke, the sculptor and stained-glass artist, who, with his wife Bill, also stayed for a time, laying out his designs for the new windows for the recently re-built Coventry Cathedral on my living room floor.

Noni Jabavu's tenure was equally entertaining in a different way. She was a honeypot for a great many of London's male and married literati who were forever turning up to take her out. On September 1st, the first day of the new oyster season, supposedly one of nature's great aphrodisiacs, she was asked to both lunch and dinner several times over. I cannot imagine now why any of them trusted me to remain discreet about their assignations, the more especially when I knew some of their wives, but I did.

I first met Roger at a dinner party in January, 1963 – literally on the way back from crossing the Berlin Wall between East and West Berlin. I was visiting close friends in Prague at the time and therefore comparatively on the spot, so I was asked by *The Sunday Telegraph* to fly back via Berlin to cover Kruschev's visit – having previously interviewed him in Moscow in 1960 when I had been sent by the paper. But Prague was then, of course, in the Eastern Bloc which meant flying into East Berlin, which curiously I do not think the paper had realised, whereas the Summit was in the West. I was not able to get any East German money so could not get a taxi: the airport was covered in thick snow; I was slipping and sliding humping my own luggage, plus a suitcase full of Czech glasses that I had been given, and I really had no idea about how to even get to the Wall, let alone get across it. Happily, the Moscow correspondent of the leading West German newspaper had also been on the plane, and was looking much as I felt. He was not much more *au fait* about crossing to the other side than I was, but at least he spoke German, had some East German money and we were able to do it together.

The dinner was given by my old *Daily Express* boss, Joy Mathews, who had subsequently married George McWatters (at that time Chairman of Harveys of Bristol, the sherry and wine importers), and because it was black tie and I had no time to go home to change from the airport, I remember that I had had to wriggle gracelessly into evening clothes in a taxi on the way to their house. I was introduced to Roger before dinner. I sat next to him at the table. He gave me a lift home, came in for a coffee and we were married four months later.

Before that I had been engaged to, and amicably disengaged from, Charles Lewis, a young Editor, then with the publishers Allen & Unwin who had later transferred to Oxford University Press. He was the OUP representative for many years in both India and then Pakistan before returning to Oxford where he became a director of the firm. Prior to his publishing career, he had been ADC to the late Sir Andrew Cohen, at that time the Governor of Uganda (who some said was 'the greatest Pro-Consul since ancient Rome'). Charles had not only stayed in touch with several people from those days, notably Tom Mboya, the charismatic (at least I found him so) Kenyan politician and the Tanzanian painter Sam Ntiro and his politically active wife – who I profiled in *The Times* – but also remained firm friends with Sir Andrew and his wife Helen.

The Cohens had taken me under their wing too, and generously kept me there, having me to stay with them in New York on my first visit to that city in 1960, when Andrew was Chairman of the Trusteeship Council at the United Nations. Iain McLeod, then President of the Board of Trade in the Macmillan government was also staying, prior to becoming Minister of State for the Colonies – no doubt on that visit, learning all he could from Andrew's experience. There was talk about McLeod succeeding Macmillan as Prime Minister but he was thought too young. Then, when Macmillan blocked the succession of Rab Butler as the next leader of the Conservative party in favour of Sir Alec Douglas-Home, McLeod stepped down from the cabinet, as did Enoch Powell, and was passed over for a post in the eventual Douglas-Home regime. At the time, he seemed to me to be the model of all that one could hope for in a politician: obviously clever, liberally-minded, unstuffy, witty and able to think out of the box. He became Editor of *The Spectator* for a time, and then zoomed back into political prominence as Chancellor of the Exchequor in the Edward Heath government in 1970. Alas he died that year, all too prematurely, leaving behind a new phrase for the economists, 'Stagflation'. Many people thought that, had he lived, he would have been an inspirational leader.

Through the Cohens, I also met several other politicians and UN staff. As Roger's ex-step-father-in-law, the Australian, George Ivan-Smith – with whom Roger stayed friends – was also Director of Press and Publications for the UN (and a friend of, and spokesman for, the then head of the UN, Dag Hammarskjöld) and he had a couple of other friends and employees of the UN, Bill Henson and Michael Popovic, we had a good many acquaintances in common.

This tedious name-dropping preamble, probably more than a shoe-in for *Private Eye's Pseuds Corner,* is actually only to show how fortunate we were that our joint acquaintance at that period was both wide and eclectic. Roger and I started our married life in my old flat in Flood Street, Chelsea before moving to a large corner house in Thurloe Square, right across from the Victoria & Albert Museum in South Kensington. This was a time when people entertained very much more at home and only very rarely in restaurants. Elizabeth David's books were *de rigueur* for interested amateur cooks, as were (though not quite as strongly) those of the under-estimated Constance Spry, Arabella Boxer, Jane Grigson, Robert Carrier and Marika Hanbury-Tennyson. I was also much attached to *The Sunday Telegraph Cookery Book* written by an old friend, Jean Robertson, who had had the desk next to mine in the *ST* office.

Elizabeth David's sister, Felicity, worked in John Sandoe's eponymous book shop off Sloane Square and one year, as a joke, gave Elizabeth a publisher's bound but blank copy of the new Robert Carrier book for a Christmas present. Seeing only the cover and not yet realising the blankness, Elizabeth, according to Felicity, instantly flared up furiously at the perceived insensitivity, since she thoroughly disliked Mr Carrier and thought him pretentious.

Julia Child's books had not really reached the UK in the early 1960s and names like Delia Smith, Jamie Oliver, Nigel Slater and Nigella Lawson were as yet, of course, unheard of. In fact, Nigella's father, Nigel Lawson, one of the first employees on the then new *The Sunday Telegraph,* and the paper's first City Editor, was at that time already married to his stunning first wife, Vanessa Salmon (Nigella's mother, a member of the old Lyons Corner House family, who died rather young). Then he was a very thin, very intense and palely handsome young man, with a fine ironic wit.

As an inveterate pun lover, I still remember a weekly editorial conference at the latter paper, when the gossipy news came through that Penelope Gilliatt, who had gone off with John Osborne, whose late 1950s play, *Look Back in Anger* had caused an enormous stir, was now getting married to him. 'Good', said Nigel Lawson, 'Now John Osborne can legitimately say that "Good Mornings Begin with Gilliatt"', nicely twisting the then well-known Gillette Razors' shaving slogan: 'Good Mornings begin with Gillette'. I had absolutely no idea of course that I would also become a Gilliatt in the not too distant future. And Nigel Lawson, for his part, could have had absolutely no idea – how could he, or any of us – that, in the next couple of decades, he would become a distinguished but increasingly prosperous-looking, not to say stout, Chancellor of the Exchequer in the future Margaret Thatcher government. Just as no one from that era could have imagined that, after Lawson's resignation from the Treasury, he'd swiftly recover his youthful shape and write a best-selling diet book. Or that one of his future children, Nigella, as clever and easy a writer as she is beautiful, would wow, quite literally, the world of cooking and gain an enthusiastic world-wide readership and TV audience, not to mention the enthusiastic buyers of her licensed merchandise.

In any event, most of my contemporaries actually cooked regularly in those days, rather than doing it vicariously by watching TV cooking programmes (which, except for Fannie Craddock, did not really exist then). The 1960s however, saw the beginning of what were then called the new Colour Supplements, attached to the Sunday newspapers. The menus published in them were all too often used by the same people so that in a couple of weeks of dinner parties one might, for example, get a cold egg and anchovy mousse, followed by roast pigeons and red cabbage, followed by a Pavlova – three times over.

To counter a repeat of this, some of us, in the so-called swinging, revolutionary, but still undoubtedly domesticated 1960s, kept records of our dinner parties – not in the least for posterity but rather to prevent us repeating ourselves with the same people. I was given a red leather-covered entertaining book from the Bond Street stationery store, Smythson's (now also in Sloane Street), as a present on the first Christmas after our marriage. It had a diagram of a table for the placement, a heading to record the guests and other spaces for the menu, the wines, the flowers and the hostess' clothes. It was formulaic but, nevertheless, an easy way to keep a record, and I kept buying the books and filling in the pages as religiously as any diary in the mid-1960s and through the 1970s; then rather more sporadically – rather like the photograph albums that start out with such good intentions but get less and less attended to – both for London entertaining and for our small cottage and then small house in the country.

After that, my life changed radically as I commuted more and more to the US for my books, eventually living there in the mid-1980s, and finally ending up in France. I might easily have lost sight of these records if my elder daughter, Sophia Gilliatt, a determined family archivist, had not preserved them. And they have served me well as the basis of this anecdotal record of those days.

# Mary Gilliatt's Fabulous Food and Friends

Because I was quite a lot younger than many of my friends of the 1960s and 1970s I seem to be, towards the end of the first decade of the Twenty-First Century, one of the dozen or so survivors of that particular circle. (Having dinner a year or so ago, with the splendid journalist and writer Druscilla Beyfuss, widow of Milton Shulman, the film critic and mother of Alexandra Shulman, the current editor of British *Vogue*, she said, 'We *must* stop saying "Isn't it sad that he or she has died, or even remarking that they are still *alive*,''. It's *so* depressing'). Although a good deal has been written and televised about the period and its chief protagonists, both the love-ins and the hate-ins as it were – as well as the various bitter rebellions that followed at the end of the 1960s – I do not often recognize the description of those decades as I had experienced them – at least domestically – nor of the protagonists – at least the ones I knew. I had long wanted to redress the balance but did not quite know how to do it or how to provide an appropriate framework for my anecdotage – this last an all too easy condition in which to fall with advancing years.

The entertaining records therefore, suggested by my daughter Sophia, seemed to provide just such a framework in a fairly elastic way. I could, I thought, describe some of those dinners and lunches year by year; the menus – rather too-well sauced, quite souffléed and tarted out and not all that well-balanced or calorie-conscious by today's standards (some of these recipes can be found at the back of the book, see p. 219). I also list the wines we drank – which now, of course, often sound stupendous, although I stupidly did not record the various producers. Looking back for the first time in years, I was surprised to see that Italian and New World Wines were never mentioned, although some Spanish wines crept in here and there, and how many German wines we *did* drink, which do not seem to be much drunk now. It is interesting too, how I had forgotten how difficult it was in the early and mid-1960s to get things we now take for granted: a choice of potato varieties (and my husband did not think a dinner was really a dinner without potatoes), vegetables like fennel, endives and aubergines, all sorts of herbs and different salads; good olive oil, Parma and Serrano ham, balsamic vinegar, unsalted butter, crème fraîche and good vodka. And cheese at almost every meal? Like most of my generation, and the generation or two before, we were blindly following the esteemed French chef, Brillat-Savarin's homily ('Tyrannical maxim', Elizabeth David called it with her usual fierce felicity) about the bleak deficiency of a meal without cheese.

But, most of all, I wanted to write about the guests. Some well-known, some going to become well-known, and some happily obscure and all the happier for that. Just as there are recipes at the end of the reminiscences, so too there is a glossary of names, and information about those names, in the front of the book. I am embarrassingly conscious that so much of this memoir as I said earlier (but feel the need to repeat) must seem like one long blatant, name drop. But the fact is, that not only were those people our real (and sometimes life-long friends) and not just collected human trophies, but at that time there was no so-called Celebrity Culture. I was quite jolted to see from the dinner books, when I looked at them again, that we entertained some of these 'names' several times a month and went back to their homes just as much. In any case, distinguished as some of them were, they were very different from the current 'celebrities' – not that they would ever have thought of themselves in that way – who are mostly in sports or music, pop culture, movies or modelling and, one way or another, almost always on TV. But in any case, caught in the moment, or a moment, one often forgets the monumental truth of *sic transit gloria*. So come to think of it, I suppose only my own generation and possibly the next one would know what I was going on about. I doubt that many young people today have even heard of, and certainly not registered, most of the people mentioned. I was startled recently to hear an intelligent woman in her forties ask who Spike Milligan was? 'Was he a star of the silent movies?' Spike, a huge admirer of Buster Keaton may even have been delighted, if rather bemused, to hear it.

The time was sociologically very different from now. It was still quite normal for all sorts of people to gather around the radio to listen to a Reith Lecture or a Royal Albert Hall Prom concert, as opposed to religiously watching TV reality shows today. A great deal of the entertaining was totally different too and somehow – I cannot now imagine why – there seemed to be more time to regularly eat and chat with one's friends and family and still get one's work done. Roger had grown up in large London houses with nine indoor servants. After the war, my parents had first a live-in maid and then a couple working in the house. Once I had children, I was lucky enough to have a nanny. I also had a cleaning lady and early on, in Thurloe Square (before we had children), a young Portugese worker, a refugee from the enforced military service of the Salazar regime. But, otherwise, I was the working mother replacement for my parents-in-law's former nine helpers.

Incidentally, I realise that I wrote the menus down in a peculiar mixture of English and restaurant French, sometimes one, sometimes the other and, sometimes, a mixture. But that was how so many menus seemed to be written in those days: not just what may now seem a pretentious *folie de grandeur* on my part. Or maybe it was. Or maybe

I just wrote the first thing that came into my mind. Anyway, one hopefully gets less pretentious with age when it's mostly too late to pretend about anything.

Writing about so many of our then friends with the advantage of hindsight and the benefit – or sadness – of knowing their future so many decades later was a curious, nostalgic, and sometimes upsettingly disturbing experience. But at the very least, it seemed to me, it could be a good social record of the food and mores of those years, entwined with the various events of those decades just as they happened. A little way through starting to write tentative notes around these gustatory and anecdotal reminiscences that rereading all the old menus released, I read Nigel Slater's engaging and deservedly best-selling memoir *Toast* (Fourth Estate, 2003) which is also based around food. Unlike Mr. Slater's memoir, this book is not based around my life engendered by reminiscences of food, or only a small incidental part of it, but it is definitely based around dining and lunching *occasions*, long gone but re-remembered, which in turn, engendered other good and not so good memories. How curiously patchy and frustrating our minds become as we get older with such clear long-term memories and such frequent short-term temporary blanks. How I wish there was some sort of pocket modem or a WiFi memory stick for the mind that would be as useful and as quick for dredging up facts from our memories as 'googling' on the internet or smart phones.

Finally, I could not resist ending this reminiscence of those meals with friends with a dinner I gave just before one Christmas for the occupants of the very small street in the village in France where I now live – again thanks to my elder daughter, Sophia. Their métiers and their lives were and are altogether different from my English, American and Antipodean friends, but their conversation, I have to report, was every bit as good.

# CHAPTER TWO

# THURLOE SQUARE, 1964

IN JANUARY 1964, I was six months pregnant with our first child, Sophia, and we gave several small dinners, rather than any large ones, mostly for various family members, close old friends and visiting neurologists and colleagues of Roger. In fact, I see from the dinner books that, pregnant or not, this turned out to be a regular pattern interspersed occasionally with larger dinners and the odd party. We very, very rarely took anyone out to a restaurant or went to a restaurant ourselves. Our roomy mid-Nineteenth Century house in Thurloe Square was excellent for entertaining with a large dining room which had a working fireplace – much-used on cold evenings – a good-sized kitchen, utility room and cloakroom on the ground floor; a pleasant book-lined study halfway up the stairs; and a graceful aquamarine-painted L-shaped drawing room with French windows plus a balcony overlooking the leafy square garden and, to the right, the Victoria and Albert Museum. Another long window at the other end of the room overlooked our own paved garden to the side of the building.

This room took up the entire first floor and was a natural party space. Opposite the door as you entered the room, was a very large gilt mirror behind a grassy-green Victorian *chaise longue* that I had bought, as an early and precocious teenager (at least as far as antique furniture was concerned). I had used my weekly pocket money on a ridiculously reasonable 'never-never' arrangement with an obliging and extremely trusting antique dealer. Opposite it was a pretty Regency cabinet which I had obtained in the same way. In front of the window, overlooking our garden, was the black lacquered Steinway baby grand piano that Captain Scott had reputedly, and somewhat curiously, taken on board his ship *The Discovery* to the Antarctic. It had belonged to Wayland Young (Lord Kennet of the Dene though, at that time, he rarely used the title) the son of Captain Scott's widow, who had later

55

married Lord Kennet, Wayland's father. He had sold it to Roger before our marriage for £50.

On the back wall of the fireplace-end of the room, a decorator friend of the 1960s, Paul Anstee, had designed us a large, pedimented bookcase with cupboards underneath for the sound system and drinks. There was also both a club fender in front of the fireplace and a large upholstered stool for extra seating between the fireplace and the long sofa, which did double duty as a coffee table. There were arm and occasional chairs and a good-looking early-Nineteenth Century sofa table behind the sofa, as well as some side tables. The aquamarine walls looked cool in summer – when I always used several large plants, as well as white flowers and masses of leaves on the *Bonheur du jour* desk between the French windows – and warm and sparkly in winter (when I swapped the white flowers for red and used plenty of candles along with the firelight).

The dining room was dramatic in a 1960s way, with a white vinyl tiled floor, mossy-khaki covered hessian walls, and black lacquered James II chairs around a large, round green marble-topped table. The lighting, even then, consisted of early recessed ceiling spots on dimmers, many candles and the flickering firelight when appropriate. The spectacular Eighteenth Century green and white marble fireplace had been installed by the previous owners who, to their dismay, were not allowed to take it with them when they left since it had inevitably become a fixture. This was sad for them but undoubtedly fortunate for us. I loved the house. In fact, it was the first London house ever to be featured in *Country Life* – an unexpected honour, especially as they ran the feature over two issues.

### JANUARY 16th, 1964

**DINNER:** *Dr John Walton (later Lord Walton of Detchant)*

One of the small dinners we gave in early January was for a neurological colleague of Roger's who had a most distinguished academic career. He later became, first, the Professor of Neurology at Newcastle University and then the second warden of the original Green College, Oxford, now called Green Templeton College, the graduate school first named after Dr Cecil Green, founder of Texas Instruments and his wife, Dr Ida Green.

At that time though, many years earlier, John was a full-time academic neurologist working with Professor Henry Miller at Newcastle

# Thurloe Square, 1964

University and had already published an impressive number of books on his subject. I particularly remember the freezing – but bracing – walks taken during a weekend spent at John and (the now late) Betty Walton's cottage in Detchant, Northumberland in that stunning moorland landscape with the Duke of Northumberland's Alnwick Castle, looming in the misty distance. It was the perfect place to choose as the setting for Hogwart's 'School of Witchcraft and Wizardry' in the *Harry Potter* movies and clever of the producers to think of it.

But my chief memory of that first recorded dinner, in the first of the dinner books, was of John, the proud moustached author, looking more like a banker than a doctor, standing in front of the fire in the drawing room at Thurloe Square, ruminatively swirling a glass of wine and saying: "It's a curious thing looking back, but do you realise I wrote all my first nine books in longhand?"

**The Menu was:**

*Jerusalem Artichoke Soup* (p. 219)

*Escalopes of Veal Panées*

*Spinach with Lemon, Olive Oil and Garlic*

*Soufflé Potatoes and Tomatoes stuffed with Duxelles of Mushrooms*

*Cheeses*

*Fruit*

The wine was an impressive – and probably meant to impress – Chambolle-Musigny 1949, even then, handsomely aged.

## FEBRUARY 13th, 1964

**DINNER:** *Elizabeth and Guy Scott*
*Constance Green*

Elizabeth (Betty) and Guy Scott were old friends of my parents who, to their children's advantage, were determined, or perhaps just instinctive, mixers of the generations, and I had known the Scotts since I was 10-years-old or younger. Guy was a stockbroker in his family firm. The still glamorous Elizabeth, in a 1940s way, had first been one of

Sir Anthony Eden's administrative assistants and then a long-standing speech writer during his time as Foreign Secretary during Churchill's wartime coalition government as well as during Churchill's 1951 government and finally during his brief but tumultuous period as Churchill's successor as Prime Minister. Eden's Premiership had encompassed the Suez Crisis in 1956 when he took the contentious decision to bomb Egyptian forces and to deploy British troops after Colonel Nasser's abrupt nationalisation of the Suez Canal. In effect, this invasion was as hotly and bitterly disputed in 1956 in the UK as the Iraq War. The Americans, along with most of the world, were strongly against the British action.

The Scott's had a large and beautiful Eighteenth Century house in Polstead, West Suffolk, near where I grew up, in what was known as 'Constable Country' after the painter, John Constable who painted so many memorably green and tranquil landscapes under the great bowl of the East Anglian sky. However, peaceful Polstead had more sinister connotations in that it was also the village where 'The Red Barn' was situated, the site of the famous Nineteenth Century murder of a village girl, Maria Martin; a bloody legend (always known as 'The Red Barn Murder') which I saw re-enacted with gory relish as part of a Harvest Festival in that very barn.

Although well this side of discretion, Elizabeth nearly always had delectable political gossip to recount, the more particularly after Anthony Eden's abrupt resignation from the premiership for health reasons after less than two years in office. This was, in some ways, unsurprising because his health had already been seriously undermined by overwork during his wartime Foreign Office appointment. After his retirement, Elizabeth felt able to tell tales of his apparently frightening, hysterical rages and increasingly eccentric behavior. As I mentioned, the whole business of the Suez Canal had been extraordinarily divisive for the country.

Constance Green was my mother: a strongly religious, humorous but shy woman who, along with my father, Arthur Green, were generous hosts who had given their three children not only an excellent education but a strong schooling in, and enjoyment of, entertaining, Shy as Constance was, she was nevertheless an ardent feminist and, in 1943, had proposed for the first time the motion 'Equal Pay for Equal Work' at the Women's Institute Annual Conference at the Royal Albert Hall in London. Alas, though hard to believe now, she was constantly heckled during the speech which was also regularly interrupted by demands for her to speak up. It was an experience which gave her nightmares for the rest of her long life. When, just before she died in

2001, she was approached by the historian of the Women's Institute for an interview about this now historic occasion, she categorically refused a meeting and remained depressed by the resurgence of memories of the event for the next few days. She was, however, rather interested in the fact that, years later, her elder daughter helped Gloria Steinem, the much admired feminist writer and founder of *MS* magazine, with her apartment in New York.

Interestingly too, I heard recently from a feminist historian that the W.I. was, at that time, a strong advocate in the campaign for a 'family wage'. That is to say that it was no use a women expecting equitable wages because wages were supposed to reflect family responsibilities of which a working woman had none, since she should not be in the work place anyway when her correct role was running the home. This was tough on any women who wanted, or had, to work, and particularly widows and the unmarried. 'She must have been a brave young woman', the historian concluded.

**The Menu was:**

*Spinach Soufflé with Anchovy Sauce* (p. 220)

*Carbonnade de Boeuf* (p. 221)

*Baked Potatoes and Sour Cream*

*Salad of Red Pepper, Endive and Avocado*

*Cheese*

*Syllabub* (p. 222)

**FEBRUARY 23rd, 1964**

**DINNER:** *Bill and Maria Henson*
        *Claudie Worsthorne*

Bill and Maria Henson were an odd but interesting couple. Bill, later a godfather to our son, Tom (born 1967 and currently Director of Non-Fiction at Pan Macmillan in Australia) was at that time the urbane, lanky, always elegantly dressed and constantly pipe-smoking head of Public Relations at the UN headquarters in New York. Enigmatic, very short, very nervous, slightly plump Maria was a hugely talented freckled and red-headed Russian photographer, also attached to the UN. Their liaison, during what was, after all, the height of the Cold War, was regarded with alarm in many quarters. Living in New York, they were conscious of constant and irritating surveillance, from both Russians and Americans and probably English too, although they went on with their day-to-day life determinedly undeterred. Bill, a stalwart socialist, had a ready, risqué wit, as sharp as Maria's black and white photographic portraits and was unashamedly non P.C. when the irresistible opportunity came to make a joke. He was also a dedicated punster. At a time when there had been some newspaper comment about untoward homosexual behavior in St James' Park with some of the inhabitants of the Guards' Barracks, Bill drawled through his pipe 'Oh my *dear*, I hear that there are fairies at the bottoms of our guardsmen.'

Claudie Worsthorne, then married to Peregrine Worsthorne, the consciously foppishly elegant political columnist – and at that time Assistant Editor of *The Sunday Telegraph* – was French, and had originally come to London in World War Two as a member of de Gaulle's Free French staff. After the war, she stayed on in London and joined the late Michael Wharton's team on the hilarious Peter Simple column in *The Daily Telegraph*. Small, with a fringe almost covering her brown, quizzical eyes, the dedicatedly cynical and memorably husky Claudie, had a mordant sense of humour, made even more mordant-sounding by her smoky Edith Piaf voice. Claudie had become a particularly dear friend after a trip she, Roger and I had taken to Egypt with the ICA (The Institute of Contemporary Arts) in 1963, soon after Roger and I met, and just before the historic moving of Abu Simbel.

On the paddle steamer, on the way down the sluggish Nile to the site of the temple, Roger and I, as yet unmarried, were not allowed by the Egyptian owners to share a cabin. Therefore, Claudie and I crowded into a miniscule four-bunk space with the equally mordant and equally husky-voiced legendary American beauty, Lee Miller, a brilliant photographer, peripatetic lover and ex-*Vogue* war correspondent. In fact, although the words War and *Vogue* seem totally antipathetic, Miller was the only female combat photo-journalist to cover World War Two and was at the liberation of Buchenwald – which must have caused her nightmares ever after – as well as the destruction of Hitler's Bavarian home. There is a well-known photograph of her lying triumphantly in Hitler's bath, I'm not quite sure why. But, like most soldiers with bitter combat experience, she rarely talked about her war memories.

# THURLOE SQUARE, 1964

Lee, a little raddled by now, but none the worse for that for someone who had not seen her in her glory days, had been the mistress and muse of the American Dadaist-Surrealist Man Ray in the late 1920s, as well as his assistant and collaborator, and been painted several times by Picasso. After the Man Ray period and marriage with an Egyptian during the 1930s, she had met, in 1939 in Paris, Roland Penrose, also a friend of Man Ray and the co-founder, with Sir Herbert Read, of The Institute of Contemporary Arts. Roland was well-known as a British Surrealist painter as well as an avid Collector of Modern Art. Lee finally married him after the War in 1947. But he was currently unavoidably absent from the trip. Instead, she was travelling with her American friend, the rather beautiful – and on that boat – appropriately Nefertiti-like, Bettina McNulty, wife of the gregarious and equally unavoidably absent, American publicist, Henry McNulty. I hope the often caustic, cynical but generous and witty Lee Miller would have been gratified to be the subject of a much admired retrospective exhibition of her photographic portraits at the National Portrait Gallery 42 years later in the Spring of 2005, and the long running retrospective of her works and life at the Victoria & Albert Museum, as well as, of course, the several biographies. Neither she nor Roland Penrose had thought to promote her former work and she apparently became very depressed after she gave up photography, took up cooking, and started to drink. Her son, Anthony, single-handedly revived her image and her work, and the V&A, in its introduction to her retrospective, called her one of the leading female icons of the Twentieth Century.

Bettina too, worked with Condé Nast and was an American *House & Garden* alumni ('Have you put your children down for Condé Nast?' used to be the jokey catchword for both contemporary and ex-Condé Nast writers. In fact I think my daughter Annie and I still share the record for mother/daughter Condé Nast Talent Contest runners-up). Like Lee Miller, Bettina was an outstanding cook. The McNulty's often cooked and entertained together with the Penroses at Farley Farm, the latter's farmhouse in Sussex. Together, too, they cooked an extraordinarily delicious Middle-Eastern dinner in the Penroses' London home some months later in a get-together of our ICA group.

Claudie was to become the god-mother of one of our future children, in this case, our daughter Annie (now Constantine). The previous November, only three months or so before this particular evening (and long before mobile phones, of course) Perry and Claudie were coming to dine when the telephone rang. The call was for Perry who had been out of the office all day, from the news desk at *The Sunday*

*Telegraph.* I asked if I could give him a message as soon as he arrived and the caller had said 'Yes. Tell him President Kennedy has just died in Dallas. We have to talk to him.' Like almost everybody who first heard that news and can remember vividly what they were doing at that precise moment, I can remember standing shocked and devastated in the hall. Busy cooking for the dinner, I had not even known that Kennedy had been shot.

**The Menu was:**

*Shrimp Cocktail* (pp. 223–224)

*Fillet de Boeuf Roti*

*Sauce Béarnaise*

*Pommes Dauphinoise*

*Cheese*

*Mont Blanc en Surprise* (p. 224)

And the wine was Nuits St. Georges, 1949.

**MARCH 1st, 1964**

**KITCHEN SUPPER:** *Terence and Caroline Conran*

Like the dining room, the Thurloe Square kitchen was generously-sized with a battered old pine table and old pine dresser and good for informal suppers and lunches as well as purely family eating. The window looked out over our garden which was separated from the house at the back by the railinged area surrounding the basement-flat like a deep, dry moat. I mention this because, a few nights later, after another dinner party, we had taken a car-less friend home after our charming new Portuguese worker, José – a refugee, as I mentioned in the introduction – had gone out after washing everything up, leaving all the glasses to dry on the window sill. (Roger felt happier having a helpful guy around the house when he was away and, in any case, we had been asked to give him a job).

When we returned to the house, we found we had both forgotten our keys. Luckily, the garden door had carelessly been left unlocked and we saw that the kitchen window was open a crack from the bottom. Intrepidly, Roger took the ladder out of the garden shed, balanced it between the railings and the outside windowsill, crawled across it and gingerly pushed up the window (to the accompanying tinkle of most of the glasses breaking). He then climbed over the sink, miraculously avoiding the broken glass, went through the kitchen and opened the front door. I, meanwhile, had watched terrified, knowing that if he fell off the ladder to the area below, there would be no way, at eight months pregnant, that I could get to him and would have to try to summon help from someone in the square at 2am. Not for the first time I could easily understand how he had been intrepid enough to win the Military Cross and Mentions in Dispatches during World War Two, although he always said that he just got so furious and upset after friends had been killed that he simply did not care what he did.

At that time, Terence Conran was about to open the first of his Habitat chain of stores selling his young, fun, affordable furniture and versions of the fashionable Italian designer furniture by Magistretti and others, all made in his factory in East Anglia. Before the furniture manufacturing, he had been running his first restaurant venture in the form of down to earth 'Soup Kitchens', presumably little imagining, as the furniture retail mogul he was beginning to be then, that he would also have an extraordinarily successful second career as a restaurateur so many years later. Caroline, Terence's third wife – as Caroline Herbert – was a blithe, funny and immensely attractive general writer as well as writing on food for *Queen* Magazine, prior to it becoming *Harper's and Queen*. (A fact that, curiously, Terence seemed to have forgotten about in their rather public divorce hearing over 25 years later, when he announced – hopefully, because he was flustered – that all she had done in their partnership 'was cook a few meals' – not mentioning the many books she'd written or her terrific and selfless early support for him in every possible way).

Roger had known Terence during his second marriage to Shirley Conran, the fabric designer-turned-journalist and novelist (I still remember how good her designs were) – and I had read, just before I met Roger, that she had become engaged to him – which was not at all true according to Roger. But she *had* held her most recent marriage reception in his flat in Lowndes Square. Purely fortuitously, as he was driving by one evening, Roger managed to scoop Terence and his car off an unfortunate collision with the Cadogan Square railings – a rescue that evidently Terence never forgot because he brought up the whole incident, greatly dramatised, with my daughter Sophia at a meeting, only quite recently, some 50 years later. I knew and admired

Caroline as a journalist and was very fond of her as a friend: I was fond of them both. She and Terence had married at much the same time as Roger and I and we were both imminently expecting our first children. Terence already had two young sons, Sebastian and Jasper, by Shirley. In fact, I had been having supper with Terence and Caroline in their then Fitzroy Square flat when an envelope was pushed under the door announcing Shirley's forthcoming marriage to John Stevenson, Terence's then Managing Director, so rather too close to home. It was not a happy end to the evening.

**The Menu was:**

*Hard Boiled Eggs Stuffed with Tuna* (p. 226)

*Breaded Lamb Cutlets*

*Mashed Potatoes with Olive Oil*

*Puréed Spinach*

*Cheese*

*Blackcurrant Leaf Sorbet* (p. 226)

And the wine was Moulin à Vent, 1959.

**MARCH 15th, 1964**

**DINNER:** *Wayland and Liz Young*
*Elaine Dundy*

Wayland Young (Lord Kennet of the Dene – such a romantic-sounding title) and his wife, Liz, were passionate nuclear disarmers, passionately involved socialists, had a great many children and lived in J.M. Barrie's old house at 100, Bayswater Road. At that time, Liz used to arouse a good deal of attention when she breast-fed one or other of her many babies in public whenever and wherever she happened to be – a very common occurrence now, but absolutely not then. It was Wayland who had sold to Roger the previously mentioned Steinway grand piano that had improbably accompanied Captain Scott on his voyage to the Antarctic, which now stood in the corner of our drawing room evidently none the worse for its freezing maritime adventures. When we subsequently bought a small house in the country and a smaller house in London there was no room, alas, for the piano, and it was sold back to Wayland and Liz for the same peripatetic £50 which was typical of Roger's determinedly gentlemanly code. Wayland, like Tony Wedgwood-Benn when in government, and Prime Minister, Gordon Brown, had a then well-known aversion to dinner jackets. I can even remember meeting Tony Wedgwood-Benn actually going back to change into a corduroy suit one night when he was due at a black tie dinner.

American Elaine Dundy, waifish and wry (a little like Carson McCullers, I always thought), had recently had a tempestuous divorce from Ken Tynan (the very clever, very controversial *Observer* Theatre critic, a friend of Roger's from his Oxford days, and a particular friend of his ex-wife, Penelope). But it was hard for both of them to let go of a marriage that had happy highs as well as bitter lows. The Tynans were known by some as the 'Zelda and Scott Fitzgerald' of their day because of their renowned and exausting fights and Elaine was the author of the best-selling *The Dud Avocado* which had been a huge success on both sides of the Atlantic and had a lot of resonance for me. I had read it admiringly when a student in Paris, never imagining for one moment of course, that I would ever be friends with its author.

Elaine's new novel, *The Old Man and Me* had just been published in London and she celebrated the occasion by dolefully drinking a very great deal of champagne all on her own with us one Sunday morning. Prior to their on-off divorce and this rather mournful occasion, she and Ken, when they did occasionally come together, gave what seemed to me at that time, wonderfully raffish parties at their flat in Mount Street, right by the Connaught Hotel. These parties had as their backdrop a huge blown-up reproduction of an especially macabre Hieronymus Bosch painting, which covered one whole wall, and were continued by Ken with his new partner, Kathleen Halton. In fact, we saw in the election of the first Harold Wilson government under the very same Hieronymus Bosch later that autumn.

I always remember that election because, as one of the very small group of Labour voters in the Royal Borough of Kensington and Chelsea, I had volunteered to help (yes, I know, I know. Talk about Latté Liberals). In one council block, trying to get an answer from someone with a line of milk bottles outside the door, a neighbour popped out and said quite matter-of-factly, 'I 'aven't seen her in days dear. But she's very old ain't she. Just look at all them bottles. She's probably dead, dear.' And she shut her door firmly. One hectic morning, just before Election Day, I was asked to drive a particularly articulate young man around to bestir possible voters. I was not given his name and, thinking he was just another volunteer, I said to him in the course of the day 'You know so much about politics, are you thinking of standing yourself one day?' 'I *am* the candidate' he replied to this obvious dolt of a woman.

**The Menu was:**

*Oeufs Mollets on a Bed of Buttered Spinach* (p. 227)

*Tourte Bourguignonne* (p. 228)

*Salad of Lettuce Hearts with a Warm Butter and Tarragon Dressing* (p. 229)

*Cheese*

*Glacé au Melon de l'le St. Jacques* (p. 230)

And the wine was a simple Moulin à Vent, 1960.

**MARCH 29th, 1964**

**DINNER:** *Terence and Caroline Conran*
*Bill and Maria Henson*
*Mary Brogan*

Looking in the dinner book for that March, I see that we seemed to have had a couple of old friends or colleagues to dinner almost every night up until the end of the month, culminating in a final dinner with the Conrans, the Hensons (over for a week or two from New York) and Mary Brogan, a fellow journalist, a good friend and daughter of the Catholic apologist and writer, Colm Brogan. I say final because both Caroline and I gave birth to our first children a few days later: Caroline to Tom Conran and I to my daughter, Sophia Gilliatt, now a successful wine consultant and entertainment maven in her own right. Clearly, judging by the Schnapps and most especially the stunning wine listed, there were not too many strictures on alcohol for pregnant ladies in those days. Maybe we were both circumspect, though I doubt it. Caroline and I were both so pregnant that I longed for a table with the practical semi circles cut out to accommodate larger stomachs like those the 'Fatty Puffs' had in that memorable 1930s book by André Maurois, translated as *Fatty Puffs and Thinifers*.

66

# THURLOE SQUARE, 1964

**The Menu was:**

*Taramosalata with Schnapps* (p. 231)

*Roast Contrefilet with Sauce Béarnaise*

*Pommes Anna* (p. 231)

*Cheese*

*Salad*

*Fruit*

And the wine was a Château Calon Segur, 1937.


## MAY 3rd, 1964

**DINNER:** *Eden and Marston Fleming*
*Peregrine and Claudie Worsthorne*

This was the first actual dinner party we gave after the birth of our daughter, Sophia on April 6th and her subsequent christening lunch for family and godparents on April 24th.

Marston Fleming, born in Canada, had the Chair of Mineral Engineering and was also the distinguished-looking and distinguished Dean (and later Pro-Rector) of Imperial College in London. His wife Eden, was a well-known Primitive painter of the time who worked under the name of E. Box. They were a deeply devoted couple who had both considered themselves happily married enough until they happened to meet each other and had a mutual *coup de foudre*. They entertained generously and eclectically in their totally wisteria-covered house in Montpelier Square. (Among other people we met with them were Leslie Caron, the actress, and her then husband, Peter Hall – the founder and director of the Royal Shakespeare Company in 1960 at the age of 29 and later Director of The National Theatre from 1973 to 1988). Eden's best friend, the writer and traveller, Lesley Blanch and the great political novelist Arthur Koestler and his wife, who also visited us, as did Lesley Blanch and, sometime later, Warren Beatty with Leslie Caron, who had by then moved on from Peter Hall. On that particular occasion, my wonderfully absent-minded Professor husband sat next to Leslie Caron and hardly addressed a word to her although she was looking ravishing. He was much too engrossed in an across-the-table scientific chat with Marston. I, on the other hand made the most of sitting next to Warren Beatty.

The Flemings later moved to a graceful Regency house and garden overlooking the Thames in Strand-on-the-Green where they hung a Monet water lily painting (inherited from Arthur Jeffries, Eden's gallery owner), on top of a green-painted trellis, over a sky blue painted wall, in a kind of conservatory addition off their drawing room. It was a memorable juxtaposition mostly occasioned however, by the fact that they wanted the painting to meld in with its background because they could not afford the hideously expensive insurance.

Eden's previous surname had been Van Dyke which was not a particularly apposite signature for a new painter or indeed, for a painter of her deliberately naïve style. So since Marston often, for some unexplained reason, called her Box she chose E. Box as her alias. Her paintings of melting-eyed lions and other animals in appropriate Garden of Eden-like settings were wholly original and she knew several gallery owners including Arthur Jeffries. She was a modest, though idiosyncratically attractive, and rather bold-looking woman in a slightly gypsy-ish way and did not want to put any of her art dealer friends in the embarrassing position of feeling they should take her on, or turn her down for that matter. She was not, however, unambitious. On a night when Arthur Jeffries was coming to dine, she left out one of her latest paintings and showed it to him fibbing that it was by her local green grocer – or perhaps butcher – who was something of an amateur painter and what did he think? What he thought was that he liked it very much indeed, but he had just finalised the hanging of an exhibition of Primitive painters. Perhaps, if her grocer – or butcher – agreed, he could take the painting and put it on a centre table in the gallery?

A day or so after the show opened, Mr Jeffries called Eden to say that the painting had sold almost immediately and that there was much demand from visitors to the gallery for more paintings by the same artist. Could she get some? She hurried to the gallery with several more which sold quickly in their turn until she was cleared out of her stock and was reduced to painting others in a hurry, the paint still damp, especially for the show. In the end, of course, she was forced to confess the subterfuge and she always exhibited in the Arthur Jeffries Gallery from then on.

Perry Worsthorne wrote his political columns and comments, we used to think, like an angel, whatever one thought of those politics – and I was always interested when we went to their parties by the number of friends he had, clearly very fond of him, who had utterly opposing views. I was also interested by the fact that everyone in his immediate family had a different last name. His father, born with the Belgian name Koch de Gooreynd, had apparently anglicised the surname to Worsthorne in the early 1920s – though he was the only family member to change it back. When he did so in 1937 *before* the Second World War, many people with purportedly alien, but not necessarily German, names were rushing to get them anglicised. His first wife, from whom he was divorced only a few years after Perry was born, became much involved with local government in London and was President of the Women's Voluntary Services (WVS) as well as the World Federation of Mental Health. She was also a granddaughter of the 7th Earl of Abingdon, and her mother, Perry's grandmother, inherited part of their Towneley estate in Lancashire. Some years later, it passed to Simon Worsthorne, Perry's older brother, on the condition that he changed his family name to Towneley. In the early 1930s, his mother was remarried to Sir Montague Norman, later Lord Norman, who became the Governor of the Bank of England. Voila, a different name for each family member.

(I cannot, by the way, imagine why I served two wine and honey sauces.)

**The Menu was:**

*Taramosalata with Schnapps*

*Roast Young Ducks with Wine, Orange and Honey Sauce* (p. 232)

*Young Peas and New Potatoes*

*Salad of Lettuce Hearts*

*Pears Poached in Red Wine, Honey and Cloves* (p. 232)

And the wine was Château Clinet, 1953.

## MAY 9th, 1964

**DINNER:** *Spike and Paddy Milligan*
*Liz Young/Kennet (Wayland was away)*

The late Spike Milligan, member of the popular *Goon Show* of the 1950s and 1960s, and much admired comedian and writer, was married to Paddy, a beautiful, forthright, statuesque former singer from Yorkshire whom he had met when she was singing in the chorus of *The Sound of Music*. Though Spike had bipolar disease and suffered greatly from depression – and others suffered horribly from his bouts of disconcerting behaviour when he was not being manically funny – Paddy was funny all the time, sometimes howlingly so, a great mimic and a dear, dear friend. I remember her putting on one of my children's toy Viking helmets and belting out a Wagner Brünnhilde solo at the top of her voice with everyone collapsing in helpless giggles all around. And I remember a very tussled Spike turning up in his pyjamas and dressing gown on our doorstep about 3am one morning having escaped from some nursing home or other. As Roger opened the door after some maniacal ringing of the bell, Spike said, 'I just came to say that if anyone wants to know what I want to be in the after life, tell them it's dead'. And stalked off again. Not so very different from the purported message on his gravestone: 'I told you I was ill.' In fact, the Chichester Dioscese in charge of the Parish of Winchelsea, Sussex, where he was buried, had refused to allow any such inscription.

Spike became a godfather to our second daughter, Annie Constantine, along with Paul Reilly and Kenneth Bradshaw and I became godmother to Spike and Paddy's daughter, Jane. We saw a great deal of each other until Paddy heartbreakingly died of cancer in the mid-1970s and Spike finally married again. When Spike's parents (old music hall devotees, who lived in Woi Woi, New South Wales, just up the coast from Sydney), came over from Australia for visits, Spike and Paddy often used to bring them over for Sunday night suppers, which almost invariably ended with Spike's father playing Captain Scott's piano and everybody standing around singing old music hall numbers.

Liz Young was a full-on partner for Wayland and managed to serve on a creditable number of committees despite her large family. I always felt that they both regretted that I had replaced the brilliant Penelope. They never could remember whether I wrote about cooking or design – or anyway something boringly domestic. And here I am, after all these years, finally writing about food, though I was asked to do a stint on a long-departed magazine called *Nova* when Elizabeth David gave it up. Coming after Elizabeth David would be like coming after God, so I said I would do it until they got someone proper – which, luckily, they did very quickly.

**The Menu was:**

*Pâté de foie gras truffé*

*Veal Goulash* (p. 233)

*Baked Potatoes and Sour Cream*

*Lettuce Salad*

*Cheeses*

*Fruit*

# THURLOE SQUARE, 1964

And the wines were (Spike was a known wine-lover and I obviously wanted to please him): Château Climens, Sauternes, 1953 with the foie gras and Château Pontet-Canet, Bordeaux, 1937.

## MAY 22nd, 1964

**DINNER:** *Max and Joan Reinhardt*

I was interested to meet Max because I knew he had been married to Margaret Leighton, an actress whom I much admired but who had died early of cancer. Max and his new American wife, Joan, the daughter of a leading American industrialist, were at that time just neighbours down the road and this was a return, getting-to-know-each-other-better, quiet little dinner for their initial welcoming hospitality. Like Marston and Eden Fleming they had a large and eclectic circle of friends and were generous hosts. As it turned out, this was a significant evening for me because Max was a publisher, and now ran the distinguished old firm of Bodley Head which published such luminaries as Solsynitzen, Graham Greene, William Trevor and Charlie Chaplin. In fact, a year or so later, Max and Joan asked us to dinner with the last three. I was in awe of both Graham Greene and William Trevor but Charlie Chaplin (looking unexpectedly well-dressed, moustache-less, dignified, shaggily white-haired and a bit taller than I had imagined), apparently adored pregnant woman and, as I was pregnant with our next daughter, kept caressing my burgeoning stomach. But that future evening is indelibly ingrained in my memory because the Reinhardts had just moved to this practically all white and pristine house and, after dinner, I spilt a whole cup of black coffee all over the white sofa and white carpet, to my horrified embarrassment.

I sent flowers with an abject letter of apology. I offered to have the carpet and sofa professionally cleaned. I would have replaced the wretched sofa and carpet if I could have done so. But I know that Joan never forgot the incident (and I probably would not have done so either in her place) because, some 20 odd years later, on a visit to London from New York, I saw her in a local South Kensington shop. We had a pleasant enough chat recalling old friends when I said again how bad I had always felt about making such an awful mess in her new drawing room. Her face clouded. 'Uhmmmm,' she said. 'Goodness. I did not realize the time. Must rush. Lovely to see you'.

But, on that particular dinner with them in Thurloe Square on a warm early Summer evening, Max saw the inside of our house for the

71

first time and, talking about my journalistic work, began, apparently, to consider the possibility of asking me to write a book on decorating – at a time when very few such books existed. He did not actually commission me to write a book until the next year, but that book was *English Style*, which was taken up in the US by Viking, by Mondadori in Italy and Pont Royal in France (mostly, I suspect, because Princess Margaret had actually asked if I would like to include their newly decorated part of Kensington Palace, especially her beloved rose pink bathroom with the tongue-in-cheek loo inset into an old throne on a dais). I remember that bathroom so well because, one evening after a dinner at Kensington Palace with just the four of us, she asked me if I wanted to come up stairs to freshen up. When we were in the bathroom she asked if I wanted to go to the loo. I said yes but, to my bourgeoise horror, she just said 'Well, do use it then,' pointing to the throne but showed absolutely no sign of leaving. 'Go on,' she said, brushing her hair. But although I obediently sat there, I simply could not do it, so had to pretend and flush quickly.

That aside, this was the book which launched my career as a writer, decorator and consultant and, indeed, the whole list of country and city 'style' books that have been with us ever since. It was the first decorating book, and maybe the last, to get a whole half page review in *The New Yorker*. But I always suspected the hidden and generous hand of Penelope Gilliatt for that honour. I actually suggested, to both Bodley Head and Viking in the US, that we should go on and create a whole such series on other countries' styles but, in spite of *English Style's* success, both publishers rejected the idea saying there was no call for books about other country's decorating ... As indeed did my next US publisher, Pantheon. I always did have a penchant for being too early with ideas, whereas people like Terence Conran seemed to have an enviably impeccable sense of timing.

**The Menu was:**

*Iced Cucumber Soup* (p. 234)

*Lobster Mayonnaise*

*Tomatoes and Basil*

*Salad of Lettuce Hearts*

*Cheese*

*Fruit*

And the wine was a Puligny-Montrachet, 1959.

# THURLOE SQUARE, 1964

## MAY 31st, 1964

DINNER (in the garden): *Perry and Claudie Worsthorne*
*Giles and Anne Playfair*
*D'Arcy and John Howell*
*Jim and Robin McLeod*
*James and Edith Bull*

This was a good mix of friends and neurological colleagues. The Playfairs, an old theatrical and literary family, were neighbours of ours and very close to the Worsthornes with whom we had met them. Giles was the son of Sir Nigel Playfair, the actor, who had been in the original cast of Oscar Wilde's *Lady Windermere's Fan*. Giles himself was a writer, TV scriptwriter and hard-working penal reformer.

D'Arcy and John Howell were two of my best friends from earlier days. D'Arcy, a former colleague from *House & Garden* with whom I had also shared a flat, had ended up as Chairman of East Sussex County Council. This seemed a very dignified position when I could remember having to stand guard in front of her, in our shared office at *House & Garden*, to disguise her from the Editor, then Michael Middleton, after she drank rather too much wine at a tasting we'd both been to. John was an immensely attractive and eccentric inventor, engineer and collector of vintage cars, who had grown up in Hollywood with his aunt, actress Benita Hume and her first husband, actor Ronald Colman.

Jim and Robin McLeod were visiting from Sydney. Jim was, at that time a craggily, handsome ex-Rhodes Scholar and promising young Neurologist whose work Roger much admired. He later had a personal chair in Neurology at Sydney University (where he still remains as Emeritus Professor, still handsome, with his equally attractive wife, Robin.)

James Bull was Dean of the Institute of Neurology at Queen Square and his wife, Edith, was as immersed in local politics in London as D'Arcy Howell was in Sussex. James had the horrible distinction of having to dig what was supposed to be his own grave when he was a prisoner of the Japanese in World War Two. He fell, or was pushed into it, and broke his neck. Only his knowledge of neurology and the last minute capitulation of the Japanese saved his life. John Howell's father, Miles, uniquely captained the Oxford, and Oxford and Cambridge cricket teams and finally the MCC. His mother, Billie Howell, was one of the then famously beautiful Hume sisters. Her sister, Benita was by that stage divorced from Ronald Coleman and married to a fellow actor, George Saunders. I vividly remember staying with the Howells in

73

Sussex one weekend, along with the Saunders, while George Saunders lounged in his deckchair and expounded on his unlikely plans to open a sausage factory. Why sausages, I wondered. It did not sound very glamorous. Anyway, he didn't.

As a small boy, during the war, John and his sister had been sent out to LA to live with the Colemans and, far from being in the least excited about being in Hollywood, they had, not unnaturally, bitterly resented being parted from their parents. However, John grew up to be splendidly idiosyncratic; amassed an extraordinary collection of vintage cars which he raced, and built himself a gyrocopter which he promptly crashed, breaking both legs. He tried to disguise the fact from D'Arcy who had been away in Scotland, by going to the station to meet her, letting his trousers cover his casts and walking horribly stiffly without his crutches which he hoped she would not notice in the crowds. However, his bravado was blown when she gave him her cases to carry, which he simply could not manage. He was tender-hearted about all animals and birds, including a pair of peacocks whom he used to lure back when one or other escaped the property by blowing the horn of his 1930s De Dion-Bouton, which sounded usefully like a peacock mating cry. When one of the peacocks developed a nasty and prolonged avian illness, he brought it inside the house and had the living room floor turfed with grass so that the peacock would feel more at home.

**The Menu was:**

*Cold Chicken with a Creamy Curry Sauce* (p. 235)

*Rice Salad with Red Peppers, Cucumber and Sultanas* (p. 236)

*Lettuce salad*

*Cheese*

*Strawberries with Balsamic Vinegar* (p. 236)

And the wine was a Provençale Rosé, Vaumartin, 1963.

**JUNE 3rd, 1964**

**DINNER:** *Princess Margaret and Tony Snowdon*
*Anthony and Annie Nutting*
*Ken Tynan*
*Virginia Makins*

This was the first time I had had the Snowdons to dinner and I was nervous. It was also a bitterly and unseasonably cold and wet Derby

Day. I did not know whether I was shivering with cold or nerves. In any case, it was so chilly and damp that I lit both the drawing room and dining room fires; an unusual thing to be forced to do in June.

We had already been to dinner at Kensington Palace a couple of times and I was charmed the first time we went to hear Princess Margaret impishly singing – under the crucifix hung between the drawing and dining room – the Harvard mathematician and ironic song writer Tom Lehrer's *Vatican Rag* 'Ave Maria, Jeez it's good to see yer'. It was not in the least what I had expected. Roger said that, actually, PM was rather religious, in spite of her good time girl reputation. She had adored her father, who was certainly a religious man and, after his death, she had a kind of nervous breakdown. At that time, she was pregnant with her daughter, Sarah, who had been born at the beginning of May, only seven weeks before this dinner. Not long after, we had been invited to Sarah's Christening at Buckingham Palace and I had found what I thought was a fabulously appropriate present at the invaluable Stephen Long's shop in the New King's Road. It was a large black and white printed china mug, obviously *very* Victorian since it had a font in the middle with Queen Victoria and Prince Albert either side, each with a trail of their children encircling the mug. Tony and Princess Margaret seemed very gratified with it and immediately put it on display in their drawing room where it remained, though goodness knows where it is now.

These were the Snowdon's glory days when they entertained happily and eclectically and delighted in meeting new people – though they seemed to like keeping some favoured ones strictly to themselves. Noel Coward was heard questioning plaintively why he was *always* asked all by himself like a one man cabaret. During the rest of the 1960s and 1970s, we dined quite often with the Snowdons and later, after the divorce, with Princess Margaret on her own. Although she certainly could be spiky – and, if in the mood, deliberately, I thought, difficult – she could be equally kind and sensitive and sometimes touchingly vulnerable as well as witty and a marvelously irreverent mimic. She was also a surprisingly good photographer. I have found it hard to stomach the subsequent and often malicious stories and TV programmes made about her. Many years later, just after Roger died, she very sweetly phoned me in my office in New York where I was making the first American TV Decorating Series for the PBS Channel. The secretary came in to say that 'Some mad woman calling herself Princess Margaret' was on the line. 'I told her', she said, 'that I was the Queen of England but I'd see if you were in.'

We had met Anthony and Annie Nutting quite by chance in Aswan, Egypt in 1963. As I mentioned previously, Roger and I had joined a tour organised by the Institute of Contemporary Arts to visit Egypt and, most especially, to see Abu Simbel, before it was shifted a little way up the Nile from its historic site. We were with Roger's old friends, fellow travellers (in both senses of the word according to US Senator Joe McCarthy), the black-listed Hollywood screenwriter Donald Ogden Stewart and his Australian wife, Ella Wheeler Winter. There we were, lazing in deckchairs on the front lawn of the Aswan Dam Hotel with the Nile flowing slowly by, lulled by the mixed sounds of the chittering monkeys, parrots and birds and chatting desultorily in the stifling heat, when four truly beautiful people, got off a boat and walked up the path, all dressed in white and looking as if they'd stepped straight from the days of the British Raj.

They turned out to be Anthony, one of the youngest Under Secretaries of State ever at the Foreign Office, who had famously put integrity before a potentially brilliant political career and resigned from the Eden Government over the invasion of Suez, aged only 36; his stunning wife Annie (formerly Gunning), whom I had known slightly as a model along with Barbara Goalen, when I was on *The Times*; and Annie's Aunt Gunning and her husband, who had brought Annie up and were both equally – but more frailly – decorative to look at. The Gunnings, interestingly, had always had a reputation for family beauty ever since various Gunning women had been painted by Thomas Gainsborough in the Eighteenth Century. Now the family was on its way to stay with Colonel Nasser, who had remained a Nutting friend and admirer, the more particularly, since Anthony had resigned his job in the Cabinet mostly for him. Ella Winter – who loved to shop but hated to carry – and was thus wearing four hats one above the other, had apparently once met Anthony and boldly got up to introduce us all. After they were settled in their room, they came back to join us for a drink undeterred by the many-hatted woman.

The dashing Anthony, one of the best-looking men I have ever met, kept his own pack of hounds when at Cambridge, and had apparently been expelled from Eton for conducting a gambling cartel. He had gone through the war, not in the army, because of a steeple chasing accident, but as a sort of Scarlet Pimpernel rescuing people in sardine boats and so on. He had also happened to rescue the author Ian Fleming, who, it is said, subsequently used him as one of the models for James Bond. After finally returning from a particularly hairy mission, he had rung up his father, Sir Harold Nutting, at his splendid house, Quenby Hall, Leicestershire, to announce his safe arrival home. He spoke to the butler who told him that Sir Harold was dining and thus difficult to disturb. Anthony, lucky to be alive, persevered in wanting to speak to his father who finally came to the phone showing an interesting sense of priorities: 'Good Lord, boy' he said. 'What's all the panic about? Didn't you hear that I'm in the middle of dinner?' Anyway, we became fast friends, the four of us, and shared Christmas Eve dinners with them for several years.

Ken Tynan, the immensely influential theatre critic for *The Observer* – many say *the* greatest theatre critic of the Twentieth Century – had by now entirely split up with Elaine Dundy. He was tall, thin, pale, and totally different from, but equally as dashing as, Anthony, in his flamboyantly dandyish way. He was a pithily articulate character, despite his slight and sometimes not so slight stutter, who appealed enormously to the Snowdons who had never met him before. In fact, Ken extracted a very deep love (and consequently very deep pain) from both his wives and his various girlfriends. The year before, he had been appointed Literary Manager of the National Theatre and, determinedly refractory, he kept a much remarked on notice on his desk: 'Rouse tempers, goad, lacerate, raise whirlwinds'. Much has been made of his sado-masochistic tendencies and his intolerance of the boring and of boredom, but Ken was also the most generous of men, who always pulled his wallet out after a restaurant evening, however broke he was – which was frequently – and who wrote the most tender poems for Tracy, his first child by Elaine Dundy, and his subsequent children – Roxana and Matthew – on their birthdays. It was the beginning of a long friendship between the Snowdons, Ken and, later, Kathleen Halton who became his second wife. Furthermore, that particular dinner propelled Ken, who much liked our house and the square, into leaving his flat by the Connaught, buying the house that was for sale across the road to us, and thus becoming our next door neighbour.

Virginia Makins had been a colleague on *The Sunday Telegraph* although, by then, she had moved on to *The Times Educational Supplement*. She was one of the three daughters of Lord and Lady Sherfield, then Sir Roger and Lady Makins. Sir Roger had been British Ambassador in Washington during the time of President Kennedy and had been a good friend of Kennedy's. (Another daughter, Molly, was then married to Hugo Phillips, the son of Rosamund Lehmann, the novelist, and Lord Phillips, the 'Red Peer', as he was called. Molly subsequently married the historian and writer John Julius Norwich surely one of the most graceful writers and best conversationalists in Britain, though Molly herself is no slouch).

Virginia and I had been sent all around the country writing reports on all the universities, new, old and red brick for *The Sunday Telegraph* for a comparative series of articles that we were jointly assembling. One nail-biting night – since we had been to see the new University of Sussex and it was not so far away – we stayed in her parents' house during Kennedy's historic standoff against Kruschev during the Cuban Missiles Crisis. We stayed up nearly all night listening to the news, interjected by Virginia's several telephone calls to her parents in Washington, until we heard first-hand that the Russian ships had finally turned around. Soon after we were married, Roger and I went to a dance the Makins gave in Hampshire and stayed with the neighbouring son of Hermione Gingold, the actress and comedienne, and his wife. Rather curiously, they kept a python and a boa constrictor in a glass cage next door to their Aga. Playing croquet the next morning, we were all forced to step over the python sunning itself whilst lying stretched across the lawn. They fed it on mice, often resorting in a grisly way to buying them on account from Harrods' Pet Department until the inquisitive Pet Buyer found out about the reason for their rather too frequent purchases of pet mice and firmly refused to sell them any more.

As often, the guests were very disparate although they seemed to get on well. I had made for a first course, small tartelettes with Dover sole and asparagus in a delicate white wine and cream sauce as made by the Restaurant Lasserre in Paris and the main course was *Rognons au Porto*, an Elizabeth David recipe. (I cannot imagine why I made that risky choice because now I would be very wary of serving offal to people, let alone HRH unless I knew they liked it). The tartelettes seemed to be a success except for the disconcerting fact that HRH, a fast eater, having been served first, had started and finished hers before Roger and I had even been served. Since it was customary in those days on no account to start to eat before royalty, nor to go on eating after they had stopped, some of us had a pretty meager entrée to the dinner.

Even worse, as our Portugese helper brought in the main course, I noticed, with horror, a lot of marooned little sliced kidneys on the dish without the sauce that I had made before to my (unusually) complete satsfaction. Despite my – I thought, explicit instructions – he had drained it all off. I managed to get him and the dish back into the kitchen as inconspicuously as possible to find out whatever had happened. He said I had always taught him to drain the vegetables well so he thought I had meant him to do the same thing with the meat. Thank goodness, by some miracle he had not thrown the sauce away so I was able to retrieve the situation, quickly heat it up again and toss the kidneys in it before re-arranging them. Somehow they had not toughened-up and no one seemed to have noticed my sudden absence. The good thing was that every time HRH stopped for a cigarette, which was frequently, the rest of us we were able to catch up on our eating.

Still it was better, I was told by Roger later that night, than dinner with the late King, as his father, William Gilliatt, described it. As the Queen Mother's obstretician and gynaecologist, until he died in a motor car accident on the way back from Ascot races, the Queen's William had been invited to stay at Balmoral one summer. There he was equally disconcerted to discover that, if the King turned to speak to his right-hand neighbour, everyone had to turn and speak to their right-hand neighbour, turning to their left as soon as the King did, which was often in other people's mid-sentence. They too, could not eat another morsel once the King had finally put down his knife and fork.

**The Menu was:**

*Cassoulettes Lasserre* (p. 240)

*Rognons braisé au Porto*

*Tiny New Potatoes*

*Salad of Lettuce Hearts*

*Cheese*

*Small Ogen Melons stuffed with Raspberries and Kirsch* (p. 241)

And the wines were Kreuznacher, St. Martin, 1961 and La Tache, Burgundy, 1959.

## JUNE 11th, 1964

**DINNER:** *Mark and Vita Baring*
*Nick and Sandy Fletcher*
*Anna de Goguel*
*Rev. A. de Zulueta*

Mark and Vita Baring were our left-hand neighbours and Mark, a member of the banking family, was Chairman of the Thurloe Square Garden as I was the secretary. He had quite a pronounced stutter and, only a week or so before, he had called me one afternoon and began his conversation by saying 'Now, you're a m-m-married woman. I can t-talk to you about these things'. And proceeded to tell me a rather shocking story that the Square gardener had once told him.

Sandy Fletcher and his very nice wife, Nick, were old army friends of Roger's. Anna de Goguel was a painter and a good friend of mine. The Rev. Alphonse de Zulueta was the parish priest of The Holy Redeemer Church, Chelsea to whom we had first gone to see when we decided to get married. He had also been the Roman Catholic Chaplain when Roger was up at Oxford and was a fearful old snob, not much disguising the fact that he thought Roger was making a poor choice. There were complications because Roger, born a Catholic, as I had been, had been divorced which was a big no-no for getting married in a Catholic church again. This would have been a tragedy for my mother, though not so much for my father who was more relaxed about these things. It was, apparently, better to live in sin, as it were, than to have a church wedding with a divorced partner.

There is an apocryphal story about three girls who returned to see the Reverend Mother of their old Convent School. One said she had become a lawyer, which delighted the nun. The next said she had become a doctor which also very much pleased her. The third announced that she had become a prostitute. '*What* did you say?' asked the Reverend Mother unbelievingly. 'A prostitute' repeated the third girl. 'Thank *Goodness*,' said the Mother Superior 'For one moment I thought you said a Protestant'. This story is relevant because with the wonderful casuistry, which seems something of a specialty with the Catholic Church, Father de Zulueta managed to work out that because Roger was a born Catholic, his first marriage to Penelope in an Anglican church did not count, therefore, his divorce did not count either. We were, therefore, free to have a church wedding but only a very small one and in a very small church in the country somewhere, certainly not his church. In the end, the wedding took place in a tiny Catholic chapel hidden away in Suffolk near where I had grown up and we were married by a dear Jesuit, Father John Murray from Farm Street, London.

**The Menu was:**

*Eggs stuffed with Tuna with Tomatoes and Basil* (p. 237)

*Filet de Boeuf, Sauce Béarnaise*

*Sautéed New Potatoes and Courgettes*

*Salad of Lettuce Hearts*

*Cheese*

*Iced Coffee Mousse* (p. 237)

And the wine was a Château Neuf du Pape, 1959.

# THURLOE SQUARE, 1964

## JULY 6th, 1964

**DINNER;** *John and Penelope Osborne*

Unsurprisingly, Roger had seen very little of Penelope since their divorce, though window- shopping the previous Christmas just outside what was then the avant garde store of Woollands in Knightsbridge (now and for many years, Harvey Nichols) I had observed a mink-slung Penelope stepping out of a chauffeur-driven Rolls Royce and sweeping into the shop. Successful playwrights, particularly John, were well rewarded in those days. However, we and the Osbornes had both been to the (disappointing we both thought) first night, a week or two earlier, of *Camelot* (and how wrong we were about its staying power). Unknown to each other, we had both left at the first interval. We had then unavoidably met each other standing in the vestibule of *The Ivy* restaurant waiting for tables much earlier than those we had both – coincidentally – booked. We chatted, decided to share one table, and there we were, ill met by candlelight so to speak and friends once again, though it was certainly my first meeting with John, who, I have to say, was always particularly nice to me. After this rapprochement, Roger devolved into a sort of wise elder brother for Penelope, to whom she came with many of her subsequent worries.

I found it interesting, considering his horribly difficult reputation – he is credited, after all, with making contempt an acceptable emotion – that John Osborne seemed to have been as much loved as hated by his various, apparently horribly mistreated, wives. His first, Pamela Lane; the actress, followed by Mary Ure, also an actress; followed by Penelope, the writer and critic; followed by another actress, and, astonishingly, Penelope's former best friend, the actress, Jill Bennett; and, finally, the journalist and critic, Helen Dawson, who really seemed to gentle him up into an unlikely Shropshire squire. A clue for this anomaly might be found in a sentence from the playwright David Hare's memorial speech about him. 'John Osborne,' he said, 'devoted his life to trying to forge some sort of connection between the acuteness of his mind and the extraordinary power of his heart.' John had always argued, David Hare said later in the address, for 'the cleansing wisdom of bad behaviour'.

When John had his first major illness, Roger was sent for and he later described all of his wives, and I believe some of his lovers, clustering worriedly around his bed though I am not sure about Pamela Lane. He and Penelope had the most charming big brown-eyed daughter, Nolan, named after the Captain who was a principal character in the Tony

Richardson film *The Charge of the Light Brigade* for which John had just written the script. After their divorce, Penelope took Nolan to live in New York with her and the director, Mike Nichols, with whom she lived then. Nolan came back every summer to stay with her father in his house in Sussex. As she grew older she was able to travel by herself and, when she was in her mid-teens, Penelope went eagerly, as arranged, to Kennedy Airport to meet her at the end of the summer only to find that she had not been put onto the plane. John, according to Penelope, had virtually kidnapped Nolan and she was devastated. Of course poor Penelope had been drinking a great deal which could have been one good reason for John's action but it appeared that, unforgivably, he treated Nolan abominably when she was under his care so that she eventually ran away, aged 17, never to talk to him again. I do not think Penelope ever recovered from that and many other woes, including the ridiculous or certainly inadvertent plagiarism charge when she was at *The New Yorker*. She was far too much of an original and had much too brilliant a mind to need to plagiarise deliberately.

But all that misery was in the future. In 1964, John was at the height of his fame, Penelope was still on the love side of the love-hate relationship and all was well with their world.

**The Menu was:**

*Avocado Mousse*

*Lamb Cutlets Farcies in Puff Pastry, Tomato Coulis* (p. 238)

*New Potatoes, Courgettes and Chopped Tarragon*

*Cheese*

*Apple Snow* (p. 239)

And the wines were Château Nuits St. Georges, 1959 and Château Climens, Sauternes, 1960.

**JULY 18th, 1964**

**DINNER:** *Bill and Maria Henson*
*Norah Sayre*
*Perry and Claudie Worsthorne*
*Kenneth Bradshaw*

# Thurloe Square, 1964

This was really for the benefit of Norah Sayre who had arrived for a week or so from New York and was staying with us. Her father Joel Sayre, had been an early staff writer and war correspondent for *The New Yorker* and one of the Algonquin hotel round table members along with Don Ogden Stewart (who had first introduced her to us), Dorothy Parker *et al*. Norah herself was then a dark, lively and immensely articulate *New Statesman* correspondent in the US and, like her father, a great friend of the Stewarts who had first introduced her to all the black-listed Hollywood exiles in London. She subsequently became well known as a perceptive radical writer, with a graceful, easy style that momentarily disguised her strongly held political beliefs, as well as a sometime daily film reviewer for *The New York Times*. However, at that time, and somewhat superficially, the biggest impression she made on me was for her packing. As one who, after all these years and all this travel, still cannot pack lightly, I was deeply impressed that she invariably managed to arrive anywhere with nothing but a plastic shopping bag carrying the merest essentials. I was also struck by the story she told me of *The New Statesman* who, she said bitterly, paid by the inch from which they subtracted the measurement of any quotations.

The Hensons were also over from New York on leave from the UN and we thought it a good idea to introduce them to Norah. Kenneth Bradshaw was, at that time, one of the Clerks to the House of Commons, the legal men who know all about parliamentary procedures and Select Committees and so on and keep the House of Commons on the straight and narrow. He eventually became *The* Clerk and was credited with doing much of the work to modernise The Commons. He was an old-fashionedly gallant and charming perennial bachelor, suave, attentive, outrageously flirtatious and devoted to opera. He put much effort in his retirement to start an Opera House at Compton Verney, the lovely early-Eighteenth Century house in Warwickshire, extended by Adam in the 1760s, who also redesigned the interiors. The landscaping was designed by 'Capability' Brown and Kenneth had tried very hard to turn it into a kind of second Glyndebourne and was deeply disappointed that it never really came into fruition. He used the Garrick Club as his second home and, despite his ebullience and almost exhausting sociability, he was a most loving and loyal friend to so many people. Like Spike Milligan, he was godfather to our second daughter, Annie. Unlike Spike, he was a great cook. The year before, we were having dinner with him in his flat where Enoch Powell, then the Minister of Health, was also one of the guests. Roger, who always smoked elegantly through a long cigarette holder, as did HRH and many other people at the time, was lighting up a cigarette as he chatted to the

Minister. 'I thought you were a doctor?' said Mr Powell, fixing him with his darkly gimlet look. Roger never smoked another cigarette.

**The Menu was:**

*Cheese Soufflé*

*Veau Marsala* (p. 242)

*Salad of Lettuce Hearts*

*Strawberries with a Raspberry Purée* (p. 243)

And the wines were Nuits St. Georges 1959 with a Sauternes, Château Suduiraut 1957, for the fruit.

**JULY 30th, 1964**

**DINNER:** *Spike and Paddy Milligan*
*Terence and Caroline Conran*
*Ivor and Jan Burt*
*Perry and Claudie Worsthorne*
*Margot Walmsley*
*Kenneth Bradshaw*

This was a birthday dinner for Roger for close friends and I am always struck looking over these books just how often we had all of the above to dinner then, and for many subsequent years. It's a gloomy thought that so many of them are dead, or with new partners like Perry Worsthorne, the Conrans and Ivor Burt (who is happily remarried after the early death of my dear friend Jan). And sad, but inevitable, in spite of Dr Johnson's dictum 'that a man must keep his friendships in constant repair', that you can be such close friends through one long period and either through distance or circumstances, hardly see one another the next. Happily, it seems possible to go on making new good friends long after one imagines people could do so.

Jan and Ivor Burt had been just such good friends since my engagement to the publisher, Charles Lewis, before I married Roger. Ivor and Charles were Hockey Blues for Oxford and Cambridge respectively and had met and become friends over many glasses of beer after their first match. Our friendship went on, luckily for me, long after Charles and I broke off our engagement. Ivor's specialty was shipping

84

insurance and he handled all the Onassis work and other Greek shippers, among other things. Jan was gentle and wry, exceptionally well read and exceptionally clever and had been President of the Junior Common Room at Oxford where she had met Ivor. Her grandfather, Sir Angus Watson, was a benevolent sardine tinning millionaire who had strong literary ambitions for his children. According to Jan, he bought *The Spectator* magazine for Jan's father (who was an alcoholic and made a mess of it) and Curtis Brown, the very old established literary agency, for his other son, who managed the agency for years. His daughter, Jan's hospitable aunt, also had at least some tenuous literary affiliations, and was a good friend of Vita Sackville-West and Harold Nicholson, who were neighbours. I stayed at her house once with Jan and Ivor and she took us over to meet the Nicholsons and see the renowned garden. When Jan's father died early, her mother married a man called Gough, commonly known as Goffo, who had been a Chairman of the British American Tobacco Company. A post held later by our friend Duncan Oppenheim and not then a company so often vilified for its tobacco interests. Their younger son, James, was also a godson of mine.

Margot Walmsley was deservedly one of the most loved women in London at that time and a great and frequent hostess – though a definitely *literary* hostess and not in the least one with the mostest as *The Spectator* Magazine pointed out in her obituary. She was Managing Editor of the literary magazine *Encounter* along with Stephen Spender, the poet and Editor. At that time there was much talk about the magazine being a tool of the American CIA. In fact, it was started and funded, according to Wayland Kennet, by the Congress for Culture, an organisation originally set up in France as a way for French intellectuals to combat the spread of Marxism. The organisation was then spread around the world including the UK via *Encounter* and there were plenty of left-wing contributors. But Margot was an extraordinary woman, as well as being a most efficient and, to all intents and purposes, a determinedly a-political Editor and I never heard one critical word said about her which was extraordinary in itself. For some four decades, she lived in a top flat in Earl's Terrace, one of those enclaves protected by trees from Kensington High Street. Whenever you went there and rang the bell, her living room window was opened and down would dive the front door key in a tatty old envelope or scruffy piece of brown paper. And this applied to everyone who Margot invited, many of whom had to scrabble around looking for the key by the tenuous lights of the street lamps as key and paper covering very often became separated, or failed to meet their target at her guests' feet. The everyone in this case being most of the writers, politicians, literary academics, artists and journalists in the UK. It was not at all unusual to arrive at Earl's Terrace on one of these evenings to find various distinguished upturned bums clustering around the entrance which, the right way up, turned out to belong to Kingsley Amis, Noel Annan or Lord Balogh.

Margot never had much money but it did not deter her from her very regular drinks parties which everyone was delighted to attend both because of her, and the extraordinarily varied people she managed to get together. So intent was she on being a good hostess and not letting anyone feel left out, that she went round assiduously introducing everyone to everyone several times of an evening and often to one's own partner. 'Darling Mary, have you met darling Roger. Oh yes, but *of course* you have! How silly. Come and meet darling so and so instead.' But Margot was very far from silly and a marvellous *listening* friend to so many people that, on her 80th birthday, organisers like Perry Worsthorne kept having to move the venue to accommodate all the 'friends' who wanted to come. The great sadness in her life was the death of her only child, Alaric, while still a student at Cambridge. Noel Annan, the historian, and at that time Provost of King's College, called us to tell us of his suicide, knowing that we were close friends and to ask us to take care of her. This must have been all the more painful for Margot because her husband, told he had a malignant brain tumour, had also killed himself many years before.

We took her to the country where she had became a very regular visitor and, typical of Margot, she spent a great deal of time trying to work out what best to do for Claudie Worsthorne, who was not at all well at the time, rather than talking about her own deep grief. At night though, we could hear her smothered sobbing in the guest room next door which was almost unbearable. She was a much loved godmother to our son Tom whom she treated particularly lovingly in turn and who eventually had the chance, along with my daughter-in-law, Sophie, to attend her parties himself. Margot was so particularly pleased when he became a publisher.

As she grew older and her enclave was being upgraded for new and more prosperous owners, the uncharacteristic landlords, instead of chucking her out, thoughtfully moved her whenever necessary from flat to flat and floor to floor. I went to see her one evening in one of those flats not long before she died. Her drinks table in the living room was as overflowing as usual, and we sat opposite each other in front of the flickering fire. It was peaceful and comfortable and comforting – and, as far as I remember, she had the same blue-painted walls and the same furniture as she seemed always to have had. But suddenly I felt a very slight scuffling at my feet and looked down to see a mouse scuttling away behind the fireside table, presumably disturbed by all the surrounding building work. Very soon there was a repeat performance and another. They were practically running over my feet. Not liking to remark upon it I tried to quietly shift my legs but Margot noticed. 'Oh, the darlings', she said. 'You've noticed them! Aren't they sweet? Well, at least I've come to think they are. I suppose it's a little odd and I suppose I should have reported that there were so many, but then they would have come and killed them off, and it's not really their fault poor little things.' Margot had always had the habit of being genuinely and generously nice about everyone and everything: 'Oh, he or she is so sweet' she would say about somebody palpably not sweet at all. When the listener showed some surprise at the statement, she would alleviate it a little. 'Well, perhaps not *quite* so sweet.' she would add. The mice incident was so much a part of this that it was hard to keep from laughing out loud.

**The Menu was**

*Some Crudités and Hors d'Oeuvres* (p. 243)

*Beef Wellington* (p. 244)

*Salad of Lettuce Hearts*

*Cheese*

*Rose Petal Water Ice* (p. 245)

And the wines were Kreuznacher St. Martin, 1961, Château Clinet, Pomerol, 1953 and Château Suduiraut, Sauternes, 1957 (it was, after all, a birthday).

**AUGUST 12th, 1964**

**DINNER:** *Sir Hugh and Rita Casson*
*George and Joy McWatters*
*Spike and Paddy Milligan*
*Perry and Claudie Worsthorne*

Sir Hugh Casson and his wife Margaret, mostly known to friends as Rita, were both talented and distinguished architects and also near neighbours. Hugh, who painted and drew beautifully – he later became President of the Royal Academy – always sent the most charmingly illustrated letters and was a particularly good architectural apologist given that he had a quick and felicitous way with words. He had designed the Elephant House at the London Zoo and at the well-attended opening, he stood in front of a couple of the elephants who had their rear ends turned towards the audience. Suddenly, aware that his audience were not as attentive to him as usual and, worse, were laughing rather more uproariously than he thought his wit deserved, he turned in time to see the bull elephant with a lifted tail defecating copiously just behind him. Hugh turned back. 'Oh dear,' he said, deprecatingly spreading his hands. 'Client's comment, I suppose.'

Hugh was doing restoration work in Bath, and George McWatters, still then Chairman of the sherry and wine company, Harveys of Bristol and married to my old friend and *Daily Express* boss, Joy Mathews, had much to do with the preservation and strict development of the lovely, golden city where they later lived. The McWatters also had a country house in the area, near Cheddar Gorge, where they entertained at weekends with much style and verve. George was – and remained – extremely handsome and, like Kenneth Bradshaw, was courtly, with very good old world manners and a beguilingly soft voice. He also had the gift of gathering the most talented and equally good-looking group of young men to work with him in the wine business from Harry Waugh (not *so* young, it's true but possessed of an extraordinary palate), to Colin Fenton the poet and Tim Miller, son of the former head of The World Bank, Johnny Miller, who was credited, along with the then Aga Khan, of re-discovering Sardinia as it were, and turning it into the resort it is now. I used to go out with Tim, who sadly died very young, and I had written a piece in *The Sunday Telegraph* about this thoroughly desirable group of bachelors, as they all were in those days.

When I first knew Joy on *The Express*, in the latter half of the 1950s, she was married to David Wolfers, later of the New Grafton Gallery, who was a vigorous proponent of modern British figurative art though he had an eclectic stable of painters from Elizabeth Frink to Mary Fedden, Patrick Heron and Keith Vaughan, though most of them, as far as I remember, were also with my old Sorbonne friend, Leslie Waddington in Cork Street though that sounds odd to me now. Just before I became Joy's rather short-lived assistant, I had been working as an in-house copywriter for Harrods and sharing a flat with D'Arcy McGeorge, whom I had met on *House & Garden* and who later married John Howell. D'Arcy had expressed some desire for a pet lion cub and as a rather pathetically elaborate joke I had bought a rather realistic small toy lion cub, borrowed a wooden cage from Harrods' pet department, filled it with straw, put in the cub and presented it to her. For some reason I told this story to Joy who misunderstood and went around saying that she had a new assistant who had a pet lion. For days, she asked me how I fed it, how I exercised it, how often I took it for walks, what did people say about it and so on, and I went along with it making up ridiculous answers because I thought she was just carrying on the feeble joke. When I heard back that she actually really did think I had such a pet I had to tell her that I had made it all up. She was not unnaturally, furious, and I got fired with a month's notice, but to be fair, I had also been so nervous about working at last on a daily newspaper, that I was conscious of making a real hash of the job. Harold Keeble, the then Editor, also thought very little of me since I was nothing like as good as Barbara Griggs whom I had followed after she became Women's Editor of *The Evening Standard.* In any event, it would have been hard to live up to Barbara in any way, who is one of the nicest and funniest of people and went on to become an erudite expert in alternative and herbal medicines.

Joy and David Wolfers had quite recently and tragically had a badly mentally retarded baby who they were forced to put in a home. A day after Joy had taken me out to lunch and fired me, she went off to Italy to cover the Italian collections but when she came back, David met her at the airport and told her he had left her. She was devastated. I, working out my month's notice, so still in the office and very young, had absolutely no idea how to help her. But, as my parents were away, and I felt strongly that she should not be on her own I took her home for the weekend to Suffolk. This was the start of a very long and close friendship in spite of my early inefficiency and later, when Joy herself left *The Express* I was able to introduce her to one of the Editors of *The Daily Mail* who was a current boyfriend and she started the lively *Femail* column for them. Not so very much later she went on a press trip to Spain organised by Harveys and met and fell in love with George, then a widower after a not particularly happy and childless marriage. The feeling was clearly mutual. They got married soon after. I became godmother to their only child, Christopher, and a long and good marriage it was.

Quite apart from being such a caring and supportive friend – and it was in the McWatters London house that I met Roger – Joy was a clever journalist and copy writer. I remember accompanying her as her assistant on a trip to Cornwall (still under notice, but, too late, getting rather better at my job). We kept being passed by young men in sports cars and even Bentleys, going to fish shark and she was much amused by the thought that there were all these young girls going to the Costa Brava for their Summer holidays with the hope of meeting eligible young guys – where all they met were waiters because the eligibles were all back in Cornwall fishing. She started her next page with 'All you Misses who would be Mrs ...'. But for ever after, whenever I started to tell her some story or other, she would say 'It's not one of your awful lion stories, is it?'

**The menu for a hot night was:**

*Cold Tomato and Orange Soup* (p. 246)

*Vitello Tonnato* (p. 247)

*Rice Salad, Tomato and Basil Salad*

*Cheese*

*Tea Ice Cream* (p. 248)

And the wines were Chambolle-Musigny, 1957 (I guess this was particularly for George, though a Rosé or an Italian wine would probably have been more appropriate) and a Château Suduiraut, Sauternes, 1957.

**OCTOBER 3rd, 1964**

**DINNER:** *Nicolas and Barbara Bentley*
*Bill and Maria Henson*
*Leslie Waddington*
*Lester Cole*
*Margot Walmsley*
*Anna de Goguel*

Nicholas and Barbara Bentley were more of my parent's age and they had been friends of Roger's well before I met him. Nick's father was Edmund Clerihew Bentley who invented the humorous verse form, half a parody of the Limerick, half a mock eulogy, called after his middle name and in AABB form like:

*Daniel Defoe*
*Lived a long time ago.*
*He had nothing to do, so*
*He wrote Robinson Crusoe.*

The form was often used by G.K. Chesterton, who really started its popularity but it was also used by the poet W.H. Auden. Nick, a gentle, pensive man, was a splendid cartoonist and book illustrator. He sold one of his first drawings to his godfather, G.K. Chesterton and then illustrated Hilaire Belloc's *New Contrary Tales* which started his freelance career. Probably his most famous illustrations were for T.S. Eliot's *Old Possum's Book of Practical Cats* but he actually thought of himself as more of an author and took deep pleasure in illustrating his own books. From the late 1950s, he had drawn a daily cartoon for *The Daily Mail* but had given it up as too much of a strain a couple of years before and instead, took up working for *Private Eye* and illustrating Auberon Waugh's weekly column. Barbara, his very nice wife, was herself a children's books author and was a great friend of Margot Walmsley. She was the daughter of Sir Patrick Hastings, a well-known barrister and a former Attorney General.

I had been at the Sorbonne with Leslie Waddington, before he went on to study at Les Beaux Arts in Paris. At that Parisian period, he was close friends with the rather languid-seeming and glamorous Michael White, the future theatrical impresario, who had his own flat on the Left Bank in the tiny, but aptly named, Rue Git le Cœur (Rest, or lay, the Heart Road). They had both fallen raptly in love with Sharon Buckner, the beautiful blonde daughter of an American film writer and his extremely well-dressed wife who mostly lived in Paris. Sharon, also at the Sorbonne, happened to be a good friend of mine. I, therefore, became popular with them both as a useful conduit to her. At that time, Leslie looked exactly like a charming Irish leprechaun with soulful eyes – or what I imagined an Irish leprechaun to look like. He was homesick and deeply missed his father, an art dealer and a good friend of both Jack Yeats, the painter, and his brother W.B. Yeats, the Irish poet, which intrigued me mightily. He wanted to carry on the family tradition – in which he more than succeeded since he has become a most distinguished dealer with his galleries in Cork Street, London.

Lester Cole was another one of the 'Hollywood 10', the blacklisted Hollywood filmwriters mostly exiled to London, whom we had met several times at the Ogden Stewarts. He had started as a writer and playwright and moved onto movies in the 1930s, writing some 40 of them. He had been one of the founders of The Screen Writers' Guild, now called The Writers' Guild of America (rather in the news for their protracted strike as I write this). He was affectionately known as 'the Screenwriter's Screenwriter' and after his forced departure from California, he went on writing under various pseudonyms like Gerald C. Copley which he used for his movie about lions, *Born Free*. He was an attractive man and a courageous life-long protester against any form of injustice. When he finally went back to California, he became an extremely popular teacher of film at the The University of California, Berkeley. The first time we went to San Francisco, after his return, we stayed with Lester and his wife Kay, whom we had not met before, in London, and they were generous hosts. After that, I always saw them whenever I went to SF which, unfortunately, was rather rarely.

**The Menu was:**

*Swedish Cocktail* (p. 248)

*Lamb Cutlets in Puff Pastry*

*Coulis de Tomates*

*Little Green Beans*

*Salad of Watercress and Avocado*

*Cheese*

*Blackberries with Sweet Geranium Cream* (p. 249)

And the wine was Château Margaux, 1953.

### NOVEMBER 13th, 1964

**DINNER:** *Andrew and Helen Cohen*
*Don and Ella Ogden Stewart*
*Alan and Ruth Sillitoe*
*Spike and Paddy Milligan*
*Sam Ntiro*
*Larry Adler*

Andrew Cohen, the very successful ex-Governor of Uganda, had just been appointed Permanent Secretary of the Ministry for Overseas Development with Barbara Castle as its first Minister. Andrew was very large so the Ministry became known as 'The Elephant and Castle', like the district in South-East London. He had an equally large appetite. Once, as a Governor, he had to settle a dispute about lousy work conditions: one of the exhibits on his desk was a very mouldy loaf of bread which the disputers said was the sort of inedible food that they had to put up with. The time came for the meeting but where was the number one exhibit? All that remained were a few crumbs. Absent-mindedly Andrew had eaten it. I could believe it because once, at a party I gave before I was married, I saw him pick a banana off a fruit dish when he was talking to someone, peel it, eat it and then, clearly obliviously, eat the skin.

We saw a great deal of Helen after Andrew's sudden death four years later. She was a clever and attractive woman in her own right and had been particularly generous to me when I stayed with them, the first time I went to New York in 1960 (when Andrew was head of the Trusteeship Council). However, we had one unfortunate incident with her. A couple of years before, I had given a dinner for close friends to say goodbye to Charles Lewis (ex-ADC to Andrew and ex-fiancée to me) who was going to India for Oxford University Press. I had saved up to buy some caviar which Charles loved. Helen and Andrew arrived for the dinner a little bit worse for wear after being at some reception or other. The caviar was handed to Helen first who was chatting away to Charles. Still talking, she took a helping and then kept spooning it on to her plate till she had inadvertently helped herself to almost all of the caviar. Everyone else around the table was looking appalled. No-one liked to say anything. Andrew was busy eating all the toast and looking absent. The even more tragic thing is that, while we all shared the tiny bit that was left she just sat there, talking on and on and just pushing all that ill-gotten caviar around her plate. It might just as well have been lumpy porridge.

I had first met Don and Ella Ogden Stewart on that ICA trip down the Nile in 1963 just before we were married, although Roger had met them well before with Penelope. We had been close friends ever since and had met so many other people through them who had become good friends in their turn. They were an extraordinary couple, who had left Hollywood where Don was a most successful scriptwriter (*Philadelphia Story, The Man Who Came to Dinner, Edward My Son, Life with Father, The Barretts of Wimpole Street* etc.) because politically active Don was blacklisted, along with other colleagues, for refusing to testify during the McCarthy era. In the 1920s, he had been a member of the famous Algonquin Hotel Round Table group and was friends with Dorothy Parker, Joel Sayre (Norah Sayre's father), Robert Benchley and George S. Kaufman, who were also all members. During the Second World War, he had founded the Hollywood Anti Nazi league – most curiously and illogically, McCarthy was convinced that this was really a front for Communist sympathisers.

Ella, originally an Australian, who wrote under the name Ella Winter, for the *New York Times* and other papers and who, as an ex-communist, was supposed to have been the best early interpreter to the US of Post-war Russia, as well as China, had been married, aged 17, to the very much older, radical Californian writer, Lincoln Steffens. Steffens was an early Michael Moore-type figure, then in his late 40s, who specialised in exposing governmental failures and is famous for his quote, made after returning from the Soviet Union in 1921, 'I have seen the future and it works'. He was however, disillusioned with the Communist Regime by the time he died in 1936, as was Ella. Long before that, he had decided he hated the forced ties of marriage so he and Ella divorced but continued to live together much more happily in an officially unwedded state. In fact, Don had met Ella when he attended a Memorial Service for Lincoln Steffens and heard his widow speak. He had imagined her to be elderly like her late husband so he was dazzled when this young, dynamic woman stepped up to the podium. And Ella was nothing if not dynamic. After their courtship and eventual marriage, Don took Ella back to Hollywood and bought a new house. 'The walls seemed so bare' Ella told me, 'so I went down to the nearest gallery and asked if I could borrow some paintings with a view to buying them if I liked them. 'Well', said the owner, 'I have this new young painter called Poul Klee, you could borrow a few of his'. Ella took them back, liked them, bought them and asked if he had any more or any other new painters' offerings. 'There is this guy, Picasso,' the dealer said, 'and this German called Schwitters ...'. It was the start of Ella's great collection, all of which she brought with them to London in the 1950s. (On her death, she left most of her Poul Klee collection to The Tate).

The Stewarts bought Ramsey MacDonald's old house in Frognal, Hampstead. He was the first Labour party Prime Minister (1924–27 and 1929–35). They stuffed it with Ella's art and artifacts and, as I have mentioned several times, had a sort of salon in their long living room every Sunday afternoon to which we often went, taking the children too because Ella, though a real opinionated rabble rouser in her way, loved kids. In fact the kids were always fascinated when they came through the front door to see a very large rear view of a bending woman by Schwitters on the first landing up the stairs. Their living room, with its many chairs and sofas, led onto a spacious conservatory which, in turn, led onto a large garden. There we met, at different times, a star-studded list: Katharine Hepburn, Lester Cole, Larry Adler, Charlie and Oonagh Chaplin, Dr Spock, Ingrid Bergman, Edward Albee, Graham Green, Sean O'Casey at the very end of his life and his wife Eileen, and whatever old friend was passing through London at the time. My daughter, Sophia, still remembers the embarrassment she felt at Katharine Hepburn pointing out her 'budding breasts' to the room.

Towards the end of their lives in the late 1970s, both Don and Ella suffered from depression but hardly ever together. Though they clearly loved each other deeply, if one was up, the other was generally down although the 'Sundays' valiantly continued. Ella was as much a collector of people as she was of art. The Tynans maintained that Don had said she should have inscribed on her tombstone: 'She was awful, but she was worth it'. I never thought Ella was awful – in fact, extraordinarily generous – but she was certainly bold and outspoken whereas Don was mild and very drily funny. Alas, in those latter days, going there was sadly like visiting Miss Haversham with cobwebs meandering over the peanuts and the buns being as hard as stones, though the conversation and the guests were as varied and as interesting as ever.

Ella wrote her autobiography in the early 1960s and had been invited to do an author's tour in the US. She was excited to go back after their enforced exile but also extremely nervous about being let into the country again. She therefore arranged to accompany Roger who was going to NY for a meeting in November. But Ella's tour coincided with the assassination of President Kennedy and that was really that for any publicity for her book. She and Don died within a couple of days of each other in 1980.

I had met Sam Ntiro with my ex-fiancée Charles Lewis, who had known the Ntiros in Uganda when he was ADC to Andrew Cohen, although Sam literally came from the slopes of Kilamanjaro in Tanzania. Happily, he and his wife Sarah had remained my friends too. Sam, an attractive and very merry man with a huge smile, was considered to be one of the best East African painters (I had bought one of his paintings much earlier on) and had taught painting at Makerere University, then Makerere College, and later at Dar es Salaam where he helped to found the Department of Music, Arts and Culture. But, from 1961, he had also been the first African High Commissioner in London and was just about to leave the post to go back to Africa. His wife, Sarah was, at that time, the only woman with a degree (and from Oxford at that) sitting on the Legislative Council of Uganda, the equivalent of a Member of Parliament in the UK or a Representative in the US. She was very astute with such a gentle voice and smile, that you only realised later what a peculiarly ironic sense of humour she had. She credited much of her success to Andrew who, she said, had inspired so many young people to get out and do things for the country prior to Uganda's independence.

# Mary Gilliatt's Fabulous Food and Friends

I had profiled her for *The Times* in 1959 and she had explained the huge difficulties of being a politician in a country where there were literally hundreds of different dialects and so little possibility of properly communicating. Even though she had won a Colonial Development Fund Scholarship to Oxford, she told me she only actually managed to scrape into St. Anne's College to read History by the skin of her teeth since she had no Latin, and no other languages (at that time a requirement). However, they said, they would let her in if she managed to learn one other language by the time term started the following October. Undeterred, she rushed over the Channel and ferociously and successfully applied herself to French. I felt quite sure that she would also be entirely successful in whatever field she applied herself but, that night, she was back in Uganda.

Alan Sillitoe, often called the natural successor to D.H. Lawrence (another writer from Nottingham and coal mining country, who's *Lady Chatterley's Lover* had been the subject of a famous obscenity trial in 1960), was also one of the so-called 'Angry Young Men' of the 1950s, the group of writers and playwrights led by John Osborne and including John Braine, John Wain, Arnold Wesker and Kingsley Amis. By then, Sillitoe had great success with two books which had both been made into movies: *Saturday Night and Sunday Morning* and *The Loneliness of the Long Distance Runner.* His American wife, Ruth Fainlight, born in New York, was a successful librettist and writer herself and became rather a prolific poet later on.

Larry Adler was considered just about the best harmonica player in the world though he preferred to call it a mouth organ which indeed it was. He worked with George Gershwin, Kate Bush, Sting and even Ralph Vaughan Williams but he, too, had fallen quite unjustly foul of Senator McCarthy, been blacklisted and had come to live in London. The Communist allegations, although not true, were unfortunately believed and his American career was quite ruined in the 1950s and the early 1960s, although he became enormously popular in the UK where he lived for the rest of his life. Soon after he arrived and gave his first concerts, harmonica/mouth organ sales were said to have increased by over 20 per cent and 300,000 people joined fan clubs. Aside from his musical abilities, he was another rather quiet-looking but very funny man, much enjoyed by Spike and Paddy Milligan, and made almost a sport of writing letters, particularly to the satirical magazine, *Private Eye*. Again, we had met him on several of the Stewarts' 'Sunday' afternoons, that haven for radicals and – mostly – temporarily rejected American talent, and had become friends. Like Spike and Andrew, he very much enjoyed his food and wine and actually became a restaurant critic for *Harpers & Queen* later on.

**The Menu was:**

*Borsch with Sour Cream* (p. 249)

*Roast Pheasants with Bread Sauce and Fried Breadcrumbs*

*Game Chips, Tiny Brussels Sprouts and Bacon*

*Cheese*

*Marquise d'Ananas*

And the wines were an Alsatian Reisling, 1961 and Côtes de Beaune, 1957.

## NOVEMBER 15th, 1964

**DINNER:** *Ladislas Tarnowski*
*Paul and Annette Reilly*
*Eileen O'Casey*

Ladislas Tarnowski had been a boyfriend of mine for a while when I was 17. Like many aristocratic Polish families, referenced in his cousin Andrew Tarnowski's moving book *The Last Mazurka*, they had had to flee Poland at the beginning of World War Two. His father survived internment in the Dachau Concentration Camp where so many Poles had been put along with Jews. Luckily, the family still had their old apartment in Paris and they ended up there. Ladislas had just finished at the Catholic school Ampleforth (where my brother was at the time). His parents, friends of some other Polish friends of ours in Suffolk who had been generously helped to leave Poland by Rab Butler (the Conservative politician and his wife), asked them if they knew of an English family where he could stay for the summer holidays. We were suggested and what a happy suggestion it turned out to be.

It was because of Ladislas that I decided to go to the Sorbonne rather than Oxford and he and his family fixed it all up for me, including finding me a room to rent with some acquaintances of theirs, and were really as much of an education as the Sorbonne itself, where Ladislas was a law student. His family had lost all their former money and almost all their possessions but they knew an enormous number of people from both pre-war and after. They had regular Sunday lunches and afternoons where they entertained as eclectic a group of people (on a shoe string) as the Ogden Stewarts and Margot Walmsley did in London. You might end up with only potatoes and tomato sauce and red plonk but you might also meet Sartre or Simone de Beauvoir or Méndes France, a couturier or two and even Arthur Rubinstein come to give one of his concerts in Paris, not that I did more than see them from across the room being much too shy and awkward and in any case was only just beginning to know who they all were at that stage of my life. Everybody seemed to talk different languages and one simply kept up when and where one could which was not very much.

After the war Ladislas' father had become Private Secretary to the Duke of Windsor, after unsuccessfully trying to run a laundry for which he was uniquely unsuited, and was at that time the Secretary of the Paris Jockey Club. His mother, Rosa, a distinguished-looking woman, took me to galleries and concerts and dress shows, and on the train to Versailles and Rambouillet and to every possible museum, pointing out things which I am quite sure I would never have noticed on my own. All of this was revelatory to an ex-convent girl, brought up in the country and mostly during the war – although my parents had taken us driving over much of Europe in the Summer holidays once people were allowed to travel again (from about 1948).

Every other year or so there was a students' pilgrimage to the great Cathedral of Rheims. It was called *Le Pèlerinage Charles Péguy* after the turn-of-the-Century French writer who made the first pilgrimage to plead for the life of his small son who had Diptheria, very prevalent then but mostly wiped out now with mandatory inoculations in infancy. The child recovered and, in gratitude, Péguy founded this regular pilgrimage in thanksgiving. Students walked from universities all over France and stayed the first night in the hay barns and fields on the estate of the Duc de la Rochefoucauld. Ladislas and I marched in 1954 from Paris and came back extremely tired, footsore and dirty a few days later.

In the short time we were away, the French were devastatingly defeated at Dien Bien Phu in French Indochina, by the Viet Minh Communist Revolutionary Party. This was the climactic battle of the First Indochina War and, under the 1954 Geneva Accord, the French had to agree to withdraw all their forces from their former Indochinese colonies. The accord also partitioned Vietnam into two (North and South Vietnam) which was one of the chief factors in the later American-Vietnam war. Anyway, the embittered French felt that the British and Americans had not supported them enough and Gallic feelings ran high. As a result, when the door opened to me at the house where I was staying, I was startled by a great gobbet of spit aimed full in my face (just for being English). For good measure, I was not allowed a bath or shower which were, in any case, strictly rationed in that house. Nevertheless, I absolutely adored Paris and could hardly keep from crying for days after I had to leave it.

In fact, my father, a part-time Regional Director of Lloyds Bank, as well as working with his own engineering company, had helped Ladislas to get a job in the Paris branch of Lloyds after he graduated in the 1950s and he went on to have rather a successful career in investment management and, to my sadness, a family-arranged and rather unhappy marriage to a French woman. He was godfather to my son Tom and liking, as so many Parisians, to dress as an Englishman, was then in London on his annual visit to his tailor.

I had asked Eileen O'Casey – whom we had met several times at the Ogden Stewarts with her near blind husband – because I had first seen Sean O'Casey's play *Juno and the Paycock* in a French translation with Ladislas in Paris. Sean had only died a couple of months ago of a heart attack at their home in Devon, aged 84. They had both been devastated when one of their two sons had died of leukemia in 1957, and, Eileen, 20 years younger, was now doubly sad but had moved to London. She became a close friend, very often coming to dinner and later, staying for weekends in the country. Sean O'Casey's work was popular in Paris and I thought Ladislas would be interested in meeting the playwright's wife. Also, Paul Reilly's daughter, Victoria, had married a Czech musician and had just gone to live in Prague which Ladislas knew well, so I thought he might be able to give them some advice and perhaps some contacts to help alleviate Victoria's early isolation.

Eileen had understudied the outstandingly beautiful Lady Diana Cooper (later Viscountess Norwich and the mother of John Julius Norwich) in *The Miracle* and Eileen herself was still very beautiful and wry and funny – usually at her own expense. 'Fading blue, dear', she said of her eyes to a *New York Times* interviewer, with one of her deep chuckles. 'Fading quietly like the rest of me'. She was reputed to have been much loved by both George Bernard Shaw and Conservative Prime Minister Harold Macmillan (1957–1963) and to have been at both their death beds, though I can in no way vouch for the Macmillan part.

One of my favourite Eileen stories was one she told about going to dine in the 1930s at the London house of the formidable Lady Ottoline Morrell of Bloomsbury Group fame. Eileen was nervous, she could not find anything that pleased her to wear and kept discarding things whilst Sean was becoming more and more impatient. It was pouring with rain and he was worried about being very late which indeed they were. Standing impatiently outside, he had managed to hail a rare passing taxi and insisted that they left immediately. So she put on her raincoat and rushed out. When they arrived at the Morells' the butler opened the door and went to take Eileen's coat. It was then that she realized the dreadful fact that she had not, in the end, actually put on a dress and was clothed only in her underwear and a slip. The tactful butler took one look, quickly stopped disrobing Eileen and went for Lady Ottoline. She in turn, equally quickly realised the situation, ran upstairs and tactfully got her own raincoat: she and Eileen passed the rest of the evening dressed for the wet outside.

**The Menu was:**

Oeufs Mollets en Soufflé (p. 250)

Carré d'Agneau

Pommes Lyonnaises

Braised Endives

Cheese

Pears Poached in Red Wine and Honey (p. 232)

And the wine was Chambolle-Musigny, 1957.

CHAPTER THREE

# THURLOE SQUARE, 1965

WE HAD had a lot of small and family dinners towards the end of the year and then a big after-dinner Boxing night party, at which I had managed in the nick of time to prevent the gallant but helplessly flirtatious Kenneth Bradshaw from pinching Princess Margaret's bottom. Kenneth, approaching her from the rear, evidently thought she was some other young woman with whom he was on more intimate terms. I was talking with a small group just behind her and saw out of the corner of my eye, Kenneth's wickedly predatory hand going out towards the royal buttocks. I leapt forward, practically knocking over the couple in front of me to say firmly, 'Kenneth, I don't think you've met Princess Margaret. Ma'am, may I introduce Kenneth Bradshaw?' An unusually red-faced Kenneth bowed elaborately to cover his embarrassment.

Now I had asked Kenneth to partner his great friend Margot at a post-New Year dinner, although I had also got an extra man in Michael Webb. Although many people seemed to care a lot about even numbers at that time, and it is was certainly easier with the placement, I did not really care too much if I had an extra man or woman or two.

### JANUARY 4th, 1965

**DINNER:** *Michael Webb*
*John and Sheelagh Metcalfe*
*Jo and Claude Mattli*
*Jimmy Andrade*
*Sonia Orwell*
*Margot Walmsley*
*Kenneth Bradshaw*

Michael Webb had originally been an editor on *Country Life* and wrote a lot of articles for them – as did I at that time. Like Roger, he loved old films with an ardour (Roger's particular favourites were Buster Keaton and W.G. Fields) and moved to The National Film Theatre on the South Bank then, finally, to the similar organisation in California where he also wrote occasionally – since he was a very good writer and also loved houses and architecture – for *Architectural Digest* when it started in the 1970s. Anyway, I had obviously been talking to him and suggested he came to dinner too, if he was free.

John and Sheelagh Metcalfe were generous hosts in their house near Berkeley Square; they were close friends of Margot Walmsley and always gave the most delicious dinners. John was a leading advertising executive as well as a literary critic, and Sheelagh an elegant, stylish and caring woman. We had recently been invited by them to meet Nicholas Monsarrat, author of the hugely successful wartime novel, *The Cruel Sea* which was made into an equally successful and searing movie in the 1950s, with Jack Hawkins, Denholm Elliot, Donald Sinden, Stanley Baker and Virginia McKenna. Actually, I thought that Monsarrat looked like a cruel jay (the bird) and found him rather disconcerting which was probably unfair.

The Mattlis were a sociable couple. Jo Mattli was a very good couturier. In my brief career writing about fashion for *The Times* I see, from my scrap book of articles, that I had given him high praise. I had even saved up to have him make me a party dress and he and his wife, who ran the showroom, had become our friends. Thinking of fashion writing reminds me that in New York recently I took my 17-year-old, stunning granddaughter (though I say it myself) Olivia Constantine, to meet a woman, Lydia Gordon, who has a loft filled with the most interesting archive of clothes starting from the Eighteenth Century which she now wants to sell to a museum. Olivia was considering a career in fashion and I thought she would be fascinated. I mentioned to Lydia that I had once written about fashion for *The Times* and she looked me up and down and said 'Yes, but I do see that Interior Design would suit you better.'

Jimmy Andrade had been a huge influence in my working life. He was a true antiquarian with an impressive little shop near the end of the Kings Road, Chelsea, impressive because of his very well chosen collection of early and exotic furniture and bibelots. I was on *The Times* when I was first introduced to him by John and D'Arcy Howell (John had an excellent eye for the rare and beautiful) and, from then on, I visited the shop every weekend I was in London. Soon, I started helping him in the shop on Saturdays because I learnt so much and, whenever I could get away, I used to join him on Thursday afternoons, wandering around arcane antique shops all over London. Thursday was his buying day and we almost always had dinner together afterwards. Although he was quite an old man when I first met him, he became very dependent on our friendship and was very sad when I married Roger, sure that we would never see each other much again. In fact, he went on coming to dinner pretty well every Thursday evening, either on his own or with any other people we happened to have invited, until he got ocular cancer. I used to take him for his chemotherapy, but eventually he died. Almost all my best possessions: a pair of Cloisonné jars, a Cloisonné table top, a pair of Eighteenth Century Swedish lacquered end tables, an Eighteenth Century round occasional table, a couple of marvelous pieces of ancient pottery and an early food painting which we had in the kitchen at Thurloe Square, all came from him. Terence Conran always admired the latter and I ended up by selling it to him when we moved from Thurloe Square, which I continue to regret, as I continue to regret losing my mentor, Jimmy.

Sonia Orwell was still something of a femme fatale though a dedicated drinker, not surprisingly, for she had had a wretchedly sad life, one way and another. She was said to be the quintessential literary groupie and had married George Orwell, if not on his death bed, at least very near it. He had made her his literary executor and she was unfairly accused by many of being a gold digger although the poor woman had, in fact, been extremely badly treated by the accountant for his estate, and she had never had much money. Despite this, she was always as warm and generous as she could be. Roger and I liked her very much and she was always an interesting dinner companion. I was pleased to see Hilary Spurling's sterling defence of her in her book called *The Girl from the Fiction Department* (referring to her early work on Cyril Connolly's literary magazine *Horizon*).

**The Menu was:**

*Smoked Haddock Soufflé* (p. 251)

*Cotes de Veau Foyot*

*Small Baked Potatoes*

*Spinach with Garlic and Olive Oil*

*Cheese*

*Grapes under the Grill* (p. 252)

And the wines were Ayler Herrenberger, 1961 and a St. Emilion, 1955.

# Mary Gilliatt's Fabulous Food and Friends

## JANUARY 24th, 1965

**DINNER:** *Spike and Paddy Milligan*
*Peter Forster*
*Ricki Huston*
*Lester Cole*
*Roland and Lee Penrose (Miller)*

Spike had had several mental breakdowns and, every so often, if he was not clinically depressed enough to have to go to a nursing home, he went very quiet, although he always looked benign enough – even if he went quite beserk at times. This was a quiet night for him though Paddy, as always, made up for it. Peter Forster, another old boyfriend of mine, had written a novel and was then the film critic for *The Spectator* or was it *The New Statesman*? In any event, he sometimes used to take me to new movie showings where he would promptly go to sleep, asking me to tell him the plot at the end. He wrote very well, but I was always amazed how well he managed to pull his criticisms off. Perhaps he went again, but he was fun – when he wasn't falling asleep – and articulate.

I much admired Ricki Huston, whom I had met through Leslie Waddington who adored her too. She was beautiful and idiosyncratic and warm and funny and became such a good friend, though she did not come out to dinner much because of her then small children (including Angelica) so we often had lunch instead. At the time she was still married to John Huston, the film director, but separated. She was divorced in 1969, and lived with the children in a house in Little Venice which I thought stunningly original and which I photographed for my first book *English Style*. She was killed prematurely in a motor car accident in Italy to the devastation of her many friends.

As I mentioned earlier, Roger and I first met Lee Miller, Roland Penrose's wife, on the Institute of Contemporary Arts trip to Egypt and the Lebanon. But Roland could not make that trip, though we had met together several times since and had a couple of absolutely delicious dinners with them. Lee was an extraordinary cook as well as an extraordinary photographer, and had been, as you can see from early photographs of her, a very beautiful woman loved by many men. She was still attractive to look at and also quite mesmerising with her husky voice and ironic humour. I do not think many people recognised at that time the large part she had played in the Surrealist Movement in Paris in the 1920s with her lover, Man Ray as well as Picasso, Max Ernst, Gertrude Stein and Alice B. Toklas. But she rarely talked about the past or her extraordinary experiences, just as she was reticent about her war.

Roland Penrose was a distinguished figure both to look at *and* in the arts; a well-known British Surrealist painter himself, as well as being a prescient collector of Abstract Art – about which there was much controversy before the war, particularly the Henry Moore sculpture he had commissioned for his then Hampstead House. Most of his collection was kept at their country home, Farley Farm in Sussex which was, unfortunately, burgled by evidently connoisseur art thieves who demanded a ransom for the return of the paintings. Luckily, the Tate Gallery came up with the ransom money, on condition that some of the collection went to The Tate on his death. Roland was also a writer and a great friend of Picasso about whom he wrote, as well as writing books on other friends like Max Ernst, Man Ray, Joan Miro and Anton Tapiès.

**The Menu was:**

*Oeufs Mayonnaise Verte* (p. 252)

*Chicken Pie* (p. 253)

*Petits Pois*

*Salad of Watercress*

*Cheese*

*Iced Coffee Mousse* (p. 237)

And the wines were a white Rhône, Hermitage, 1960 and Nuits St. Georges, 1959.

**FEBRUARY 1st, 1965**

**DINNER:** *Peggy Guggenheim*
*Leslie Waddington*
*Ken Tynan and Kathleen Halton*
*Michael White*
*Eileen O'Casey*

We had met Peggy Guggenheim at one or two dinner parties, including with Roger's old friend, Nick Bentley and his wife Barbara, and had become quite well acquainted. When I asked her to dine, I wondered if there was anyone else she would particularly like me to ask as well and she said 'Actually, yes. Could you possibly ask Princess Margaret? I am afraid I quite unwittingly offended her and I would really like to explain what happened myself.' It turned out that she had been at a party given by the art critic, John – and his then wife Vera Russell, and Peggy said she had been talking to a pretty little dark girl to whom nobody had introduced her. Somebody else whom she knew arrived at her side and she turned to greet them, apparently quite obviously offending the pretty little dark girl who turned out to be Princess Margaret.

Anyway, I called P.M., who said yes she'd love to come that night and enquired who else I was thinking of asking. I was just saying Peggy Guggenheim, who will be in London then, Leslie Waddington, Ken and Kathleen Tynan and so on when she stopped me in midstream. 'Peggy Guggenheim', she said. '*What* an *extraordinary* woman. Do you know I was at a party for her given by John and Vera Russell and was having a most interesting conversation when she suddenly turned on her heel and started talking to somebody else ... Oh damn! I was just going to put the date in my diary and I see that I am doing something on that night after all. I thought I was free. What a pity. But do ask me again soon!'

A perfect example, I thought, of *lése-majesté*.

Leslie Waddington, who as I mentioned before, owned and ran the Waddington Galleries in Cork Street and had been an old friend since Sorbonne days in Paris, as had the always laconic Michael White, already by the 1960s, a leading theatrical impresario. I thought that Leslie would be interested to meet Ms Guggenheim. And I knew that Peggy was enormously fond of the theatre, wanted to meet Ken and Kathleen and would be interested by Eileen O'Casey and Michael White. But alas, I had failed to persuade Princess Margaret which, I imagined, was very possibly the reason why the intensely social Peggy, had accepted the invitation in the first place. In the event, she did not seem to mind too much. When Roger and I subsequently went to Venice in early December, she asked us both to lunch at her Palazzo. It was wonderful to see the place lived in, with all her paintings and sculpture amongst the furniture and the dogs running around all over the rooms, rather than the somewhat empty place just dedicated to her collection that it seems now.

# THURLOE SQUARE, 1965

**The Menu (it was freezing cold) was:**

*Oeufs Espagnoles* (p. 254)

*Boeuf Bourguignonne*

*Baked Potatoes*

*Salad of Lettuce Hearts*

*Cheese*

*Caramelized Oranges* (p. 255)

And the wines were a white Rhône, Hermitage, 1963 and a Volnay, 1959.

## MARCH 10th, 1965

**DINNER:** *Lester Cole*
*Angela Caccia*
*Spike and Paddy Milligan*
*Max Seifert and wife*
*Dickie and Phil Dobbs*
*Jimmy Andrade*

I had shared my flat in Flood Street for a time with Angela Caccia before she got married to David, the extraordinarily attractive and then life-enhancing son of Lord Caccia, at that time the head of the Foreign Office and finally the Provost of Eton. Angela was South African and had grown up there but had gone to Oxford and joined *The Sunday Telegraph* more or less straight after graduation. As she had no permanent place to live in London, I invited her to stay with me until she had found something. She came and did not, in the end, leave till just before her wedding. I had been very happy with the arrangement and a confidante in the long-distance, dramatically up and down love affair with David who had been sent somewhere or other very far away. They were both crazy about each other. She was rather beautiful, in a Virginia Woolf sort of way, with an equally beautiful, memorable, voice and was another really graceful writer. She was also quite intrepid and, on the paper, volunteered for all of the most difficult features to write such as ascending and descending mountain slopes in Wales tied to a rope, or reporting on some thing or another in South America where she picked up a rare parasite worm. 'At least', as she said, 'It's great for the figure.' One of David's postings had been to La Paz in Bolivia, South America. Both of them were a bit vague and they managed to miss their boat, as if it were a train or plane. They picked it up in Spain somewhere, but the only pieces of their luggage to arrive on the boat were Angela's hats. When they finally got to Bolivia, the rest of their luggage finally turned up, plus all of the cases of wine they had shipped – with all of the wine siphoned out of the bottles.

An earlier posting, just after their marriage, had been Prague at the height of the Cold War when they had to go outside to talk to each other if they wanted to say something important since all diplomats' houses and apartments were bugged. I had visited them there just before I met Roger and it was so cold that tears seemed to freeze in one's eyes and mucus go all crackly in one's nose. In fact, on that particular occasion, Angela was just back from Prague. We had children at much the same time, and, luckily for us, they were posted back to London. Unknown to Angela, David became a Scientologist and the first thing she knew of it was when estate agents started to arrive to view their house which David had put on the market without consulting her. After a time in a house in Hertfordshire, they moved to a splendid great house outside Lucca in Italy. David was still behaving quite oddly and, eventually, he just left her there alone with the children, much to her deep distress and they divorced. Sadly, it turned out in the end that his increasingly strange behaviour was because he had a brain tumour and he died prematurely, having married his nurse. Angela ended up going back to South Africa and marrying a charming and very musical academic, Taffy Lloyd, who had been an early suitor. She went on writing very successfully and did a good deal of broadcasting and lecturing, for which her melodious voice and quirky sense of humour were very well suited. She became the other godmother, along with Margot Walmsley, to our son, Tom.

We hardly knew the actor Max Seifert and his Sicilian wife but we had met them at Spike and Paddy's and they had asked us to dinner not long before so it was a return, so to speak. The same applied to Phil and Dickie Dobbs who were friends and neighbours of the Ogden Stewarts and, like us, were often asked to lunch at Frognal along with Lester Cole (before guests started to arrive for the more populous Sunday afternoons). Jimmy Andrade was there so it may have been a Thursday. Anyway, it was quite casual and I had just experimented with a chicken and mustard recipe which was a success.

# THURLOE SQUARE, 1965

**The Menu was:**

*Chicken Dijonnaise* (p. 255)

*Green Salad*

*Cheese*

*Coffee Ice Cream*

And the wine was rather a lot of Beaujolais, 1963.

## APRIL 26th, 1965

**DINNER:** *Anthony and Annie Nutting*
*Max and Joan Reinhardt*
*Ricki Huston*
*Perry Worsthorne (Claudie was away)*
*Charles and Primula Lewis*

As I have mentioned I had been engaged to Charles Lewis when I was on *The Times* and had made and kept many friends through him as well as maintaining our own friendship. I had first met him when I was playing tennis after work, at the court in Onslow Square, South Kensington with an older friend, Jeanne Wilkins, a granddaughter of Sir Francis Burnand, one of the first editors of *Punch*. I had stayed with her and her family when I first came to work on *House & Garden* and was looking for a flat to rent, and she had been exceptionally kind. For some years, she worked in the Lord Chamberlain's office and had intriguing stories to tell about the under-life at the Palace and the various rivalries between the Queen's Page and the Queen's Personal Maid, who both held great power amongst the staff. It was like listening to a Hans Anderson fairy story. Jeanne had just moved to Onslow Square, was an accomplished tennis player, and we took full advantage of the Square's court. Anyway, there was this real Rupert Brooke look-alike (an exceptionally handsome blonde poet who died in World War One whose work I knew off by heart) peering through the outside wire. When we asked if we could help with anything he said he simply wanted to know how one could get to play there. However, he lingered around till the end of the game and Jeanne asked if he would like to come to her flat for a drink. He readily accepted and we started going out from then on. He had recently started working at Allen & Unwin, the publishers, having more or less hitchhiked back overland through India when he had finished his term as ADC to Andrew Cohen in Uganda. He was too gentle for me though, or more likely, I was too bossy, and later, when he transferred to Oxford University Press and was sent to India, he met and married Primula, the daughter of a well-known judge there, and an ardent social reformer. She was actually put in prison under Mrs Ghandi, for organising a rebellion of the Agricultural Workers Collective, a difficult position for Charles and his son, both personally and professionally. But I liked her very much and they are still married and living peacefully back in Oxford.

**The Menu was:**

*Dublin Bay Prawns with Aioli* (p. 256)

*Roast Shoulder of Lamb with Garlic and Coriander*

*Tiny New Potatoes*

*Courgettes*

*Cheese*

*Orange Sorbet in Orange Skins* (p. 256)

And the wines were Puligny-Montrachet, 1959 and Château La Mission Haut-Brion, 1957.

**JULY 30th, 1965**

**Roger's Birthday Party**

**Dinner:** *Princess Margaret and Tony Snowdon*
*Anthony and Susan Crosland*
*Anthony and Annie Nutting*
*Tom Montagu Meyer and Fleur Cowles Meyer*
*Ian and Susan Anstruther*
*Ken Tynan*
*Margot Walmsley*
*Terence and Caroline Conran*
*Hugh and Rita Casson*

# THURLOE SQUARE, 1965

*William and Ruth Sampson*
*John and Sheelagh Metcalfe*
*Paul and Annette Reilly*
*Perry and Claudie Worsthorne*
*Eileen O'Casey*
*Spike and Paddy Milligan*
*Allen and Ruth Sillitoe*
*John and Penelope Osborne*
*Max and Joan Reinhardt*
*Ivor and Jan Burt*
*Leslie Waddington*
*Ricki Huston*
*Sonia Orwell*
*Kenneth Bradshaw*
*Max Clendinning*
*Andrew and Helen Cohen*
*Duncan Oppenheim*
*Michael and Annabel Popovic*
*Marston and Eden Fleming*
*Wayland and Liz Young*
*Osbert Lancaster and Anne Scott-James*
*Virginia Makins*
*Nick and Barbara Bentley*
*Mac and Beth McWilliam*
*Diana Graves*

I see from the dinner books that, as usual, we had had plenty of small dinners often for the same friends and also for various medical colleagues of Roger's through the early summer. We had also spent a couple of weeks or so in America, so we decided to give a proper party for his 43rd birthday party. He had never had a 40th nor a 41st, and we had not got around to anything major the year before, nor had we had any sort of housewarming party and there were many people we owed hospitality to so, although I was about six months pregnant with my second child, we decided to have quite a lot of friends with tables all over the place and a big buffet in the dining room. I had hoped to have it mainly in the garden but the weather was not particularly agreeable, so we had tables in my study halfway up the stairs, in the hall, the dining room and even the kitchen – not so usual for a fairly formal party in the 1960s. Fleur Cowles, one of the great hostesses of the time, with her Wednesdays in her set at Albany and her weekends in Sussex, had apparently particularly wanted on this occasion to be seated at

Princess Margaret's table, although I had not known this. But I was trying to space out the bigger stars so to speak, in a remarkably level playing field, and also to make an equitable rationing of men and women. Although Fleur had Tony Snowdon and Ken Tynan and the sculptor Mac McWilliam, and other equally agreable people, sitting at her table it appeared that she was disappointed. I had read in *Queen* magazine only that week that if she was not much enjoying a party she pleaded a migraine and summarily left. And indeed, she pleaded a headache and left. But she left her good-natured husband, Tom Montagu Meyer behind who stayed till the very end.

I had actually put Princess Margaret on a table in my study with Roger, as the host, together with Anthony Crosland (then the Secretary of State for Education and Science and, later, our Foreign Secretary), a great Socialist thinker who, in many ways, was the actual founder of New Labour; his journalist and later novelist wife, Susan Barnes; John Osborne; Alan Sillitoe; Duncan Oppenheim (then Chairman of BATS, the British American Tobacco Company); Diana Graves; Ricki Huston and Eileen O'Casey. Unfortunately, Princess Margaret and Tony Crosland got into a major argument about the recent launch of the new Hovercraft. She said she had launched it. He said he had. They were equally intractable. The next day, P.M. called to thank us for the party (she was always meticulously polite and generous with her thank yous which, is more, I heard from an impeccable source, than many other more junior members of the Royal family were) and said: 'Tell me, why is Mr Crosland always so cross?' Though she pronounced it with that Windsor drawl making it Crawsland and Crawse. 'Did Roger tell you about our argument? Of *course* I launched the damned thing. I'm not in the habit of making things up.' 'Maybe there were two different launches, Ma'am.' I replied.

Luckily, the rest of the party seemed a success judging by the empty dishes, the number of empty bottles and the fact that there were still many people there at 3am.

**The Menu was: (**After Champagne etc. the choice on the central buffet table was hopefully eclectic enough for everyone.)

*Smoked Salmon Mousse* (p. 257)

*Melon and Prosciutto*

*Millefeuilles of Chicken*

*Cold Rare Fillet of Beef with Mustard Sauce*

# THURLOE SQUARE, 1965

*Curry Stuffed Eggs*

*Stuffed Tomatoes*

*Spicy Rice Salad*

*Cherry and Walnut Salad* (p. 273)

*Avocado and Grapefruit Salad*

*Cheeses*

*A huge pyramid of Profiteroles with Chocolate Sauce*

And the wines for such numbers were a choice of St. Veran, 1964, a Vin Rosé, Côtes de Provençe, 1964 and a Côtes du Rhône, 1962.

## AUGUST 5th, 1965

**DINNER:** *Princess Margaret and Tony Snowdon*
*Osbert Lancaster and Anne Scott-James*
*Perry and Claudie Worsthorne*
*Ken Tynan and Kathleen Halton*

This was a pre-summer holiday dinner party with the Snowdons (though I don't know why they came again so soon) made a little dramatic by the fact that I might easily, I suppose, have prevented the birth of Princes William and Harry. I had had a sore throat and painful glands in my neck all the week. I went to the doctor who assured me it was not mumps as I had thought it might be but, more likely, a small stone in the throat duct which he would attend to later. I told him I was relieved as I was having this dinner party the next evening and did not want to infect anybody. He said there was no worry. I took several aspirin and felt better. The party went well and it was a good mix of people with a great to and fro of conversation.

When I had worked on the *Daily Express* as Joy Matthews' assistant, we – most of us feature writers and aspiring feature writers – worked in one big office. Osbert Lancaster always came in for a short time each day, drew his Maudie Littlehampton cartoon and usually went back home by the late afternoon. When he left, there was always a scramble for his waste paper basket to see if he had discarded any earlier attempts. Anne Scott-James, his wife, was a very tall, attractive and well-known woman columnist, several inches taller than Osbert,

113

and the mother of the future Editor, columnist and historian Max Hastings. At that time, she did a column for the now defunct *Sunday Dispatch,* the then rival of the popular *Sunday Express* which had as its woman's columnist, Veronica Papworth. There was a story that Veronica Papworth had gone to see the elderly, but much respected Editor, Alison Settle, the doyenne at that time of women journalists, to complain that Anne Scott-James was being paid so much more than her. 'But Veronica dear', said Mrs Settle pithily, 'Anne Scott-James can *write.'*

Kathleen Halton, another young journalist, must have been one of the most beautiful young women of her, or any recent generation, and was then living with Ken Tynan whom she subsequently married in America in 1967. Ken seemed to be revelling in her and looked a great deal healthier.

It was a good evening but, in the morning, I woke up with what was surely mumps, whatever the smart Doctor had said. When it was definitely diagnosed as that, we had to ring up the various guests to tell them they were in quarantine. The Snowdons had already left for Balmoral to stay with the Queen, Prince Philip, Prince Charles and various other members of the family. Neither Tony nor Prince Charles, as it turned out, had had mumps which in males often had a disastrous effect. It occasioned a letter from Princess Margaret in Scotland, telling me that, 'Tony is anxiously passing the quarantine days, examining himself every morning and night and hoping to stay as the husband he is to me now'. 'Prince Charles', she added, as heir to the throne, 'was just as anxious.'

As indeed, Ken told me, was he.

**The Menu was:**

*Avocado Mousse*

*Cotes de Veau Foyot*

*Tiny New Potatoes*

*Epinard à la Crème*

*Cheeses*

*Glacé au Melon de l'le St. Jacques* (p. 230)

And the wines were Puligny-Montrachet, 1959, Château Margaux, Bordeaux, 1953 and Château d'Yquem, 1947.

# THURLOE SQUARE, 1965

## AUGUST 13th, 1965

**DINNER:** *James Morris*

I thought this small dinner worth noting, although we only had one friend, because that friend was James (later Jan) Morris who, courageously, had surgery to change his gender later in 1972. He had been an army friend of Roger's and was on his own for some reason – he had married at the end of the 1940s and had five children and is still with his then wife. He seemed a nice young man, slight and rather good-looking and, of course, he was greatly admired as a journalist and as a writer. He had a huge scoop when working for *The Times*, when he accompanied John Hunt's and Edmund Hillary's expedition to climb Everest and was able to announce triumphantly that they had reached the summit on the day of the Queen's Coronation in 1953. Alas, I do not recollect the conversation but it was certainly not about gender change though, by then, he had apparently started taking special hormones. He was godfather to Miles Bredin, the writer and journalist and son of my later, dear friend, Virginia Bredin; Miles, as a child, but like so many people, was somewhat confused when his godfather suddenly turned into another godmother. 'Mummy,' he said to Virginia, 'Why is godfather James wearing a dress and carrying a handbag?'

**The Menu was:**

*Cold Jellied Consommé*

*St. Peter's Pie*

*Tomato and Cucumber Salad*

*Cheese*

*Peaches in Sauternes*

And the wine was Gewurztraminer, 1961.

## NOVEMBER 15th, 1965

**DINNER:** *Tom Guinzberg*
*Margot Walmsley*
*Terence and Caroline Conran*
*Quentin and Angela Crewe*

I had been somewhat preoccupied over the autumn having my second daughter in October, christened Anne-Louise Constance after her two grandmothers, although as soon as she could, she changed her name to Annie. This was our first sizeable dinner since then, and it was really given for Tom Guinzberg, then the head of Viking Publishers whom we had met when in New York during the summer, for one of Roger's neurological meetings. Tom had very kindly taken us out for dinner with his wife, Rusty, because Max Reinhardt had already got him to agree to publish my first book, *English Style* which I had just started to write (writing this, I think how rare it is, nowadays, to dine with one's publisher, especially with an unknown author and *before* the book was proved a success or not, but – *autres temps, autres moeurs*).

Quentin Crewe had suffered from muscular dystrophy since he was six and was severely crippled but that in no way stopped him from his travel writing or enjoying life to the full. Roger was extremely fond of him and thought him incredibly brave and stoical and, indeed, he was a charming, sensitive, interesting and interested man. At that time, he was married to the young journalist and broadcaster Angela Huth, who later became a very well-reviewed novelist and playwright and was also a good friend of HRH.

**The Menu was:**

*Swedish Cocktail* (p. 248)

*Sweetbreads en Croûte, Sauce Madére*

*Lettuce Salad*

*Cheese*

*Strong Coffee Jelly and Cream*

And the wine was Savigny-ès-Beaune, 1959.

**DECEMBER 28th, 1965**

**KITCHEN SUPPER:** *Ivor and Jan Burt*
*Eileen O'Casey*
*Shirley Wray*

This was a post-Christmas, simple supper for good friends including one of Roger's favourite colleagues from his hospital (the National

Hospital for Nervous Diseases at Queen Square), Shirley Wray, a distinguished Neuro-Opthalmologist. But it was even harder then to be a female specialist and ascend the promotional ladder as easily as male colleagues. My mother had a great-aunt who was one of the first female lawyers in Britain. She could not get a job and eventually went off to Boston to practice where she finally became a judge. Shirley too, finally went off to Boston – to Cambridge, Massachusetts for a better chance at Harvard. It was not much better there but at least she earned a whole lot more money and eventually, having been passed over several times for junior male colleagues, she was given a Harvard Chair of her own. I was very fond of her and saw a good deal of her when I lived much more in America.

**The Menu was:**

*Smoked Salmon*

*Cottage Pie*

*Brussels Sprouts*

*Cheese*

*Fruit*

And the wines were Gerwurztraminer, 1960 and Côtes du Rhône, 1962.

CHAPTER FOUR

# THURLOE SQUARE, 1966

S INCE we had quite a busy December we were fairly relaxed over January with just very small dinners again, so we did not start doing anything more ambitious till February.

### FEBRUARY 6th, 1966

**DINNER:** *Mac and Beth McWilliam*
*Spike and Paddy Milligan*
*Mason (Jr) and Anne Romaine*

Mac McWilliam was a well-known sculptor at that time and we had met him and his gentle and sweet-looking wife with the Ogden Stewarts. They had a splendid house in Kensington with an enviably large garden and loved to entertain. We thought it fun for them to meet the Milligans but we also had some American guests from Virginia. Some years ago, my parents had met Mason's uncle, Mason Romaine Senior and his wife, Margaret, on the Queen Elizabeth, when they were going over to America with my brother. In the way that often happens on cruises, the Romaines senior had invited them to come and stay at their home in Petersburg, near Richmond, the site of one of the last and bloodiest battles of the Civil War. The families and its younger generations had been good friends ever since. They had a beautiful late Eighteenth Century house and, when I stayed there myself, on my first visit to America in 1960, I was entranced to hear how the outstanding china and silver on the dining table had had to be hung down a well during the Civil War to save it from being stolen or confiscated or just wantonly destroyed, as so many houses and possessions were towards the desperate end of the war. I was also intrigued by the fact that the silver had actually been engraved to echo the pattern of the old porcelain service.

# THURLOE SQUARE, 1966

I had taken the opportunity of seeing Mason and Margaret Romaine again for a couple of days the Summer after we were married in May, 1963, when Roger had a medical meeting in Washington. I decided to go back to that city to rejoin him on a Greyhound bus and booked a ticket. But it was the day before what came to be known as 'The Poor People's March' and there was only one seat left on the bus which was completely full of black men – not very surprising considering some 250,000 people were descending upon the Capital. Just before the bus left a young black woman holding two small babies got on and was left standing in the aisle. I looked around thinking one of the guys would surely give her a seat. Not a bit of it. In the end I got up, knowing all too well how difficult it would be for her to have to stand holding the children all the way to the City, hoping that sooner or later someone would get off. Again, not a bit of it. There were no such stops and no rebate. The guys just sat on so I stood all the way myself. No common courtesy there to any woman, or at least not then. As I have thought many times sexism might actually be stronger than that sleeping bear, racism, in the US. Although I presume that if women want completely equal rights they should certainly be prepared not to receive any particular courtesy.

The sad thing is that I heard from the younger Romaines in 2006 that that elegant old house and garden had now been completely overrun by new small housing and that nothing at all remained of that gracious and historic bit of the South.

**The Menu was:**

*Artichokes Vinaigrette*

*Maiale al Latte – Roast Pork in Milk*

*Small Roast Potatoes*

*Spinach and Pine Nuts*

*Cheese*

*Baked Bananas with Rum*

And the wine was Chambolle Musigny, 1957.

**APRIL 8th, 1966**

**DINNER:** *Don and Ella Ogden Stewart*
*Eileen O'Casey*
*Ian and Susan Anstruther*
*Paul and Annette Reilly*

Although, as usual, we had had many small dinners for family and friends for the rest of February and March, I found that two small children only 18 months apart, were, not surprisingly, a great deal more occupying, especially as I was having to travel around England a bit to write about the various houses I had chosen to illustrate the new book. None of this was conducive to more ambitious entertaining. This dinner was an exception and I had asked several friends together.

Paul and Annette Reilly were dear neighbours who lived just down the road. Paul, later given first a knighthood and then a life peerage, was the eloquent Chairman of the Council of Industrial Design and the Design Centre in the Haymarket, who then held immense sway in the design and architectural world. Annette was a stunning woman who had been married several times before, although her marriage to Paul lasted for some 40 years until his death. Like several other of our friends and neighbours they were great entertainers and gave many, many pleasurable lunches and dinner parties in their town house with its conspicuous red door.

I so wanted to photograph their house for my book *English Style*, for which Paul wrote the foreward. It was so colourful, so warm in atmosphere and so full of paintings, sculpture, furniture, objects, books and textiles executed by their various friends all over Europe, particularly Scandinavia. But it is a sad fact that, all too often, truly beautiful and interesting houses, like truly beautiful people with faces full of experience and expression, are more beautiful in the eyes of the beholder than the camera lens.

Ian and Susan Anstruther owned Thurloe Square, Alexander Square, Alexander Place, South Terrace and a good part of South Kensington known collectively then as the Thurloe Estate, as well as being our exceptionally nice, low key, neighbours. And they must surely rate in the highest rank of thoughtful, tactful, modest and generous landlords. Susan, as Susan Walker, was the square's architect and is still well-thought of as a sensitive and uniquely knowledgeable London architect. Ian was a splendidly eccentric writer, specialising in Nineteenth Century social and literary arcania, who practically lived in the London Library and funded its new wing in 1992. He did well with his aunts. His father's sister wrote the famous book and movie *Mrs Miniver* under the name of Jan Struther. Ian was purportedly genuinely surprised to inherit the South Kensington and Scottish estates from his mother's sister, with whom he had spent a very large part of his childhood.

His first book was the charmingly written *I Presume* about Dr Stanley and, when we first met him, he had just published *The Knight and the Umbrella* all about the unfortunate Eglinton Tournament in Victoria's reign – an extremely ambitious and detailed recreation of a Medieval tournament which was washed out by rain on the day. He later, uniquely, inherited two baronetcies and, when he died in 2007, because of the intricacies of British and Scottish law, managed to pass on one for each of his two sons, one of whom, is my godson, Toby (who also inherited the ancient title of 'Hereditary Carver to the Sovereign of Scotland', although I don't think he has to rush regularly to Balmoral to carve the Sunday joints when the Queen is there). A creature of absolute habit, Ian always wore a bow tie by day and a cravat by night with a velvet suit and embroidered slippers with bells on them. (Many people still dressed up – or down – in that decade, even for simple dining at home. Roger always changed into a velvet evening jacket come what may. So did many other men I knew). Ian loved cars and owned some splendid ones including a Maserati and several Porsches but he only ever drove them extremely slowly, and had actually been stopped by the police for proceeding at such a low speed.

**The Menu was:**

*Taramosalata* (p. 231)

*Salmon Trout Cooked in Foil*

*Cold Cucumber Sauce*

*Petis Pois with Lettuce*

*Tiny New Jersey Potatoes*

*Cheeses*

*Brown Bread Ice Cream*

And the wines were Pouilly Fume, 1955 and Château Mouton Rothschild, 1955 (with the cheese).

### MAY 25th, 1966

**DINNER:** *Sophia Klöcke*
*Ursula Klöcke*
*Perry and Claudie Worsthorne*
*Margot Walmsley*
*Kenneth Bradshaw*
*Bai Patel*
*Carmel Green*

Sophia Klöcke, who was staying with us, was Roger's aunt, one of his father's sisters, and dearly loved by our particular family, though love was hardly the word that could have been used in the past. Like her sister, Alice Gilliatt, who had been a determined chain-herself-to-the railings suffragette and force fed in prison (who went on to become the first woman Mayor of Fulham in London *and* the first Socialist Mayor – (there is an Alice Gilliatt Court in Fulham), Sophia was something of a radical thorn in the side of her distinguished but conservative medical brother and sister-in-law, Anne. Though the latter, happened herself to have been one of the first woman anaethetists in the UK and had actually worked with Elizabeth Garrett Anderson, the first woman doctor in the UK to qualify, way back in 1865. Incidentally, Elizabeth Garrett Anderson also became the first woman mayor in England, in her home town of Aldeburgh in Suffolk.

Sophia met and got engaged to a German from Wiesbaden just before World War One and determinedly married him when the war was over. The power of nationalism, especially during and after a devastating war, holds immense sway and even the most civilised and comparatively gentle people can turn against their close family and friends in some sort of determined siding with their country or cause. Look at the horrifying brother against brother, friend against friend syndrome during the American Civil War. The senior Gilliatts – apart from the loyal Alice – would not see Sophia, her husband and subsequent two children ever again; even though my mother-in-law herself was Austro-Hungarian – though brought up in England as were her parents since her grandparents had left Vienna and settled in England after the 1848 Franco-Prussian War. Her grandfather was reputed to have remembered being carried in the arms of his nursemaid as they escaped through the Viennese sewers.

Once, when Sophia came to visit her sister Alice in London with her small son and her daughter Ursula, the children were asked what they most wanted to do. Wrenchingly, they asked to meet Uncle William. The best Alice could do was to take them near the garage where she knew he kept his car so that, unseen, they could at least watch him drive off to work in the morning.

When Penelope married Roger, one of the first things she did was to invite Aunt Sophia to London and Roger and I continued to have her to stay, with much pleasure, whenever she visited England. This time, she brought her daughter, Ursula. She loved our children and they loved her just as much, and we are still so fond of Ursula. Her brother, alas, was killed in the German army in World War Two while Roger fought for the British. It was not such a dissimilar situation, as Roger pointed out, to Nick Mosley, son of the pro-Hitler, British Fascist Party leader, Sir Oswald Mosley, who had survived all the flack and general opposition to fight alongside Roger in the Green Jackets during the war

Baichand Patel was, at that time, a fellow law student and boyfriend of my much younger sister, Carmel Green. Bai, who was actually Fijian, was a brilliant student and Roger had introduced him to his ex-father-in–law in the UN, George Ivan-Smith and to our friend Bill Henson. He subsequently had a long and successful career in the UN and has remained a great family friend, although, in the end, he and my sister both married different people. My sister became a divorce barrister before she married John Jones, a criminal barrister and also, now, a recorder, but stopped practicing while she brought up her three children. When they were older she went back to the law as a Clerk to a couple of Courts and has ended up as an Immigration Judge. She has to take very tough decisions and is, indeed, very decisive but she is also one of the most generous people I have ever met and is much loved by her family.

**The Menu was:**

*Iced Yoghurt 'Soup'*

*Roast Ducklings with Honey and Orange Sauce* (p. 232)

*New Potatoes and Courgettes with Chopped Mint*

*Cheese*

*Zabaglioni*

And the wines were a Muscadet, 1963 and Château de Beauregard, 1959.

### JUNE 5th, 1966

**DINNER:** *Eden and Marston Fleming*
*Lesley Blanch*
*Norah Sayre*
*Billy McCarty*
*Ken Tynan*
*Henry and Bettina McNulty*

Norah Sayre was staying with us again from New York. And the writer, Lesley Blanch, was over from France and staying with Eden and

Marston Fleming. She was as blonde as Eden was dark and gypsy-ish. I think they may have first met when she was studying painting at the Slade before she took to journalism and writing. I had met her at dinner with them and liked her so much, I had in any case particularly admired her various books: *The Wilder Shores of Love* and *Around the World in 80 Dishes* (a cook book) both written in the 1950s and *The Sabres of Paradise, Under a Lilac Bleeding Star* and her then latest, *The 9 Tiger Man*, all written in the first half of the 1960s. She was certainly a good title-thinker (or her publisher was), as well as a prolific writer, and – a friend and colleague of Lee Miller – she had been Features Editor of British *Vogue* from the late 1930s till just before the end of World War Two. In that year, 1945, she had married the French novelist and diplomat, Romain Gary and, although by all accounts it had been a tempestuous marriage, she had travelled with him when he worked in the Balkans, Turkey, North Africa, Mexico and the USA. They divorced in 1962 after he went off with Jean Seberg, who had played Joan in the film of George Bernard Shaw's *St. Joan*.

Billy McCarty, an American designer, then working sporadically with David Hicks (and instigating a great many of his product designs) became such a good friend as well as a godfather to our future son. He had previously worked in Philadelphia with one of America's architectural icons, Louis Khan, before moving over to London and I had recently photographed some of his work which I much admired. He was enormously tall and skinny and always beautifully dressed with an impressive collection of Jermyn Street shirts and bow ties, though at that time he had very little money. Nevertheless, he always arrived with a bunch of flowers, even though his living accommodation for several years was a bedroom with a mattress and a couple of cases for tables. I say at that time, because his fortunes changed – literally – when he was adopted as the son and heir of the Australian collector and art critic, Douglas Cooper, another great friend of Picasso, who by then had an enviable art-filled folly of a château near Orange, in Provence. When Cooper died, Billy took much of his very valuable collection back to the USA, a move bitterly fought by France. After Billy so sadly died of Aids in the early 1990s, the collection could not be kept together anyway. Billy, in his usual ridiculously generous way, had left so many behests, the collection had to be auctioned over two days by Christies, New York, mostly in order to pay out so much to legatees. But that was all later and, in the meantime, I liked his style so much that I had arranged to work with him as often as I could so that I could learn from him, just as I used to work with Jimmy Andrade to get more knowledge about furniture and objects.

# THURLOE SQUARE, 1966

**The Menu was:**

*Hors d'oeuvres (of Mushrooms à la Greque, Broad Beans and Artichoke Bottoms, Black Olives, Salami)*

*Roast Shoulder of Veal with White Wine Sauce*

*Roast New Potatoes and Onions*

*Salad of Watercress*

*Cheese*

*Eton Mess*


## JUNE 27th, 1966

**DINNER:** *Dr William Gooddy*
*Dr Margaret Reinhold*
*Spike and Paddy Milligan*
*Dr Graeme Robertson*
*Margot Walmsley*

Bill Gooddy was a neurological colleague of Roger's who was an interesting polymath character, as much interested in different aspects of the arts and in wine as in medicine and an amusing conversationalist. We had many good evenings with him in his flat behind Marble Arch, with his attractive friend and colleague Margaret Reinholdt with whom he wrote several scientific papers. But this dinner was also for another neurologist, the Australian E. Graeme Robertson, visiting from Sydney, who was also a polymath and an expert on 'Sydney Lace', the beautiful railings and ornamental ironwork made by convicts from the ballast in ships going out to Australia, which decorated the exteriors of so many old houses in Sydney. He had written several books about it, aided and photographed by his daughter Joan, and ended by writing the seminal *Cast Iron Decoration: A World Survey*, also greatly helped by his daughter, because he felt that the exquisite cast iron decoration of the Ninteenth Century was not sufficiently appreciated for its aesthetic value and was being destroyed wholesale. In fact, Graeme Robertson and his daughter were hugely responsible for the preservation of all the cast iron work that we see around the world today.

Spike – who, though born in India had mostly grown up in Australia – and was also, in many ways, dedicated to the preservation of old things – was interested in talking to him. Australians always particularly valued Spike and his zany humour. Moreover, there was

125

talk in Woy Woy, near Sydney, where Spike's parents lived, of naming the suspension bridge on the cycle path from Woy Woy to Gosford after him. Not quite the Sydney Harbour Bridge, but still.

I always giggled at the names of Spike's imaginary characters and their doings in *The Goon Show* and later. I am not sure that some of them ever hit the light of day, like Pontius Cack and his *Grandmothers Hurling Contest* where the idea was to take your grandmothers to Land's End and see who could throw them furthest out to sea. I was amused whenever we were taken to a restaurant by the Milligans, which were invariably Italian, at the way he purportedly spoke the language. He had not actually learnt Italian at all, but he was such a good mimic of the accent and the cadences that he completely fooled the waiters even though he was generally talking rubbish. Before they latched on, Paddy tactfully launched in with the orders in English. It did not occur to them that it was not they who had misheard. In a BBC Poll in 1999 he was voted 'The Funniest Man in the last *1,000* years'. A very well deserved award but a *thousand?* What listeners were still around, I wondered.

**The Menu was:**

*Smoked Trout Pâté*

*Crown of Lamb with Béarnaise Sauce (with Mint not Tarragon)*

*Courgettes, New Peas and Jersey New Potatoes*

*Cheese*

*Charentais Melons Stuffed with Raspberries with a Coulis of Raspberries*

And the wines were Château Croizet-Bages Pauillac, 1953 and Raventhüler Steinhaufen, Auslese, 1953.


**JULY 2nd, 1966**

**LUNCH IN THE GARDEN:** *Bettina McNulty*
*Penelope Gilliatt (Osborne)*
*Mary Jane Poole*
*Lee Penrose (Miller)*
*Billy McCarty*

This was a somewhat Condé Nast lunch. Mary Jane Poole, the Editor of American *House & Garden* was over in London and Bettina, who was a good friend and ex-colleague of hers, thought that I should meet her. Both Lee and Penelope, as I have mentioned, were distinguished British *Vogue* alumnae, Lee as a photographer (both as War Correspondent and for fashion) and Penelope as Features Editor. And I wanted Billy – who did not in the least bit mind being the only man with five women – to meet with Mary Jane who I thought might be interested in his work -- and mine too, I suppose.

**The Menu was:**

Cold Breast of Chicken in a Tarragon Chaud-Froid

Tomato and Basil Salad

Blackcurrant Leaf Water Ice (pp. 226–7)

And the wine was a Provençale Vin Rosé.


**AUGUST 8th, 1966**

**DINNER:** *Princess Margaret and Tony Snowdon*
*Spike and Paddy Milligan*
*Max and Joan Reinhardt*
*Ian and Susan Anstruther*
*Ken Tynan and Kathleen Halton*


Here was another dinner just before the Snowdons decamped to Balmoral and they were delighted to meet the Milligans, as always, as was everyone else. Spike was on terrific form and the Milligans became favourites of the Snowdons and introduced them to Peter Sellars, who became another Snowdon favourite.

It was also good for Ken and Kathleen to meet the Anstruthers, their new landlords, since they had finally moved just across the road from us, to the other corner of Alexander Place leading into Thurloe Square. It was apposite for the Tynans and Reinhardts to meet too, as other near neighbours.

However, I had one rather scary moment. I had heard from Tony that he had taken Terence Conran to see what they had achieved with the renovation and decoration of their part of Kensington Palace and that Princess Margaret, still very proud of her rose bathroom, had insisted on showing it to him. According to Tony, she had told Terence there was a great view from the bath. 'Oh yes, Ma'am,' Terence had replied, who most uncharacteristically that day, was wearing a formal pin striped suit. 'You should try it', said the Princess, 'but you will need to get into the bath'. Terence started to demur, but she insisted. 'You *must* get in, right in,' she said. And poor Terence – again according to Tony – had to clamber in, and sit there in order to get the exact view she wanted him to see, all in his smart suit.

I was talking to her before dinner and foolishly said that I thought the story about her persuading Terence Conran to climb into her bath was very funny. She fixed me with her occasional haughty look. 'What *are* you talking about?' she demanded. '*Who* is this Terence Conran? Are you really saying that some strange man got into my bath? *Who* told you this?' I did not dare tell her it was her husband who had told me and I was just starting to stumble away and mumble, erroneously, that Terence had told me when, luckily, Spike, feeling bold, came to divert her and she miraculously appeared to forget about it.

Still, Tony assured me it was true and I never got around to asking Terence. Tony also told me that she had taken the whole business of decorating their home with utter seriousness. She had even climbed up a ladder in the kitchen clutching an egg to make sure that the wall colour was the exact shade of its brown shell.

Apart from that, it was a very pleasant evening. Not too hot, not too cold and a dinner that seemed just right although I did not often enjoy my own cooking. Though not in the least a perfectionist, which, as a designer I probably should have been, I was genuinely very critical of my own food. My children find this extremely irritating, thinking I am just looking for compliments when it is just that I know what everything *should* taste like.

**The Menu was:**

*Hors d'Oeuvres of Mushrooms à la Greque, Fèves au Lard, Black Olives, Rice and Pimento Salad, Shrimp Vinaigrette*

*Roast Contre Filet, Sauce Madère*

*Pommes Pont-Neuf*

*Stuffed Tomatoes*

*Salad of Tiny French Beans*

*Cheese*

*Small Charentais Melons filled with Blackcurrant Leaf Water Ice*

# Thurloe Square, 1966

And the wines were Château Lanessan, 1953 and Raventhüler Steinhaufer, Auslese, 1953.

## SEPTEMBER 1st, 1966

**LUNCH:** *Paddy Milligan*
*Anna de Goguel*
*Eileen O'Casey*
*Penelope Gilliatt (Osborne)*
*Claudie Worsthorne*

This was a real girls' lunch though I have no idea now, what occasioned it. But I did put a note that it was considerably enlivened towards the end by a ring at the door and, when I went to answer it there, to my astonishment, was Sir John Gielgud rather curiously holding a small, familiar women's umbrella. I had met him once with my friend, the designer Paul Anstee, and, the day before, I had been lunching at Sheeky's, the fish restaurant in Soho. True, it had been raining, and, true, I had seen Sir John at a corner table with some other people, and he had given a lordly wave of his hand, so I was flattered that he even remembered me. 'You left your umbrella behind yesterday,' he said in his mellifluous voice which, as Sir Lawrence Olivier had once remarked, was 'The voice that woo'd the world'. 'I saw you had forgotten it when I passed by your table soon after. I meant to bring it back to you yesterday afternoon but I got involved in something else and then there was not time.'

I was immensely touched that he had bothered to pick it up in the first place (I had not missed it since the rain had stopped by the time we got outside), let alone to then find out where I lived and deliver it. But he would not stay for a coffee, much as I, and everyone else, would have liked it. That was a real 'Knight and the Umbrella' incident, aka Ian Anstruther's *The Knight and the Umbrella* book.

**The Menu was:**

*Artichokes with Sauce Hollandaise*

*Breaded Veal Cutlets*

*Puréed Spinach*

*Junket and Compôte of Cherries*

And the wine was a White Hermitage, 1959.

# Mary Gilliatt's Fabulous Food and Friends

## SEPTEMBER 11th, 1966

**DINNER:** *Helen Cohen (Andrew was tied up)*
*George McWatters (Joy was away)*
*Billy McCarty*
*Terence and Caroline Conran*
*Claudie Worsthorne (Perry was away)*
*Anthony Nutting (Annie was away)*

Clearly, this was a dinner for mainly left-behinds rather than left-overs since I'd noted that various spouses were not around. Except for Billy McCarty whom we were now feeding pretty regularly, they had all met each other at one time or another and mostly with Roger and I. Terence's *Habitat* shop, just down the road (at what is now known as Brompton Cross) was doing extremely well (though I was surprised to read somewhere quite recently that he had described its original location as in a really run-down area which had been made fashionable by the shop). I have lived on and off in South Kensington for years – ever since 1955 in fact – and at no time could I have described the corner of the Brompton and Fulham Roads and Sloane and Draycott Avenues as really run-down.

**The Menu was:**

*Melon with Prosciutto St. Daniele*

*Late Summer Chicken*

*Pommes Anna*

*Little Green Beans*

*Cheese*

*Blackberries and Sweet Geranium Leaf Cream* (p. 249)

And the wine was a St. Emilion (Rothschild), 1955.

## OCTOBER 5th, 1966

**KITCHEN SUPPER:** *Claudie Worsthorne and her son, David*
*(unexpectedly)*

I'm not quite sure why Claudie had arrived around drinks time with her son by her first marriage, though I suspect she might have been dropping in a present for her goddaughter Annie (then still Anne-Louise) whose first birthday was the next day. Anyway, we persuaded them to stay for a kitchen supper since it was just Roger and I.

**The Menu was:**

*Oeufs en Cocotte à l'Éstragon*

*Shepherd's Pie*

*Cabbage with Sour Cream and Paprika*

*Cheese*

*Fruit*

And the wine was Côtes de Beaune, 1959.

### OCTOBER 22nd, 1966

**DINNER:** *Ivor and Jan Burt*
*Terence and Caroline Conran*
*Winefride Jackson*
*David and Angela Caccia*
*Jeanne Wilkins*

An old friends get-together again but also a reunion for Angela Caccia and I, and to a certain extent, Caroline, who also knew Angela, because Winefride Jackson, our former Editor of the Women's pages on *The Sunday Telegraph,* had joined us. In the late 1950s and 1960s there had been a powerhouse of Sunday Women's Page editors: on *The Sunday Times,* the tiny, always beautifully dressed, American, Ernestine Carter who almost always wore little pill box hats and always gloves; Winefride on *The Sunday Telegraph* and Katherine Whitehorn, the much-admired and very witty columnist on *The Observer.* On *The Daily Mail* there was Shirley Conran, on *The Evening Standard,* Barbara Griggs, Felicity Green (later to get in the Press Gazette Newspapers Hall of Fame) was on *The Daily Mirror,* Jill Butterfield, I think, on *The Daily Express* (who had followed me as assistant to Joy Mathews/McWatters) and had taken over from her. On *The Times,* there was Prue Glyn and on *The Daily Telegraph* was Winifred Carr and her side kick, Alice Hope, who also wrote about design. I had heard that the latter had gone around saying 'that of course I had *had* to get married to Roger' but I confounded her by having my first child, Sophia, bang on time 11 months after we married. Almost all the women working in what was then known as Fleet Street, knew each other and got on pretty well. I say this because I have recently sometimes been astonished, particularly in the USA and the Antipodes, by some editors refusing to communicate with others on different publications, or even to let journalists mention other publications – as if the reader was stupid enough not to notice that there were any competitors.

This was certainly not so in the UK at the time. When I was on *The Times*, my boss, Muriel Forbes (or Mary Delaney as she was known before when she was on *The Sunday Times*) had sent me out to do a survey of all the ladies' cloakrooms provided by the various London stations and to try out both the lavatories and the washing/bathing facilities. This was after a series of complaints from readers about revolting conditions. I obediently went around, religiously tried them all out, and wrote my reports, Euston being particularly frightful. I remember rather trepidatiously asking the Scottish woman attendant if I could have a bath in the disgusting-looking bathroom at that station, only to be asked for my long distance rail ticket. I made up some excuse, since it was a very cold winter, about my pipes being frozen and she looked me up and down. 'Ye look alright on top,' she said, 'but it entairely depends on what yer like underneath.' She did not, however, inspect me and I, for my part, felt I needed another bath after the loathsome station one. I am happy to report that the station upgraded not too long after.

In the meantime, Mrs Forbes had gone off for a holiday in Rome, leaving me in charge. I wrote the piece and it was duly published on our Monday pages. The next morning I received a telegram from Italy saying 'Today, you have made *The Times* the laughing stock of Europe. Most disappointing.' This was a bit of a downer but, luckily, in the same in-basket were two congratulatory notes from the Editor, Sir William Haley, and the blind, but talented Features Editor, Frank Dobson. And that day too, there was a banner headline on *The Daily Mirror* right across the front page saying 'THE TIMES SPENDS A PENNY' (spending a penny being a uniquely British euphemism for peeing, because that was what it then cost in any public lavatory). Later in the week, Katherine Whitehorn, who also wrote for *The Spectator*, added that wasn't it apt that the woman who wrote the, by now famous, *Times* article on public lavatories lived in St. Loo Mansions, Flood Street in Chelsea. (*The Times* allowed no by-lines then. You were either 'A Correspondent', 'Our Correspondent' or our 'Special Correspondent').

Mrs Forbes however, back from holiday, remained not in the least bit pleased and insisted that I had made *The Times* look as 'if it had clay feet'. Stung – she had asked me to do the report after all – she was now making me feel like Anne Baxter in Bette Davis's 1950 film, *All About Eve*. I was unkind enough to show her the congratulatory notes from Sir William and Frank Dobson which I had not intended to, given her telegram. 'Huh,' she said bitterly, 'It's just because you're a pretty face.' 'But Mr Dobson's blind.' I could not resist. Anyway, Winefride had been a very caring and encouraging Editor, such a refreshing change, and in those early days of the paper, before we had produced its first issue, we had had a riotous time preparing a whole series of dummy papers writing more and more improbable features. Once the paper started, we most often had to stay till the early hours of the morning on Thursdays to get our part of the paper 'to bed' – nothing was really automated then – and we had to mark up the pages ourselves. At 6.30 pm or so, out came Winefride's gin and tonics and crisps for us and she would send out later for something for supper to eat at our desks. On Fridays, we had to take it in turns to work with the printers, to correct proofs on the stone, as we had done on *The Times* when it was still in Printing House Square. She was one of the godmothers of our eldest daughter, Sophia and lived a long life, dying when she was 90 in 1999.

**The Menu was:**

*Prawn Cocktail* (pp. 223–4)

*Baked Ham*

*Baked Potatoes, Creamed Leeks*

*Cheese*

*Iced Honey Soufflé*

### NOVEMBER 13th, 1966

**DINNER:** *Ken Tynan and Kathleen Halton*
*Spike and Paddy Milligan*
*Peter Sellers and Britt Ekland*
*Jonathan and Rachel Miller*

Spike was a very close friend and *Goon* colleague, of course, of Peter Sellers, at that time married to the actress Britt Ekland. Britt was actually the second of Peter's four actress wives, with actress Anne Howe, just before her, Miranda Quarry (now the Countess of Stockton and married to Prime Minister, Harold Macmillan's grandson), just after her, and finally, Lynne Frederick (who later married Sir David Frost). In fact, irreverent Spike, referred to a 'Peter Sellers Discarded Wives' Memorial' in a radio show in the next decade.

We had actually had dinner with Spike and Paddy and the Sellers, which Peter had insisted on hosting, after a performance of the long-running *Son of Oblomov*. We had been to the first night at the Lyric Theatre in Hammersmith when it was just the classic Russian play *Oblomov* by Ivan Goncharov. Spike, who, I suppose, did rather look like a lugubrious Russian, thought it a good part for this rare foray into live theatre, because he could spend so much of the play performing from his bed. But he was rather nervous on the first night and he could tell the audience was getting restless. When we were all back in our seats after the interval there was a much longer wait than normal for the curtain to go up. When it did, Spike, deliberately left the script behind and started to ad lib. He was very funny. The audience loved it. The unfortunate rest of the cast tried heroically and with some success to keep up. Result? *Oblomov* turned into the *Son Of Oblomov* and ran to packed audiences in Hammersmith, eventually transferring to the West End.

After it transferred, Spike and Paddy asked us to go to the show again and have dinner afterwards. Very soon after the curtain went up, Spike interrupted the performance and said 'Is that Sellers in the audience? I'd know his laugh anywhere.' He was right and the Sellers joined us in Spike's dressing room after the performance and insisted on taking us all out to dinner. So my dinner was a return.

Unfortunately, Peter had recently had a massive heart attack, aged only 38, and his damaged heart affected him until his early death in his fifties. His charm and wonderfully funny gift for various accents was legion and he simply could not help using them in his conversation. He was voted by fellow comedians and comedy insiders as 'The Comedians' Comedian' and was listed in the top 20 all-time greatest comedy acts. His then wife Britt, a stunning blonde, seemed nice but hardly got a word in edgewise.

Dr Jonathan Miller was basically a neurologist before he reinvented himself so many times and proved himself a real Renaissance Man. He seemed to become an opera, theatre, movie and TV director, scientific historian, actor, comedian, arts show host, writer and latterly a sculptor all with equal ease, occasionally retreating back into neurology. He had worked in Roger's Clinical Neurology Department at Queen Square between 1959 and 1961, before making a resounding hit with Alan Bennett, Peter Cook and Dudley Moore in *Beyond the Fringe* at the Edinburgh Festival. This started a whole new wave of irreverent comedy culminating in the Monty Python shows. As a result of Miller's Edinburgh success, he had been asked by the BBC to present its arts programme, *Monitor*. That year, he had just released his own version of *Alice in Wonderland* and it was good to team him up with Spike and Peter, not to mention Ken and Kathleen, though I found him fairly intimidating.

**The Menu was:**

*Leeks Vinagrette*

*Osso Buccho with Gremolata*

*Risotto Milanese*

*Salad of Watercress and Avocado*

*Cheese*

*Profiteroles (Spike's favourite)*

And the wine was Château Grand-Puy-Lacoste, 1959.

### NOVEMBER 15th, 1966

**DINNER:** *Brigadier and Mrs Hardy-Roberts*
*Annie Nutting (Anthony was away)*
*Patrick and Susan Dean*
*Kenneth Bradshaw*

Brigadier Geoffrey Hardy-Roberts, an ex-army officer, was then the Secretary-Supervisor of the old Middlesex Hospital in London, Roger's other hospital at that time – in tandem with the National Hospital for Nervous Diseases at Queen Square. He ran the hospital like clockwork as I could attest from having had my children there. In those days, London teaching hospitals often had someone in the Brigadier's position and a small administrative office, a matron, theatre and ward sisters, staff nurses and regular nurses, plus cleaners, and it seemed to work very well. Along with the then Minister of Health, Aneurin (Nye) Bevan, Roger's father, William Gilliatt as President, respectively of The Royal Society of Obstetricians and Gynaecologists and The Royal Society of Medicine, as well as the Queen's obstetrician and gynaecologist, was one of the original architects of the National Health Service – bitterly opposed in its setting up, by the majority of the British Medical Association. As Roger had occasion to remark very often in the future, he would have been horrified by the top heavy administration of today. In fact, as far as I can see, he had courageously gone out on a limb so to speak, on several occasions. Most particularly, when he successfully defended in court an abortion he had given to a rape victim; a rare thing for a medical man to do in those days.

As it happened, the following year, Geoffrey Hardy-Roberts was made Master of the Queen's Household – just as effectively running everything 'below stairs' in the royal residences. For this, he was given a charming 'Grace and Favour' residence in St. James' Palace where he and his wife entertained, I hope happily, for many years.

Patrick and Susan Dean were staying with us for a few days. Patrick was another old army friend of Roger's from the 60th Rifle Brigade or Green Jackets, so-called because in the 1760s the regiment was provided with a uniform of dark green and black for camouflage when they fought in the dark green forests of America during the War of Independence. He was also very handsome on one side of his face. The shock was seeing the other which, in spite of numerous plastic surgery interventions, had been very badly scarred when he was shot in the face during the war. As it happened, Patrick was such a flirt and had such verve, energy and irreverence that soon you did not notice any discrepancy. He was also very shrewd. He farmed a large chunk of Lincolnshire producing huge amounts of peas for freezing and was also a director of Hutchinson, the publishers. That night, he was able to divert his considerable attention to the always beautiful and elegant Annie Nutting. I liked his equally good-looking wife, Susan, who had learnt to make a self-preserving habit of ignoring Patrick's frequent attempts at female conquest. She was a member of the Benson Lonsdale banking family, part of Kleinwort Benson. When Terence Conran was trying to raise finance to buy himself out of an early alliance with Ryman, the stationery chain, we introduced him to Patrick and Susan among other people, but Terence finally found his own merchant banking help anyway.

# Thurloe Square, 1966

**The Menu was:**

*Egg and Anchovy Mousse*

*Carbonnade de Boeuf* (p. 221)

*Baked Potatoes and Sour Cream*

*Salad of Lettuce, Watercress, Pear and Avocado*

*Cheese*

*Pineapple Ice Cream with Pineapple*

And the wines were a White Hermitage, 1960 and Côtes de Nuits, 1959.


## DECEMBER 9th, 1966

**DINNER:** *Ella and Don Ogden Stewart*
*Bill and Maria Henson*
*Michael and Annabel Popovic*
*Spike and Paddy Milligan*


Not quite the same old, same old, because we had Michael Popovic and his very pretty wife, Annabel to leaven the mixture. Bill and Maria were over from New York and looking for a house in the UK for when their term at the UN was finished and Michael and Annabel were also over from the UN, though they too, moved to London not so very long after – as far as I remember because Michael had been appointed Director of the UN Information Office in London. They bought a house in Notting Hill, not at all the smart place then that it is now, but they made their house extremely airy and nice. I remember it was the first Nineteenth Century London terraced house I had seen where the dividing wall between living room and narrow hallway had efficaciously been taken down to hip level. This provided some sort of separation between the two spaces while gaining a generous amount of light and at least a feeling of more room.

I notice that we had fried Scampi as the main course. Someone must have made a special request, probably Roger, who loved it. I cannot imagine it was Spike or Paddy who ate at restaurants such a lot, or Ella and Don who were not particularly interested in food anyway. I had also made yet another mousse for the first course because they were so easy to make in advance.

# Mary Gilliatt's Fabulous Food and Friends

**The Menu was:**

*Smoked Salmon Mousse* (p. 257)

*Fried Scampi and Sauce Tartare*

*Salad of Green Beans and Walnuts*

*Cheese*

*Bread and Butter Pudding*

And the wine was Gerwurztraminer, 1959 (which Spike particularly liked) and Volnay, 1959 (with the cheese).

### DECEMBER 18th, 1966

**DINNER:** *Spike and Paddy Milligan*
*David and Susan Hay*
*Annette Reilly (Paul was away)*
*Kathleen Halton (Ken was away)*
*Billy McCarty*
*Ian McDonald*

The Milligans again, at this pre-Christmas dinner. It's hard to believe now. Maybe they were our own private cabaret, or more likely it was because Roger was such a calming and cheering presence for Spike who had always loved him. Anyway, Paddy and I were always on the phone and they knew they could come whenever, whoever else was there or not there – just as the Reillys did.

David Hay was our very good general practitioner and Susan his very nice wife and receptionist. Kathleen Halton and Ken had finally left their flat in Mount Street and moved into their new house in Thurloe Square, just across the way from us, which she had made very handsome. Like a lot of exceptionally beautiful, exceptionally well-dressed people, who you would presume to have excellent taste in houses too, she, at that time, lacked confidence in her decorating ability and had asked practically every well known decorator in London for advice – including Billy McCarty. But unlike a lot of people she followed the advice well.

I was beginning to have – if not a love-hate relationship with Kathleen – at least a love-irritation one. I had recently come back rather late one evening after a photographic session and hurried to put the dinner together only to find the fridge stripped of the pâté and chicken pie I had made the day before (in anticipation of the next day's lateness). And, because I had had no time to do other food shopping, and the

138

shops were not open late then, anyway, there was nothing else with which I could really compromise. I asked our nanny what on earth had happened and was told that Kathleen had come round saying that she suddenly had Sir Lawrence and Lady Olivier coming unexpectedly for dinner with Marlene Dietrich and did not have any food in the house nor any time to get any. She said she was sure, the nanny reported, no doubt somewhat influenced by the Tynan's guest list, that I would not mind. She was very convincing, the Nanny added. She must have been. From that time on I have always tried to keep the makings of emergency dinners in the larder.

Another time, a few months later, we had been over to a party with the Tynans with masses of other people, many of them sitting up and down the stairs. I noticed that there were a lot of discarded but beautiful engraved glasses on the floor and stairs, many of them with air twist stems, scattered dangerously about – in the sense that they could so easily get accidentally kicked over and broken. Being a collector of old glasses myself, including some rare Jacobite glasses (engraved by Stuart supporters after the House of Hanover, in the person of William III – of William and Mary fame – who deposed the Stuart dynasty in 1688. Such supporters continued to engrave glasses with symbols like six-petalled roses, rose-buds, oak leaves and thistles engraved on glasses well into the Eighteenth Century to show their discreet – but ineffectual – loyalty to the Stuart cause), I was nervous about their possible fate.

I suddenly had an awful suspicion and examined one more closely. Sure enough, Kathleen had again been over in my absence and told the poor nanny that I had said she could borrow some glasses for the party that night (although she had conspicuously failed to ask me). The nanny showed her where I kept my glasses in the kitchen and was surprised when she ran upstairs and also scooped up all my glass collection from the display in the drawing room, though the nanny had not liked to query it. Apart from, and in spite of, these infuriating foibles, Kathleen had become a good friend and I really think that for some reason, she was supremely unaware of doing anything inconvenient or aggravating. Also, I was guiltily conscious – and discussed it with other friends that knew her and felt the same thing – that it was very easy to be envious of Kathleen's great beauty, so maybe one was more critical than one should have been.

However, as I was to discover, she was not especially caring about her more ordinary women acquaintances. She had invited both ourselves and Don and Ella Ogden Stewart to dinner one night – evidently forgetting that we were old friends and had actually introduced them to each other (although Ken had known Don's son, Donald Ogden

Stewart Junior – commonly known as 'Duck' from *The New Yorker* office). She had apologised to each of us in advance, as we later discovered, saying, 'I am afraid there are only some rather boring, rich people coming!' The Ogden Stewarts might have been rich but they were certainly not boring. We might well have been boring but were certainly not rich. When we both saw who these intriguing rich, boring fellow guests were, it was hard not to burst out laughing.

As an irresistibly bitchy little last word, in spite of all the time the Tynans spent with us in London and the country, and the fact that I helped her decorate her new NY apartment for nothing after Ken died, I noticed in Kathleen's biography *The Life of Ken Tynan*, published in 1987 (seven years after Ken's death from emphysemia), that she mentioned Roger only once, and then as 'the neurologist husband of Penelope Gilliatt'. I was not mentioned at all. Not, I hasten to add, that there was much reason to mention either of us, among all the glitterati. But that again, was much into the future and this was then. Kathleen herself died – of cancer – in 1995, 15 years after Ken.

Ian McDonald was another polymath neurologist. He was a Rhodes Scholar from New Zealand, a lyrical pianist and now worked with Roger at Queen Square. Indeed he eventually took over Roger's chair after Roger retired, although there were a couple of professional appointments in between. They had begun to be very good friends as well as close colleagues and we began to see a good deal of him from then on.

**The Menu was:**

*Courgette Soufflé*

*Roast Partridges*

*Game chips, Bread sauce, Little Brussels Sprouts with Bacon*

*Cheese*

*Petits Pots de Chocolat*

And the wines were Rudesheimer Riesling, 1953 and Volnay, 1959.

### DECEMBER 23rd, 1966

**DINNER:** *Anne Gilliatt*
*Eliza Gilliatt*

Anne Gilliatt was my mother-in-law and Eliza my sister-in-law and this was another pre-Christmas dinner because we were going to Suffolk the next day to spend the actual Christmas with my family. I had not met my gynaecologist father-in-law, who had been killed in 1956 in a motor car accident coming back from Ascot to see a horse run – which he owned jointly with the then Duke of Norfolk. Anne Gilliatt, his widow, who had evidently loved him very much and absolutely haloed his memory, always referred to him as 'Nephew' for some reason, was a doctor in her own right and had been a very early anaesthetist. However, she was very deaf and had had several small strokes before I had met her and she was consequently both somewhat aphasic and dysphasic which meant her speech was affected to the extent that she got both genders and tenses muddled, which made conversation not only slow but a matter for conjecture. She made up for this with a slightly toothless but sweet and questioning smile. By that time, it was very rare for her to venture out from her flat in Bryanston Square, so this was an honour.

Eliza, unmarried, had been personal secretary to Winston Churchill from 1945 to 1955 when he finally stepped down as Prime Minister, and was the soul of discretion though she had an unexpectedly lusty sense of humour. When Churchill died in 1965, he had left her a little money in his will. Her parents had, at one time, lived next door to the Churchills and once they were both widowed, my mother-in-law and old Lady Churchill used to go for afternoon drives together, though both were already as deaf as posts so there could not have been much chat. At that stage, although Eliza had been asked by Sir Anthony Eden, the next Prime Minister to continue on with him, she had decided to take the quite different job of Permanent Secretary to the annual Lord Mayors of London. I was very fond of her and all three of my children cherished her dearly and went on cherishing her till her death in 2004. She was a most generous aunt and her job at the Mansion House afforded her the opportunity to give her small nieces, future nephew and friends a grandstand view of the annual Lord Mayor's Procession in the City of London.

**The Menu was:**

*Salmon Caviar, Sour Cream and Blinis with Vodka*

*Roast Fillet of Beef, Sauce Béarnaise*

*Pommes de Terre Rissolées*

*Salad of Watercress*

*Cheese*

*Bitter Orange Tart*

And the wine was Nuits St Georges, 1953.

# CHAPTER FIVE

# THURLOE SQUARE AND TOSTOCK, 1967

THIS was a very mouvementé year. In the Spring, we started to rent an unfurnished cottage for weekends and holidays in Suffolk outside the village of Tostock, about five miles from Bury St Edmunds and some 20 from my parents. My son Tom was born on October 6th – exactly two years to the day from his sister Annie – and my first book, *English Style*, was published about two weeks later.

We had a lot of guests in this very small cottage where, if you were one half of a couple you more or less had to climb over the bed in the guest room to get to the far side. Any spare guests had to sleep on sofa beds in the nursery. Because I had grown up in the county and my parents and brother and sister-in-law still lived there, we had a good nucleus of friends. From here on, I kept two dinner books, one for each house. But as usual, I list them chronologically.

In January, we took the two girls to stay with my parents and went to New York for a couple of weeks. Roger for medical meetings and I to meet with a couple of Editors of publications who were interested in taking extracts from my first book *English Style* – which was coming out the following October – and doing a bit of other advance publicity. Barbara Plumb, then Editor of the home pages for *The New York Times* had written to me before Christmas to say that Viking Books (the US Publishers) had shown her some sample pages from the book and she would like to print an extract in *The Times'* *Sunday Magazine*. She wondered if there was any hope of my coming to New York any time soon because she'd like to meet me. And Sarah Tomerlin Lee, the then Editor of *House Beautiful,* also wanted to do an extract and also wanted a meeting if I came to NY. Bryan Holmes, my Editor at Viking, and their publicity team were early on the job. Obviously, authors are often absurdly proprietorial about their books, but marketing and publicity seemed to be treated with much greater verve in those days when PR budgets were considerably larger than they are now and, as a result, sales were too. Anyway, I had written back to both of them giving the January dates but, of course, had no idea that both these women would become such lifelong friends.

I was impressed because, when I rather tentatively called Barbara Plumb as she had asked, she turned out to be just home from hospital after having her son, Christian, although she had not previously mentioned her imminent baby. Nevertheless, she invited me to tea at her apartment and was, as she told me later, expecting a much older woman and not someone in their early-thirties, just as she was. I too, thinking nervously, 'Hmm, an Editor on the great *NY Times*', was agreeably surprised to be greeted by this smiley, lively, very attractive young blonde woman. After a long lunch a few days later, where we could not stop talking, Roger and I invited Barbara and her then husband Bill, a talented industrial designer with a pithy taste in form-fitting Italian clothes (he had worked with Gio Ponti, the great Italian architect in Milan where he and Barbara had both lived soon after their marriage), over and we all got along very well. When Barbara later left *The NY Times* and moved over to publishing she became my Editor for a time and wrote some very successful books of her own. Later, she moved to *Vogue* as their Design Editor where she remained for 13 years before moving on to write more books and articles for different publications.

Sarah Tomerlin Lee was something of a legend. She took me to lunch and asked me to write an article defining style for *House Beautiful* as well as taking an extract from the book. I thought her an extraordinary person. She had grown up in Tennessee in the South and had, as I was soon to discover – and heard for the rest of her life – an unlimited fund of stories about her family and her early working days in New York. At one time, she had been the right-hand to Helena Rubinstein and almost always wore a huge brimmed hat, gloves and very often an impressive necklace of uncut emeralds that Ms Rubinstein had given her, otherwise it was pearls all the way. She had also been Managing Editor of American *Vogue*, the first woman on the board of Lord & Taylor, a well-established NY Store, and the first woman on the board of any major store for that matter. She was married to Tom Lee, a popular hotel designer, and the Lees too, subsequently took Roger and I out to dinner on that trip. Later, that year, and quite coincidentally, both the Plumbs and the Lees visited England at different times. We saw them in London and both came to stay in Suffolk. We, in our turn, stayed with them later in New York and Greenwich. When Tom Lee was tragically killed in a motor car accident a few years later, Sarah took over his hotel design business and went on to design several hotels for Hilton, the Parker Meridian in NY and completely restored and revamped the old Willard in Washington DC, as well as designing for other hotel groups all over the US.

I was delighted, years later, when she asked me to lunch to meet the ex-manager of the Plaza, who had figured prominently under his real name in Kay Thompson's much-loved book *Eloise: A Book for Precocious Grown Ups*. When, later still, two of my small granddaughters were staying with me in NY and the elder, an *Eloise* fan, was about to have her fourth birthday, I managed with Sarah's connivance, to hire a child actor to play Eloise, and have her to a small birthday tea in the Plaza. All dressed up as Eloise and looking astonishingly like her, the small actress met us in the Lobby. Olivia, my granddaughter, shyly said hello – as if it was entirely normal to have Eloise to tea with her in the hotel where she lived. But she happened to glance up at the portrait of Eloise that hung on the wall of the lobby, and then back at the purportedly real Eloise. 'Your hair is very tidy today,' she remarked questioningly. Quick as a whip the savvy little girl said, 'My Mother is here. She made me brush it for you.'

Sarah was still working, still wearing her wonderful hats and gloves, still telling her anecdotes, when she died aged 90.

Because of this American trip we did not do any particular entertaining in January. Kathleen Halton seems to have come several nights running in early-February so I guess Ken was away. Our first real dinner party then, was the second week in February, by which time I was just pregnant for the third time.

## FEBRUARY 15th, 1967

**DINNER:** *Princess Margaret (Tony was away with Paul Reilly on British Council business)*
*Billy McCarty*
*Tom and Fleur Cowles Meyer*
*Roger and Moira Bannister*
*Ian McDonald*
*Michael White*

Billy was always easy and urbane with people and was at his charming best with HRH although he towered over her. Ian McDonald too – whose good looks were much as I had imagined Heathcliff's to have been, and who became Roger's particular friend – had a great love and knowledge of music and the ballet so he also kept her well-entertained, the more particularly as she was President of The Royal Ballet and so musical herself. I had asked Michael White, actually *because* he was an extra man since I had the feeling both HRH and Fleur would appreciate that fact as well as him – and indeed he was as attractive and laconic as ever. I was aware that HRH kept eyeing him, and even before dinner she asked me if I could ask Michael to drive her home when it was time

Finally, I had been able to get the 'infinitely creative and indomitable' (as I read a few years ago in NY) Fleur Cowles to dinner with Princess Margaret, so no headache for Fleur that night. In any case, Fleur was always full of stories and no wonder. She was a naïve painter somewhat in the style of E. Box, wrote well, was an energetic and generous hostess – her Wednesday salons were legendary, as were her weekends and Sunday lunches – and an equally legendary Editor when married to Mike Cowles, then one of America's biggest magazine publishers whose stable included *Life* Magazine and *Look* (which Fleur had edited). Her triumph though, 'Her Memorial' as she is on record as saying, was *Flair* magazine which she first conceived and directed in 1950. According to *The New York Review of Magazines*, quoting a professor of journalism specializing in US magazines, this was 'The most magnificently designed magazine ever produced in this country.' It had articles by Jean Cocteau, Eleanor Roosevelt and Tenessee Williams, interviews with people like Salvadore Dali and the Duchess of Windsor – who gave useful decorating tips – and stunning photography and lay-outs. Convinced that everyone was enticed by a little mystery, Fleur (who rarely went swimming without wearing a kaftan or decorative overshirt over her bathing suit) insisted on a cut-out hole in different shapes on each issue's cover, giving a mini foretaste of whatever she judged of particular interest inside. *Flair* had a cover price of 50 cents and cost $1.20 to print. Nothing very much in today's terms but a lot then and I cannot imagine that it was allowed to be crammed with ads. It only lasted for one memorable year but its legend lives on. In 2000, Rizzoli published *The Best of Flair* with a new edition in 2003 which costs $250 a copy.

After her divorce from Mike Cowles, Fleur met and married the amiable, agreeable and amenable Tom Montagu Meyer, another good army friend of Roger's, and has lived between London, her house in the country and her castle in Spain ever since. That Autumn, when my first book came out, she generously gave a party for it.

Roger Bannister, literally a legend in his own lifetime, was the first man to run a mile in four minutes the decade before, in 1954. He had gone on to become a neurologist, working, at that time, with Roger at Queen Square. He bore his fame lightly, as they say, and always seemed, on the surface, a beaky, rather diffident and studious-looking man with floppy hair who nevertheless achieved much distinction in medicine as well as in the field of sport, ending up as Master of Pembroke College, Oxford. His wife Moira, was a daughter of Per Jacobsen, the Swede, who had been a distinguished head of the International Monetary Fund from 1956 to 1963. Most fellow neurologists who had done their almost mandatory stint with the much-admired Professor Denny Brown in Boston, found the Bannisters memorable for being, though junior at that time, able to afford to live in a comfortable hotel instead of the usual rather grotty digs the rest were generally forced to inhabit. Actually, I had been a bit wary of having Moira. Soon after Roger and I had been married, when we were still living in my flat, I had all the Queen Square colleagues and their wives, or husbands, to dinner and I cooked rather good party food I thought – and I'd been cooking for a long while after all – so I was somewhat taken aback when she told me that she knew a very good place where I could learn to cook… and it had gone on rankling. I cannot remember whether she made any such remarks that night. It was, after all, four years later.

**The Menu was:**

Fish Terrine Suédoise

Lamb Cutlets in Puff Pastry with a Tomato Coulis

Château Potatoes

Salad of Tiny Green Beans

Cheese

Highland Flummery

And the wines were Wurtzburger, 1953 and Château Grand-Puy-Lacoste, 1959.

**MARCH 3rd, 1967**

**DINNER:** Marston and Eden Fleming
Ken Tynan and Kathleen Halton
Teddy and Denise Obolensky
Bimby and Daphne Holt

# Thurloe Square and Tostock, 1967

The Obolenskys lived just along the way from us in Thurloe Square and Teddy was a cousin of the well-known New Yorker, Colonel Serge Obolensky, born Prince Obolensky, who grew up in Russia and first married one of the many daughters of Czar Alexander II who later divorced him. It all seemed very pre-revolutionary, Tolstoyan and romantic. Thanks to Teddy, an aptly-named rotund teddy bear of a man, we had met this intriguing guy in New York. He was in his late 70s by then but still charming and indeed had been a noted World War Two hero in his 50s but nevertheless still parachuting. He had revived well-known New York hotels like the Plaza and the St. Regis and had married again, this time to Alice Astor, a daughter of Col. John Jacob Astor who had gone down in The Titanic in 1912 but before that had built the Astoria Hotel next to the Waldorf which then became the Waldorf-Astoria. I mention Serge Obolensky's potted history because he seemed such a link with those extraordinary, heady and extraordinarily opulent Edwardian days in NY.

Teddy himself was in the film business and the main things I remember about their house were not only the magnificent saved Russian icons, Fabergé boxes and objects but their guest loo. This was either a replica, or perhaps even a preserved compartment in all its resplendent glory, from Czar Alexander II's personal train.

Bimby was another old army friend of Roger's and Chairman of Hutchinson, the publishers as well as a Governor of Harrow School where he later established a fund for bursaries. He had also, in his youth, been Racquets or Real Tennis Champion of the UK, I don't recall which. I liked him and his wife, Daphne very much. They were kind and thoughtful and extremely pleasant to deal with. I know, because later I helped decorate a new London house for them and they were model clients. This was a return dinner for them.

**The Menu was:**

Coquilles St. Jacques (p. 258)

Lemon Chicken (p. 259)

Pommes Anna (p. 231)

Spinach with Olive Oil and Pine Nuts

Cheese

Coffee Jelly

And the wines were Puligny-Montrachet, 1960 and Côtes de Nuits Village, 1957.

147

# Mary Gilliatt's Fabulous Food and Friends

## MAY 2nd, 1967

**DINNER:** *Sharon and Pierre Courtoux*
*Pierre Normand*
*Claudie Worsthorne*

We had given a lot of small dinners since March but Roger and I had also been busy decorating the small cottage in Suffolk that we had rented and trying to get it habitable for the summer, as well as cutting down the towering weeds in order to make some sort of garden. This was more or less a French evening because my diverting friend, Sharon Buckner – who had been the Zuleika Dobson of Paris in her day – had come to stay for a weekend with her second husband, a complete contrast to her first. He had been the, to me, glamourous Jacques Grangier de la Marinière, a nephew of Charles Heidsieck, the head of the Champagne family. His parents had a small Château near the Heidsieck house in Rheims, where Sharon and Jacques had had their wedding and I remember staying with them for a week and being taken over to the Heidsiecks for dinner one night. It was all very *cossu* as the French say (a convenient one word for the compendium of chic, comfortable, glossy) in a handsome *hotel particulière* (I always loved the way that French phrase for substantial townhouse tripped off the tongue). We had an excellent dinner although I noticed with interest that we drank Taittinger rather than Heidsieck champagne. But the *piéce de résistance* came after dinner in the grand salon to which we had repaired for coffee. The butler came in ceremoniously carrying a large silver tray on which were not only coffee cups but a spirit stove, a silver-plated kettle and a large tin of Nescafé. In Paris, I was often invited to Sunday lunch in the family house in the 16th Arrondissement, where a very large table would seat several generations.

Jacques was tall, well-built, nice-looking, sophisticated and amusing. He and his family had been trying to make some wine of their own on their property and, once bottled, had laid it down in their cellar. They decided to try it the following year and had labelled each one *Horrible, Épouvantable (awful), Éncore Plus Epouvantablé etc*, not in the least in the grand Heidsieck tradition. When they had a baby girl, I became godmother and I thought it was so sad that they had split up.

Pierre, on the other hand, was a passionate and very active Socialist and Trade Unionist; rather small, skinny, dark, intense and stubbly and clearly a very great deal less well off than Jacques. It was a change to see Sharon in much more work-a-day-clothes than I remembered her wearing. Her elegant mother – who had also lived in Paris at the time I was there, had mostly taken Sharon with her to Jacques Fath or J. Suzanne Talbot (famous for her hats but who made clothes as well then). I could not imagine how the two had met, given the milieu that Sharon had hitherto inhabited, but she seemed to really love this man and he her. She had had a most unusual arrangement with Jacques, in such a notoriously chauvinist country in that he would take my goddaughter and give the rearing of their small son to Pierre and Sharon.

Pierre Normand was another old Parisien admirer of Sharon's when we were students, but was then living and working in London. I remember that he had had a most vigilant – and irritating – eye for quality, telling Sharon that her nylon stockings (no tights then) were not of a good enough quality if she happened to be wearing an inexpensive pair. God knows what he thought of my sloppy, un-stylish student clothes. I had nearly always run through my small allowance by the middle of the month and was reduced to eating baguettes and cheese by the end, let alone buying best quality nylons.

Since Pierre spoke very little English, I had also asked Claudie as an amusing and wholly French woman to make him feel more at home. (The *Oeufs en Gelee au Madèrè* were especially for Sharon who I remembered had liked them very much in our Paris days).

**The Menu was:**

*Oeufs en Gelée au Madère*

*Poulet à l'Éstragon* (p. 260)

*Tiny New Potatoes*

*Salad of Lettuce Hearts*

*Cheese*

*Caramelized Oranges* (p. 255)

And the wine was Château Ducru-Beaucaillou, 1959.

## MAY 26th, 1967 – TOSTOCK

**DINNER:** *Angela and David Caccia*

This was out first entertaining weekend at Tostock (what used to be known as Whitsun and now the spring bank holiday) and the Caccias had come to stay on the Thursday night, with their two children, Alexander and Arabella, much the same age as my two girls, then three and 18 months, so all the kids piled in together in a long lean-to that we had made into a nursery. We had a big kitchen with a capacious refectory table and an old pine dresser – very 1960s country – and a small beamed living room next door which I had painted white – on the premise that beams had always originally been painted – with the walls in between a dark green. I also had a red-stained Habitat desk on red trestles and the floor was covered in coir matting, as were the stairs. In fact, the stairs were so narrow and steep, we literally had to cut our bed in half to get it up to our bedroom and the same with the bed for the guest room. The bigger room at the end held two lots of bunk beds as well as a cot for Tom, to give room for the children to have friends to stay as well.

I had noticed a small unillustrated ad for a farm cottage in West Suffolk, to let for reasonable rent, in the back of *Country Life*. And when we went to see it, what had especially attracted us to the place was its position. It was up a long – but easily walkable – cart track – which wound its way from beside the old stone village church and up through ancient oak trees, coppices and buttercup-drizzled meadows to this long Suffolk-Pink painted cottage and tiny orchard. There was not another house in sight, there were peaceful walks to be had over the meadows grazed by a few cows and the odd horse, and it seemed a perfectly safe place for the children to play and to grow up knowing what real unsullied country was like. The straggly one street village had a good little general store and Post Office as well as a triangular village green. It was in easy distance of Bury St Edmunds, a civilized old market town with a beautiful Medieval abbey and best still, England's oldest theatre, restored by energetic friends of ours, Martin and Jean Corke with the aid of Martin's brewing company, Greene King. This little theatre was used as a try-out for many new productions before they ended up in London.

**The Menu was:**

*Little Tuna fish, Green Bean and Red Pepper Tarts* (p. 261)

*Chicken Paprika with Rice* (p. 262)

*Salad of Lettuce*

# Thurloe Square and Tostock, 1967

*Cheese*

*Junket with Brandy and Cherry Compôte*

And the wine was a Rioja Crianza, 1960.


## MAY 29th, 1967 – TOSTOCK

**LUNCH:** *Margot Walmsley*
*John and Ailsa (Garland) Mason*
*David and Angela Caccia*

Margot was staying with the Masons, who were good friends of hers, in nearby Lavenham, a very pretty Medieval village with an old wool hall and splendid church. And we had invited them over for lunch. At that time Ailsa, who had been the Women's Page Editor on *The Daily Mirror* – had just become Editor of *Vogue*, in between Audrey Withers and Bea Miller. Her tenure was rather short-lived because she had been accustomed to the very different *Mirror* Group, but she was a warm, friendly, open woman, quite unlike the dignified and intellectual Audrey Withers of whom most people were rather scared. When I was with Condé Nast – and I had had a brief period being Sub-Editor on *Vogue* as well as working on *House & Garden* – everyone, both on *Vogue* and *House & Garden*, had to sign a book when they arrived in the morning with the *exact* time of their arrival and God help you if you were more than five minutes later than 9am – unless you had a *very* good excuse. Nor were working mothers allowed any flexibility. I think my later great friend, Helen Robinson (Preston) who had been working on American *Vogue* under Jessica Daves – because her then husband, a banker, was working in NY – was, on her return, the first mother to be allowed any kind of elasticity. But then she was the first to do many things. She later left *Vogue* to become the first woman director of the Debenhams Group. However, she said the rule of Jessica Daves in New York was even worse. She had gone to tell her that she was having a baby and to ask for some time off for the birth. 'What day is it due, dear?' asked Miss Daves, opening her agenda. 'Well,' said Helen rather doubtfully, 'It's actually due around August 8th (or whenever it was) but it isn't, obviously, for sure. It c——'. Impatiently Miss Daves interrupted her. 'I've made a note of the day. So that's all set then.' Helen always swore she was so frightened of annoying the presumably

151

childless Miss Daves that she actually did have it on the allotted day and even then, Miss Daves sent work to the hospital.

I forget what John did, but he was equally friendly and always very supportive of Ailsa.

**The Menu was:**

Salade Niçoise (p. 263)

Cheese

Fruit

And the wine was Muscadet, 1964.

### MAY 29th, 1967 – TOSTOCK

**DINNER:** Arthur and Constance Green
Anthony Green
Carmel Green
David and Angela Caccia
Bill and Cesca Pearson-Rogers

This was the first time my parents had seen the cottage finished and my father, born in 1900, was particularly delighted that we now had a place near them. He had started an engineering business making generating sets before the war and had joined the army when the war began, having moved his family from London to a rented house in Suffolk in 1938 with the intention of staying there until we found the right house to buy. He thought Suffolk would be safer for us if war began. He had been in Germany on business during the rise of the Nazis in the 1930s and, curious to see what this Hitler was like, had actually heard him speak at a rally; so he had seen – and heard – first hand, the extent of his forceful, frightening charisma and consequent power and he was under no illusions that war would almost certainly come. The only thing was, as it turned out, that the East Coast of England was right in the flight path of the German bombers. And we indeed were the recipients of a couple of bombs ourselves: one incendiary bomb which set fire to the barn we used as a garage, and one V2 rocket towards the end of the war which fell at the bottom of our, luckily long, garden. It knocked out not only all of the windows, but hurled my mother and small brother right down the stairs from the landing where they had been standing. When we got on the bus to school the next morning, people were relieved to see us. From a

Princess Margaret and Tony Snowdon at Buckingham Palace, just after their wedding. Roger Gilliatt, my late husband and Tony's Best Man, is in the background. The bridesmaid standing to the right of Princess Margaret is the young Princess Anne. Roger, who had known Tony for some six years, was by no means Tony's first choice for the post. But in the end he was deemed the most respectable... Tony was given his title – the Earl of Snowdon – some time later.

(This image and the one of Princess Margaret on the front cover, courtesy of Rex Features)

Myself in the 1960s.

The party for the publication of my first book, *English Style* at the Design Centre in the Haymarket two weeks after the birth of our son, Tom Gilliatt. From left to right are myself, Susan Crosland (Barnes) writer and wife of the late Anthony Crosland, a distinguished former Labour Foreign Minister and Michael Boys, who did all the photography for the book.

Menu

Cassoulettes Laissenor
('Sde, mushroom e asparagus)

—

Medaillons de Veau a
la Russe -
salad

cheese

Summer Pudding

Wines

Puligny . Montrachet
Château Haut - Batailly -
1960

Flowers

Guests

Sir Robin e Lady Darwin
Gen. Sir Brian e Lady
Horrocks

Anthony e Susan Crosland .
Spike e Paddy Mulligan .

Gown & Jewels worn :

Notes

A sample page from one of my 1970 Smythson dinner books. All the men, listed among the recorded guests, including Roger Gilliatt, served under General Sir Brian Horrocks during World War II. Smythson, the stationers in London's Bond and Sloane Streets still sell these leather-bound dinner record books in a slightly updated version. I filled in the books as religiously as a diary in order not to repeat myself too much – though I see that I often did repeat favourites, hopefully not to the same people unless they wanted them.

Spike and Paddy Milligan at a party. Paddy became a very dear friend to both Roger and I, and an excellent foil to Spike. She managed, for the most part, to lovingly keep Spike in good order except when he became really depressed. She was also a warm and caring stepmother to Spike's children by his first wife but her life was by no means an easy one.

Spike and Paddy Milligan at their wedding. Both look happy. Paddy, originally from Yorkshire, was a professional singer with, we all thought, a beautiful voice, though she much enjoyed sending herself up, which she did with alacrity and always very funnily. Spike had first noticed her in *The Sound of Music*.

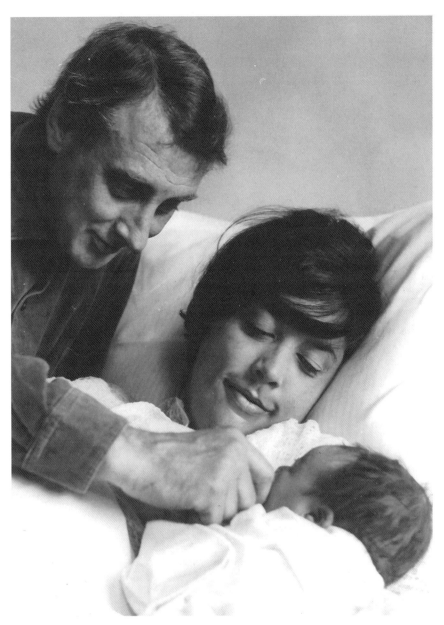

Spike and Paddy Milligan just after the birth of their daughter Jane, my goddaughter. My daughter Annie (now Constantine), was Spike's goddaughter. Alas, Jane, herself now a singer and musician, and looking very like her mother, was very young when Paddy so sadly died of breast cancer. Although driving extremely cautiously one snowy day, her car skidded slowly but uncontrollably into an old man on the pavement, pinning him against a railing. To Paddy's very deep distress, and she visited him in hospital and did everything she could, he died some weeks later, although apparently he was already seriously ill. Nevertheless, Paddy was blamed by his widow, who kept calling in the night to heap abuse on her. Many people thought the stress brought on her illness.

Paddy and Spike fooling around. She was just as funny as he was. Although not
so zany with words, names and accents as the Goon at his best, she had an equally
ingrained sense of the absurd and a splendid sense of timing.

Spike and a small Jane Milligan. Spike was very good with children and his book, *Bad Jelly the Witch* was very popular with them. Once, after he had met my Australian friends, the Lances, when they were all staying with us in London, the next time he visited his parents in Woi Woi, an hour or so away from Sydney up the coast, he took a taxi to their house in Vaucluse and kept it waiting outside while he signed copies for all five kids – the youngest was to become my daughter-in-law.

Paddy, Jane and Spike Milligan. It was always particularly good to see Spike in a really light-hearted mood.

A birthday party for Jane Milligan in the Milligan's house in North London. Tom Gilliatt, my son, is sitting at the end of the table. Paddy is holding the enormous birthday cake she had made. She was an excellent cook, though Spike loved to eat in restaurants during the week.

(All images of Spike and Paddy Milligan kindly supplied by their daughter, Jane Milligan)

Ken Tynan, the most brilliant theatre critic of the 1950s and 1960s, and Literary Director of the National Theatre, looking pensive. His words in *The Observer* could excoriate or uplift, make or break a play or a performer.

Although seemingly the most urban of creatures, Ken Tynan always seemed happy and carefree in the country. His boredom threshold was low but he was a much kinder, gentler man in many ways and situations than his public persona gave him credit for. He was also extremely generous and was pretty well always the first to reach for a bill in restaurants.

Ken Tynan standing on his balcony at Thurloe Square, the square's garden behind him. Ken bought the house just across the road from us when it came up for sale because he liked ours so much. He and Kathleen entertained there a very great deal. I guess we all did in those days. In fact, such houses were at their best full of people. He looks healthy here but his almost non-stop intake of tobacco gave him emphysema which killed him far too young. He died in California where he had gone for the benefits of its better climate.

Ken and Kathleen Tynan with their daughter, Roxana. Ken wrote his children a poem for each of their birthdays. One would not much have suspected his *pater familias* role from his writings, his long-running somewhat lascivious show *Oh Calcutta*, his sometimes excoriating public utterances or his reported sado-masochism. I was particularly fond of Ken as was my predecessor in marriage to Roger, Penelope Gilliatt who was also a theatre then a film critic who ended up doing half the film critiques on *The New Yorker* – for which Ken did long profiles.

Luncheon/Dinner

Date July 2nd

Menu

Guests

Asparagus Mousse

Lord & Lady Limerick
Anthony & Anne Nutting
Comte Dominic de Grunne
Fleur Cowles Meyer
Tom Meyer
Susan Stern

Poulet à l'estragon
Courgettes
New potatoes
Salad
Cheese
Blackcurrant leaf water ice

Wines

Pouilly Blanc Fumé 1964
Château Lalande - Pomerol 1900

Flowers

Gown & Jewels worn :

Notes

Two more sample pages from my dinner books.

Luncheon/Dinner

Date November 2nd 1970

Menu

Guests

Crèche Rosea Ailor

Professor & Mrs Fred Plum
Professor & Mrs Butterfield
James & Cork Berk
Sir Hugh & Lady Casson.

Medaillons de veau printemps

Salad
Cheese

Raspberry cream chou tail

Wines

Sauvignon blanc de Graves 1959
Château Lalande Pomerol 1960

Flowers

Gown & Jewels worn :

Notes

Leaving the tiny rural church at Withermarsh Green, Suffolk after our wedding in May, 1963. From left to right: My sister-in-law, Eliza Gilliatt, my mother, Constance Green and my father, Arthur Green escorting my mother-in-law, Anne Gilliatt.

Roger and I about to leave for our honeymoon. We actually just had a long weekend in Paris as we had already been on the trip to Egypt, the Lebanon and Jordan.

The christening lunch for our son Tom in the Thurloe Square dining room with its black lacquered James II chairs. From left to right, myself, Monica Parsons, godfather Bill Henson, and my young sister, Carmel Green (now Jones, and an Immigration Judge).

More scenes from the christening lunch (there were several tables). From left to right: Billy McCarty, godmother Margot Walmsley, my sister-in-law, Eliza Gilliatt and myself.

In the garden of my parents' Suffolk home after our very small wedding: from left to right: Guy Scott, my great friend D'Arcy Howell and Gillian Willison, wife of Robin Willison, Roger's Best Man.

n the garden of Chilton Priory after our wedding. From left to right: my sister, Carmel Green (Jones), Margaret Hitchcock, my mother, Constance Green, one of my mother's sisters, Irene Hornsey. Margot Walmsley later rescued our then two-year-old son, Tom, from that pond. Sitting on the porch, left to right: Robin Willison, Roger's Best Man, Anne Gilliatt, my mother-in-law and the Jesuit priest who married us, Father John Murray.

Our lovely Portuguese nanny, Gracia helping to clear the garden at our Tostock, Suffolk cottage with our younger daughter, Annie (now Constantine). The long lean-to in the background served as both playroom and extra guest room and was much better-looking inside than out!

Just before we had to change for our wedding in 1963. From left to right, John Howell, my brother, Anthony Green and myself. John was marvellously idiosyncratic and had an impressive collection of vintage motorcars some of which he still raced. He also built a Gyrocopter for himself which he crashed. He and D'Arcy, his wife (with whom I shared a flat when I first came to London to work) lived in Sussex and kept peacocks. If one of them strayed John always managed to coax them back by blowing the horn of his old De Dion Bouton which sounded exactly like a peacock's mating cry.

From left to right, Tom, myself, Sophia and Annie in 1970. All three of the children are wearing sailor suits which I think my grandchildren at similar ages would have totally refused to do. No wonder the children are looking somewhat soulful.

In the garden at Thurloe Square after Tom's christening, 1967. From left to right: Sophia, godfather Billy McCarty, godmother Angela Caccia (now Lloyd), Annie and Mrs Crowe, the maternity nurse, holding Tom. In those days it was customary to have a maternity nurse for around a month if one was able to do so, especially if there were older small children to look after. Such a luxury. I remember that we all especially liked Mrs Crowe.

Also in the garden at Thurloe Square after Tom's October christening at Brompton Oratory just up the road. From left to right, Maria Henson, my mother, Constance Green, my sister, Carmel Green (now Jones), godfather Bill Henson, godmother Margot Walmsley holding Sophia, godfather Billy McCarty holding Annie, my father, Arthur Green, Father John Murray S J, godmother Angela Caccia (now Lloyd), myself, Monica Parsons, Mrs Crowe. We all seem to be wearing unnaturally tall-crowned hats. Monica Parsons was Jeanne Wilkins' sister and also a good friend. I cannot recollect where Jeanne was, she was one of Sophia's godparents. Perhaps Monica was representing her.

Roger and I on the balcony with Annie after her christening. The Victoria & Albert Museum is in the background and Brompton Oratory conveniently just up the road for the christening ceremony.

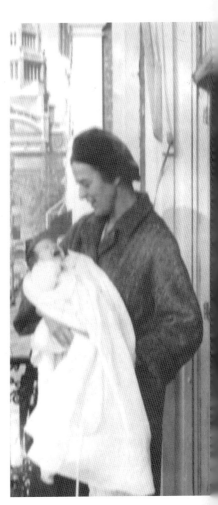

My father, Arthur Green and myself holding Annie after her christening, exactly two years before Tom's. Coincidentally, they were both Libra children, born on October 6th. The long balcony opened out from the drawing room and was a very useful adjunct to parties on warm or warmish days. (We did not have pictures of Sophia's christening because it took place at my parents' church in Suffolk).

Nanny Clarke also having a turn at holding Annie. She was best friends with Nanny Sumner, the Snowdon's nanny, the right-hand to Princess Margaret (but the scourge of Tony Snowdon) and was really only with us between very much grander jobs to kindly show our young Portuguese nanny, Gracia, what to do. Spike Milligan gave both the nannies tickets to his Son of Oblomov and stopped the show at one point to welcome them.

Godmother Claudie Worsthorne, then wife of Sir Peregrine Worsthorne, and godfather Terence Bradshaw, later Sir Terence Bradshaw, Chief Clerk to The House of Commons, having his turn at holding Annie. (Spike Milligan was the other godfather). Actually, Annie was christened Anne-Louise but changed it to Annie as soon as she could. All Annie's christening photographs were taken by Maria Henson, the Russian UN photographer wife of Bill Henson, then Head of the UN Information Service. Both US and UK surveillance services (and no doubt the Russians too), were somewhat wary of this marriage.

Roger and I with Sophia, Annie and Tom in our garden at Thurloe Square.

Godfathers, Bill Henson and Billy McCarty and godmother Angela Caccia (Lloyd) holding Tom after his christening. Bill Henson almost always had a pipe in hand except when he had to drop it for eating and other purposes.

Tom, Sophia and Annie outside our house in Douro Place, Kensington in 1972. Tom was almost a perfect but smaller clone of Sophia at that period, especially if Sophia was wearing jeans or shorts. Since their hair style was much the same style and length too, people who knew Tom were always stopping if Sophia was with me and remarking 'Hasn't Tom grown tall'. Or stopping for Tom and saying 'I somehow thought he was a little taller'.....

Me, winding Annie aged a few months in the nursery at Thurloe Square, 1965. I particularly loved that nursery which seemed to me the very model (to paraphrase Gilbert and Sullivan in *HMS Pinafore*) of what a large old-fashioned nursery should be, right down to the nursery fire and a rocking horse. *Country Life* took some very nice pictures of the whole house including that room. It was the first time they had featured a London house, and they used the pictures over two weeks.

Myself and baby Annie in the nursery at Thurloe Square, 1965. These pictures were also taken by Maria Henson.

My mother, Constance Green with Annie in Devon, 1966. We used to rent houses in Devon and Cornwall for summer holidays with the children, before we had our Suffolk place.

Myself with Tom and Sophia outside the cottage at Tostock, Suffolk, 1968.

Great Aunt Sophia Klöcke with her husband and daughter, Ursula in Wiesbaden, Germany. It must have been wrenching for Aunt Sophia to have her son fight in, and be killed in, the German Army in World War II, whilst her nephew and her son's cousin, Roger Gilliatt, was fighting in the British Army.

Sophia and Annie playing in the garden at Tostock, Suffolk in 1968.

The rear façade of our house in Rattlesden, Suffolk in 1970. The house was mostly early Seventeenth Century with a Victorian front.

The back and front façades of the Tostock, Suffolk cottage when we first moved in.

Roger and I outside our house, 19 Thurloe Square in 1963. It was right on the corner of Alexander Place.

Thurloe Square under scaffolding before we moved in at the end of 1963.

Menu                                   Guests

Salade    Niçoise                      Princess Margaret.
                                       Tony Snowdon
—                                      Lord Lady Lindsley shaw
                                       Lord & Lady Davidson
Pancakes stuffed with veal escalope    Frank & Helen Dawson
& mushrooms                            Ben Nicholson (Rose)
                                       Germaine & Hugh Carlend...
purée of brussel sprouts               Sir Duncan Oppenheim
New potatoes                           Sir David & Lady Barran
                                       Max Clendinning
Cheeses                                Paul White
                                       Gerry & May Cookson
Iced grapes brulée                     Tony Shribling
                                       Kit & Marna Wynne-Parry
Wines

Muscat Hugel 1969

Cotes de Beaune Villages 1967

Flowers

_____

Gown & Jewels worn :


Notes

A party listed in a dinner book soon after we moved into Douro Place, Kensington in 1971. I cannot imagine why I would have made a Salade Niçoise as a first course for a dinner (as opposed to a lunch) in the early spring (as opposed to the summer). Nor why I would have served a purée of Brussels sprouts. Maybe because it was easier to do beforehand for a large party. Still, it was an odd choice.

distance, they had seen where the rocket had cut out and feared we might be all dead. Other bombs had fallen all around and we used to play in the deep craters they left which rapidly got overgrown with weeds and wild berry bushes. Still, my father was right. Suffolk was a whole lot safer than the London Blitz. In the end he was recalled from his very brief stint in the army for necessary war manufacture and went on producing generators and so on throughout the war, coming home at weekends whenever he could.

One of my first clear memories was of all four of us having to scramble under the kitchen table when the first warning sirens started (we ended up not taking much notice) and another was seeing a German pilot bailing out of a shot bomber and his parachute going up in flames as a bit of burning matter from the plunging aircraft struck it. He fell dead into our next door field and the wreckage of the plane scattered all over the place. We had a searchlight camp just down the road and, later, a Prisoner of War Camp. Since we had no electricity and were not on the mains water, we used candles and oil lamps behind the blacked out windows, and heated the house with wood fires. Water had to be pumped-up from the well twice each day and we all learnt to take our turn to do the 500 or so to and fro pumps that it took. Luckily for our blistered hands, the guys from the searchlight camp used to come round and pump the water for my mother, in return for a meal or some extra pocket-money. They used to take my brother and I for rides in their Bren Gun Carriers which we thought wildly exciting. Then, when their camp was disbanded, they were followed by the German prisoners, who seemed nice enough boys, at least they were very nice to us kids. They, too, took their turn pumping and helped my mother dig up the ground to grow vegetables and looked after the animals and garden as well. Since meat, butter, sugar, flour and virtually all staples were rationed, we grew a lot of vegetables and kept a couple of pigs, chickens and ducks as food supplements. Interestingly, years later when I was living in Wiltshire, the charming elderly guy Henry who helped me with the garden there turned out to have been an ex-German prisoner of war and presumably a Heinrich, who had gone back to Germany, married his girlfriend and brought her back to England to live.

Petrol was also rationed and in very short supply indeed, so our car was incarcerated in the garage until the war ended and we either walked, cycled or took the bus. First of all we had a governess, whom we shared with some friends' children, until she was called up for the ATS (the women's army) and then we took the regular bus to school each day – there were no schoolbuses then. I think my brother must have been ill the day it got into an accident and turned over. I was rescued from the roof by Bea Miller, another future Editor of British *Vogue*, but then a young girl of 17 or so who was staying temporarily with her aunt in the village some three miles away.

I had a pet Marmoset monkey that my father's stepfather had brought back from South America for me before the war. Since my mother was unable to get the right food for it – monkey food not being a top priority – it slowly languished and died soon after Pearl Harbour, but not before it had escaped from the kitchen one day, ventured to the end of the garden and hopped down to the meadow beyond where she followed the river down to the village. It then appeared at someone's larder window, looking for food. Unfortunately, the owner of the house went to get something from a shelf at just the wrong moment. She saw its wizened little face and, I regret to say, rushed out into the village street yelling, 'The Japanese have landed! The Japanese are here.' Most of the villagers then, had hardly visited London, let alone the big world outside and had ill-conceived notions of other nationalities.

The other pathetic little thing I remembered about war time, which was, after all, a doddle compared to the frightful sufferings of so much of mainland Europe – and in any case, I knew no other way of life – were the tantalising old Fyffes Bananas ads still pasted on walls in greengrocers. I could not recollect their taste, being only four when the war started. Soon after the 1945 Armistice was declared, I came back from school one day to hear that a little food store, about four miles up the road in the other direction to our village, actually had bananas for sale. I raced there on my bicycle only to find that they had all been sold. However, the owner kindly gave me a banana skin which I carried home triumphantly as the next best thing, and even proudly took the brown and slimy trophy to school the next morning.

After the war, my father diversified into jet plane starting engines, among other things and eventually got taken over by one of England's oldest public engineering companies and became Chairman of the combined group. But we did not actually find a permanent house that my parents liked until around 1951. My sister was born towards the end of the war. Since then my brother had been to Ampleforth, a Catholic public school in Yorkshire, become Head Boy and gone up to Oxford where he read PPE. After a stint with another engineering company he had joined my father's group, rather under duress, but eventually switched to farming and to administration for the Sue Ryder and Leonard Cheshire Homes. At that dinner, he was still unmarried. My sister had studied for the Bar in London and had become a divorce lawyer and was still just dating.

# Thurloe Square and Tostock, 1967

The Pearson-Rogers lived in the village and had been immediately welcoming to us as new neighbours.

**The Menu was:**

Consommé en Gelée Madrilene

Bollito with Salsa Verde and Spicy Tomato Sauce (pp. 264–5)

White Haricot Beans and Sweet-Sour Cabbage (p. 266)

Cheese

Strawberries and Cream

And the wine was Chambolle-Musigny, 1959.

## JUNE 10th, 1967 – THURLOE SQUARE

**DINNER IN THE GARDEN:** *Dr Graeme Robertson*
*Michael Webb*
*Ken Tynan and Kathleen Halton*
*Eileen O'Casey*
*Margot Walmsley*

Graeme Roberton, the Australian neurologist and cast-iron expert, was staying again and Michael Webb was interested in writing about decorative cast-iron for *Country Life*. The rest were there just because they were friends and were around and it was a lovely June evening.

**The Menu was:**

Hors d'Oeuvres of Baby Broad Beans, Mushrooms à la Grecque, Salami, Egg Mayonnaise, Chopped Skinned Tomatoes and Basil, Black Olives

Cold Salmon Trout, Sauce Verte

Little Jersey Potatoes

Salad of Lettuce Hearts

Cheese

Strawberry Ice Cream with Raspberry Purée (p. 267)

And the wines were a White Puligny-Montrachet, 1960 and Château Suduiraut (Sauternes), 1959.

155

# Mary Gilliatt's Fabulous Food and Friends

## JUNE 23rd, 1967 – THURLOE SQUARE

**DINNER:** *Professor James Lance*
*Dr Marion-Smith*
*Dr and Mrs Tom Sears*

This medical dinner on a very hot evening produced quite unexpected long-lasting and happy consequences. It was given for Jim Lance, Roger's opposite number in Sydney, who had come for a neurological meeting in Glasgow to which Roger had also gone. And Roger had asked some colleagues from Queen Square to meet him. There was something about Jim that I liked immediately, quite apart from his laugh and his impressive Bourbon nose. As he later told me, the feeling had been mutual, mostly because he thought I had 'woozley' eyes whatever they might be, but also because I had told him that I did not know much about Glasgow except that I thought I remembered that 'Glesga' was Gaelic for 'beautiful fields', although this was well before Glasgow's splendid revamp when the description was far from fitting. I added that I was told the square-toed shoe had been invented there so that people could get nearer the bar. He, in his turn, made excellent puns which I was bound to appreciate – and still do. Eighteen months or so later, he came over again with his wife Judy, a glamorously elegant creature, even after five children, who looked like – as somebody aptly said – a cross between Julie Christie and Jane Fonda (to which was added a laser-like mind). It was an impressive mixture and she was my age, and so unlike most of the wives of Roger's other colleagues who were much older than me. They both came to dinner at our new house in Douro Place and we immediately became friends.

After that, Roger took me with him when he went to Sydney, at Jim's invitation, as Visiting Professor, and this started my love affair with Sydney, Australia and the Lance family in particular. To add to her other virtues, Judy turned out to be a gifted and experimental cook. When they brought all five of their children for a holiday in Europe in the early 1970s, they stayed with us in both London and the country and my son Tom, aged six, fell in love with their youngest daughter, Sophie, also aged six. They were going to marry, he announced, when they grew up. They did not actually see each other again till they met in New York when they were both 21. But they have been together more or less ever since and marry they did with three most special children. Well, all grandmothers think that ... though they are.

# THURLOE SQUARE AND TOSTOCK, 1967

Jim was and remains a most-respected, loved and caring doctor in spite of his impressive international reputation. I particularly note this because so many distinguished doctors appear to think it necessary to stand so much more on their dignity. Jim, I think, would stop for literally anyone in trouble. One of his specialties was headache in all its various forms and he wrote a couple of books on the subject, one, especially for laymen, *Migraine and Other Headaches* which has gone into many editions. Once, when he and Jude were staying with us in London, I had the Snowdons to dinner, and Princess Margaret, who also suffered from bad migraines (and was later President of the UK Migraine Trust), spent practically the whole evening chatting exclusively to Jim about the subject. He and Jude made up a lullaby for their children called 'Bidie Times' which none of his many young grandchildren will go to sleep without hearing from their respective parents. This is occasionally a problem so, one Christmas, he gave them all teddy bears with a recording of his voice singing the song neatly tucked inside. He also wrote a children's book, *The Golden Trout*, in his very spare amount of spare time. Both he and Jude are equally caring and loving parents-in-law to my son.

**The Menu was**

*Stuffed Courgettes with Avgolemeno Sauce* (pp. 267–8)

*Salad of Lobster, Shrimps, and Cold Poached Smoked Haddock*

*Crudités*

*Cheese*

*Syllabub* (p. 222)

And the wines were Puligny-Montrachet, 1960 and Chambolle-Musigny, 1959 (with the cheese).


## JULY 13th, 1967 – THURLOE SQUARE

**DINNER:** *Teddy and Denise Obolensky*
*Perry and Claudie Worsthorne*
*Ivor and Jan Burt*
*Harold Leeds (over from NY)*
*Norah Sayre (over from NY)*

# Mary Gilliatt's Fabulous Food and Friends

All through the summer, we seemed to have had our usual one or two people to dinners on a regular basis both in London and the country. There is nothing new to say about the guests this night, except for Harold Leeds whom I had met in NY the previous January. He was an archetypal waspy architect and designer and Chairman of the Undergraduate School of Design at the Pratt Institute in Brooklyn. The following year, he helped establish the new Graduate School at Pratt and then became *its* Chairman. He had been very kind to me, shown me around Pratt with which I was immensely impressed (though four decades later, my loyalties are with the NY School of Interior Design since I am on their Advisory Board) and invited me to his stunning 1830s house in Gramercy Park, explaining a little of its etymological history as well as its architectural past. Gramercy was derived from the old Dutch *Krom Moerasje* which meant 'little crooked marsh'. From that, it became Crommashie Hill, and finally Gramercy, but it was still a marsh when a forward-thinking developer called Samuel B. Ruggles (sounds like a Spike Milligan character) drained it in 1831, and laid out a green and the streets around it in the model of an English Square. That achieved, he offered 66 lots for sale. Somehow, in spite of various threats over the centuries, the square has remained both intact with a lovely central garden and private, in spite of the many towerering buildings all around.

**The Menu was:**

*Tuna Fish, Green Bean and Red Pepper Tart* (p. 261)

*Veal Escalopes in a Cream and Cucumber Sauce* (p. 269)

*New Potatoes, Lettuce Salad*

*Cheese*

*Peaches in Sauternes*

And the wines were Gerwurztraminer, 1961 and Château Batailly, 1959.

## AUGUST 4th, 1967 – TOSTOCK

**DINNER:** *Ken and Kathleen Tynan*

Ken and Kathleen had come to stay for the weekend, fresh from their wedding and American honeymoon. We were both just about seven months pregnant but I had been married rather longer. Kathleen told the droll story that there had been some last-minute hitch with their respective divorce papers and, instead of getting married, where they had planned, in Manhattan, they (Norman Mailer, Ken's Best Man, Marlon Brando, a witness, and Kathleen's Matrons of Honour, Marlene Dietrich and Roger's former wife, Penelope Gilliatt), had all had to decamp over the Hudson to some place in New Jersey where matrimonial rulings were more relaxed.

This last-minute ceremony made the registrar, obviously and tetchily late for his Saturday game of golf. However, there were still typists clattering away in an adjoining office and Marlene Dietrich happened to be standing in front of the slightly opened door between the two rooms, and trying surreptitiously to close it. 'Do you Ken take thee Kathleen to be your wedded wife?' intoned the registrar, and without missing a beat, but turning to Ms Dietrich, and glancing over his spectacles, went on 'If I were you ma'am, I would not stand with my ass to an open door in *this* office.' Then went on with the 'to have and to hold.' Safely back in Manhattan for a celebratory lunch, Ken, Norman Mailer and Marlon Brando had walked up the street deep in conversation, followed by Penelope and Marlene Dietrich equally absorbed in theirs with poor, heavily pregnant but still beautiful Kathleen, stumping along behind them all on her own.

**The Menu was:**

*Tomates a la Crème* (p. 270)

*Lobster and Cucumber Salad*

*Cheese*

*Raspberries with a Raspberry Purée*

And the wine was Gerwurztraminer, 1961.


**AUGUST 5th, 1967 – TOSTOCK**

**DINNER:** *Ken and Kathleen Tynan*
*Terence and Caroline Conran*
*Angus Wilson*
*Tony Garrett*
*Martin and Jean Corke*

This was the Saturday night of that weekend. Terence and Caroline had a cottage not very far away, so did Angus Wilson, the writer and his companion, Tony Garrett whom we had first met with some other neighbours, Martin and Jean Corke. The Corke's were thoughtful, gregarious hosts, who did a great deal for the arts in Suffolk, in particular restoring the little theatre in nearby Bury St. Edmunds.

They and Angus and Tony became good friends and all the while we lived in Suffolk we saw a great deal of them. I was pleased years later, after Angus had died, to read in Margaret Drabble's biography of him, how he had several times mentioned our dinners in his diaries. We were very fond of both of them and they were especially nice to the children, having them to tea on their own in their cottage and preparing the most elaborate tea for them with cakes specially bought from Fortnum & Mason.

**The Menu was:**

*Crispy Fried Aubergine and Garlicky Yoghourt* (p. 270)

*Rognons au Porto*

*Rice*

*Salad*

*Cheese*

*Apricot Soufflé* (p. 271)

And the wines were Muscadet, 1964 and Château Bel Air, 1961. (We had been advised to keep our 1961s, given us by my father, since they were predicted to be a great vintage –which they were indeed – but we kept having to try them to see if they had yet begun to attain that stature. So much so that, regrettably, we had hardly any left by the time they did begin to mature).

### AUGUST 26th, 1967 – TOSTOCK

**LUNCH:** *Lady Barrington-Ward*
*Margaret and Witgar Hitchcock*
*Bill and Jane Neville Dawson*
*Col. and Mrs Robert Cooper*
*Basil and Bridget Porter*
*Arthur and Constance Green*
*Irene Hornsey*

These were all Suffolk friends of my parents, whom my siblings and I had grown up knowing, some much better than others. Lady

Barrington-Ward was the widow of Sir Launcelot Barrington-Ward, surgeon to King George VI, and sister-in-law of Robert Barrington-Ward, a particularly distinguished Editor of *The Times.*

Margaret Hitchcock was a most interesting woman, a leading feminist, who had stood very early on as a Liberal MP and was also a leading light in The Women's Institute. She was my mother's mentor and it was she who had asked her to propose the 'Equal Pay for Equal Work' motion at the Albert Hall in 1943, the speech that gave her nightmares for the rest of her life. She was also a most determined modernist: I saw modern 1930s furniture and one or two of the modern classics for the first time in her Eighteenth Century house. Margaret was rather short and square, she always, or almost always, wore a beret pulled down one side of her head and sensible lace-up shoes in which she strode, rather than walked. She took my mother on walking holidays and took me on a field trip to see Neolithic flint mines and was another large part of my education. Most importantly, she taught me to be curious and to think laterally. She had married a miller, a very jolly miller, called Manfred. They had a beautiful Georgian mill house straddling the River Stour, a lushly romantic garden with a large pond in front of the house, a mill race beside it where people caught eels and, best of all, for us, a grass tennis court always kept immaculately mowed – though there were the occasional poisonous adder in the long grass around the court. My brother got bitten once when searching for a ball and had to be rushed to the nearest hospital.

They entertained frequently and most memorably with summer breakfasts under the drooping weeping willows on the river bank with hot home made bread and bacon, eggs and sausages cooked over a camp fire. Writing this, I was suddenly reminded again that, on one of these occasions, when I was in my teens, they had an old gypsy fortune-teller as a diversion. When it was my turn she studied my palm and told me that I was artistic and would become an artist or do something artistic with houses but that I would have a child who would be much better. She was right. Actually, all three of my children have made impressive and idiosyncratic homes but my daughter, Annie Constantine, is now a full-time interior designer and, quite dispassionately, she is very much better than I ever was. I am very proud of her.

The Hitchcocks also had tennis parties with fabulous teas – because, even in wartime, they had their own cows – so there were cream and homemade jams and scones which you certainly could not get anywhere else. And they continued having winter dinner parties during the war and after. As I grew up, my brother and I joined some of these dinner parties where we nearly always had to play charades and all kinds of other games, whatever our ages. Witgar (an ancient name if ever there was one and well on a par with Launcelot), was their son, a tall, fair, shy, bespectacled academic who eventually took over the mill after Manfred died. He was a confirmed, as they say, bachelor, with a sly sense of humour, a disconcerting shout of a laugh (given his normal retiring academic stance), and an enduring fascination for Scandinavian girls after he had fallen deeply in love, in his impressionable youth, with a beautiful Norwegian au pair.

Bill and Jane Neville Dawson were equally instrumental in my greater education. Bill was a rather round, bald, tweed-jacketed barrister with a disarming chuckle, one of those charmingly dry and precise old English voices – now all but completely obsolete – and little gleaming wire rimmed glasses invariably perched on the end of his nose. He spent the weekdays in his law chambers in London. Jane was tall and thin and angular with wild, flying, iron-grey hair and an equally precise voice. Bill refused to learn to drive and, throughout the war, they just bicycled in a dignified, wobbly way, with very upright backs though Jane later purchased an ancient, rickety Austin which she drove in an appallingly dangerously manner. I was deeply impressed that, because their beautiful Eighteenth Century longcase clock was too tall for their hall, they just removed some tiles and dug a hole for it. Bill and Jane and my parents went on playing tennis on our court into their 80s, Bill in his yellowing long white trousers and Jane looking like an elderly Suzanne Lenglen, the French tennis star of the 1930s with, I think, equally wild hair. The most remarkable thing about the Dawsons however, was the library Bill had built up and the Seventeenth and early-Eighteenth Century paintings and furniture he had collected. He had apparently, I did not know that then, amassed a staggering collection of early first editions including, for example, *The Advancement of Learning* (1605) by Francis Bacon which he later most generously gave to me. All I knew was that I was so happy as a teenager visiting that room with its over-laden shelves, books piled all over the floor and on tables, a flickering fire and the smell of ancient paper and battered leather bindings. Astonishingly, he let us take down and handle the books whenever we wanted.

He must have been well-known in the trade because I remember Ernestine Carter's husband, Jake Carter, who ran the Antiquarian Book Department at Sotheby's, getting very excited when I mentioned his library and asking if I could ask the Dawsons if he could come and see it. He did, they all three got on, and I have no doubt that he was eagerly waiting on the side-lines for his eventual prize. But, in their 80s, the Dawsons decided to leave their friends in Suffolk and move nearer to a niece of Jane's in Somerset where they knew no one. Tragically, Bill got Alzheimer's and sold his entire magnificent library for a pittance to some glib, roving rogue of a second-hand dealer. Jane died in her bathroom and Bill did not even notice that she was missing until several days later when her niece came to visit.

I did not really know the Coopers, except that their son had won the Miltary Cross in the Korean War, but the Porter's were the very nice parents of my future sister-in-law, Sarah. Irene Hornsey was one of my mother's six sisters who had always been a generous aunt to us.

**The Menu was:**

*A Buffet of Millefeuilles of Chicken*

*Smoked Fillet of Pork and Melon*

*Spicy Rice Salad*

*Tomatoes Stuffed with Tuna and Greek Stuffed Tomatoes* (p. 272)

*Stuffed Eggs*

*Cherry and Walnut Salad* (p. 273)

*Cheese*

*Summer Pudding* (p. 273)

And the wines were a choice of Muscadet, Moulin-à-Vent, 1963, and a Provençale Rosé, 1966.

### SEPTEMBER 11th, 1967 – TOSTOCK

**DINNER:** *Margot Walmsley*
*Aunt Sophia (Klöcke)*
*Guy and Elizabeth Scott*
*Terence and Caroline Conran*
*Reginald and Cecilia Errington*

Margot and Aunt Sophia were staying for the weekend, Margot sleeping nobly on a sofa-bed in the nursery, and we had invited the Conrans over from their cottage. The Scotts, whom I mentioned earlier, were old friends of my parents as well and lived quite near, also came, as well as Reginald and Cecilia Errington who lived at the very end of the village. The latter, a charming old couple, had two daughters, Ginty and Cordelia who had married the two Vanneck brothers, Gerald and Peter, who came from a long-established Suffolk family (originally Dutch; Vanneck was a corruption of Van Eyck) with a very splendid house, Heveningham Hall, designed by James Wyatt for the family, along with most of the furniture, in the early 1780s.

Unfortunately, the younger Vannecks' father, Lord Huntingfield, who was originally an MP for Eye, Suffolk, and had been Governor of Victoria, Australia, had apparently got in a panic during the 1929 financial crash (although the family had thought their land had been sufficiently well-planted and farmed to make it self-supporting) and sold the property to a first cousin. On his father's death, Gerald, the older son, inherited the family title although without the land. Peter Vanneck, the younger son, feeling disinherited with no title and no land, decided that he would make it his business to at least become Lord Mayor of London. Cleverly, at the age of 19 he took out an insurance policy *against* becoming Lord Mayor. Naturally, at that age, and with nothing whatsoever to do – at that time – with City of London politics, he got a very advantageous deal. When he did become Lord Mayor in 1977, he received a most handsome and useful nest-egg which made his tenure at the Mansion House quite memorable. However, en route to his popular mayoralty – and it *was* popular – he had been ADC to the Queen from 1963–1973 and Deputy Chairman of the Stock Exchange, so not just a flash in the pan. He and Cordelia, his wife became good friends of ours.

We had recently been to lunch with his brother Gerald and Ginty, his wife, who also had a cottage nearby. What I most particularly appreciated was their elegant parsimony – at least with the washing up. They offered us sherry before lunch in silver mugs. At lunch we drank the wine from the same mugs and also, afterwards, the coffee.

**The Menu was:**

*Spiced Green Eggs*

*Circassian Chicken* (p. 274)

*Saffron Rice*

*Chopska Salad* (p. 274)

*Cheese*

*Rhubarb Flan* (p. 275)

And the wine was Rioja Crianza, 1963.

# THURLOE SQUARE AND TOSTOCK, 1967

## SEPTEMBER 26th, 1967 – THURLOE SQUARE

**DINNER:** *Bill and Barbara Plumb*
*Mr and Mrs Peter Cook*
*Terence and Caroline Conran*
*Billy McCarty*

I was, as it turned out, only 10 days away from the birth of our third child and Bill and Barbara Plumb whom we had met in New York in the winter, were staying with us – actually by accident. They had already been staying the weekend with us in Suffolk and were going to stay a few days at the London hotel I had booked them into at Barbara's request. But when they arrived, the front desk simply could not find their booking. I was puzzled because I had definitely booked it, so I asked the Plumbs to continue staying with us instead. It was quite a coincidence that I had met Barbara when she had only just come out of hospital having had her son, Christian, and here I was about to go into hospital for the same reason. Anyway, the denouement was that eventually the hotel called up and apologised. I had booked them in under Mr and Mrs William Lansing Plumb which was Bill's proper name but they had listed it under L rather than P. They stayed on anyway and the hotel sent around a couple of bottles of Champagne as an apology which we drank that night.

I had asked the Conrans and Billy McCarty to meet Barbara because of her design pages in *The New York Times* as well as Bill's involvement in product design. I must own up that I was agreeably surprised to see the name Peter Cook in the dinner book, who I thought, at first, must be the wonderfully funny comedian with Jonathan Miller and Allan Bennett from *Beyond the Fringe*. But I was puzzled that I had not remembered him coming to dine since I was such a fan. I still remember his acting out a hilarious audition for Tarzan as an indignant one-legged man who thought he was being victimised. Why shouldn't Tarzan be one-legged? He still, after all, had a perfectly good pair of arms ...

It turned out that this was the other well-known Peter Cook, the architect, whom I had recently interviewed. He was one of the founders of the influential *Archigram* group, and I had liked him very much and thought Barbara would be interested to meet him too. He was then teaching at the Architectural Association. He later became a Life Professor of Architecture at the Stäedelschule (or Acadamy of Frankfurt) which he helped to become one of the leading architectural schools in Germany. He ended up as Professor of Architecture at the Bartlett School in London and was given, like Terence Conran, a knighthood.

It was a lot of designy people for Roger, but then I was often the only non-medic amongst many visiting neurologists.

**The Menu was:**

Green Cheese Mousse (pp. 275–6)

Provençale Chicken with Black Olives (pp. 276–7)

Rice with Diced Red Pepper, Cucumber and Celery

Orange and Onion Salad

Cheese

Blackberries and Sweet Geranium Leaf Cream (p. 249)

And the wines were Schloss Johannisberger, 1961, Château Ducru-Beaucaillou, 1959 and Château Suduiraut, 1961 with the blackberries.

## OCTOBER 26th, 1967 – THURLOE SQUARE

**DINNER:** Penelope Gilliatt/Osborne
Professor Gil Glazer
Paul and Annette Reilly
Victoria Reilly
Charles Lewis

Our son Tom was born the early evening of October 6th, exactly the same date as his younger sister Annie two years before, and three and a half years after his elder sister Sophia who was born on April 6th. Clearly, six must have been a fortunate number for me. Annie was having her second birthday party but had, unfortunately, come down with a mild case of whooping cough that very afternoon, and Roger had to arrange for the two girls to be packed off to my obliging parents in Suffolk to stay there till the requisite quarantine was over. Whooping cough was considered very dangerous for new borns.

My book *English Style* had come out some two weeks later on October 20th and, barely out of hospital – women were kept in for much longer periods then – I went off to the Design Centre in the Haymarket where Max Reinhardt, the publisher, and Paul Reilly kindly gave it a great reception party.

Victoria, Paul Reilly's daughter from his first marriage, who had also worked on *The Sunday Telegraph*, was over from Prague where, that spring, there had been such euphoria about the (unfortunately short-lived) mini-revolution, 'Socialism with a Human Face' instigated by the new Secretary of the Communist Party, Alexander Dubček. This had been an energetic attempt to convert the constrictions and rules of the totalitarian Czech regime into a more democratic mode. (We suddenly got a great many visits from Czech neurologists and I remember Roger ringing up late one afternoon to ask if it was all right to bring six of them back to dinner that night – it was.) This brave attempt was brutally crushed the following summer with the invasion of Czechoslovakia by 7,000 tanks from the Soviet Union and its neighbouring allies.

Penelope was briefly over from New York and wanted to see the newborn Tom. Charles Lewis was over from India for a visit and Gil Glazer, a friend and colleague of Roger's, whom I met for the first time that night (and got to know much better later), was over from Newhaven, where he was Professor of Neurology at Yale.

**The Menu was:**

*Jambon Persillé* (pp. 277–8)

*Boeuf Bourguignonne*

*Baked Potatoes*

*Cheese*

*Blackberry Water Ice* (p. 279)

And the wine was Savigny-Lès-Beaune, 1960.

## NOVEMBER 10th, 1967 – THURLOE SQUARE

**LUNCH:** *My mother, Constance Green*
*Mrs Reginald Maudling*
*Marion, Lady Harewood*
*Mrs Basil Porter*
*Mrs Parker Bowles*

This was a lunch for a charity my mother and Bridget Porter, with which my brother's future mother-in-law, were involved (I forget which, though it may have been Action for the Crippled Child). I presume the three others were on the main committee. I was also surprised, when I re-read the relevant dinner book, to see that a Mrs Parker Bowles – whom I erroneously thought must be Camilla Parker Bowles – was one of the guests. I photographed her house for another book of mine in the 1980s (before all the Prince of Wales publicity) and, from a very limited acquaintance, remembered her as being pleasant, natural and amusing. But I did not recollect that I had met her before that. It turned out that, of course, she would have been far too young to have been on any charity committee at that time. The Mrs Parker Bowles in question was the mother of Camilla's ex-husband, Andrew Parker Bowles. When I had a house in Wiltshire, over a decade later, I lived just down the road from Andrew and his new wife, who were sociable neighbours – and who still saw a lot of Camilla, contrary to the supposed animosity and embarrassment promulgated by the press. If those same journalists had been around in the 1930s, they would have seen that the sophisticated attitude then was that husbands were quite flattered by the attentions of the then Prince of Wales to their wives. As was the case with the Prince of Wales, later Edward VII, at the turn of the century. Certainly that was the case with Mr Simpson, husband of the future Duchess of Windsor and earlier Edwardian husbands.

Beryl Maudling had been an actress before she married Reginald Maudling, the Conservative politician, in the late 1930s. I was particularly interested to meet the very pretty Lady Harewood, the former pianist and opera singer Marion Stein, who had been divorced from her husband, Lord Harewood – a great music lover – only that year. The divorce occasioned a good deal of publicity because Lord Harewood was first cousin to the Queen since his mother was the Queen's aunt, the Princess Royal, and he was, though way down the list, still in line to the throne. In fact it was one of the very few divorces of any one so close to the Royal Family, apart from the thrice-divorced Duchess of Windsor in the 1930s; one of Queen Victoria's many daughters at the turn of the century; and the divorce of Group Captain Peter Townsend which caused Princess Margaret such pain (such unnecessary pain, as it turned out, given the later softening of attitudes). That the Princess was not allowed to marry a divorced man and keep her rank was entirely occasioned by stuffy Palace courtiers giving self-serving misinformation. Though I cannot imagine what advantage they gained, except that of sticking to the dubious status quo.

Lord Harewood had married again the previous July, this time to Patricia Tuckwell, the Australian violinist and sister of Barry Tuckwell, the musician. And they had already had a son between them. Marion Harewood herself, got re-married some six years later to Jeremy Thorpe, the then leader of the Liberal Party who got embroiled (in the

1970s) in a homosexual scandal and subsequent trial – where he was accused, but acquitted – of trying to instigate the murder of a deeply troublesome friend, though the friend's dog was undoubtedly killed. This did, however, end Mr Thorpe's political career.

**The Menu was:**

Smoked Salmon Quiche (p. 279)

Winter Salad (p. 280)

Cheese

Crème Brulee (p. 280)

And the wine was Montrachet, 1961.

## NOVEMBER 22nd, 1967 – THURLOE SQUARE

**DINNER:** Ken and Kathleen Tynan
Margot Walmsley
Arthur and Cynthia Koestler
Kenneth Bradshaw
Eileen O'Casey
Oliver Sacks

We had met Arthur Koestler, the ex-Communist Hungarian writer, both at Marston and Eden Fleming and with Margot Walmsley. His books, particularly Darkness at Noon – as darkly warning about Communism, many people thought, as Orwell's 1984 – and Thieves in the Night about Zionism had made an unforgettable impression on me when I read them, aged 17. He had accurately and presciently remarked of the 1917 Balfour Declaration – the partitioning of the Ottoman Empire at the end of World War One, with part of Palestine promised to the Jews – that it was 'One nation solemnly promising to a second nation, the country of a third'. And look what that has led to.

Mr Koestler had quite recently married his third wife, Cynthia, slight, quiet and very much younger than him. He was a rather short man with a dark and deeply-lined complexion that to me, somehow belied his powerful books. But he was both polymath and a polyglot with an extraordinary linguistic facility which enables him to write elegantly, articulately and forcibly in several languages. He contributed to both The Sunday Telegraph and Encounter and to publications in many

169

other countries as well, whether about politics, drugs, science, capital punishment, nuclear disarmament or the paranormal. But, that night, he held forth most indignantly about the 'illogical British police' who had stopped him the night before – as they had stopped Ian Anstruther at a similar age – for driving much too slowly.

The heavily-bearded and then slightly ungainly Oliver Sacks, had worked briefly with Roger at Queen Square before moving to New York. At that time, he was just 34 and had only started working as a consultant neurologist at the Beth Abrahams Hospital in the Bronx the year before (1966). It was there that he studied a group of patients who had suffered the devastating effects of the 1920s sleeping sickness or, more formally, *encephalitis lethargica*. Many of them had spent decades unable to initiate any movement and his moving book *Awakenings* (also made into a film) describes the miraculous effect of the new drug, L.Dopa, in 1969. These patients were also the foundation for his Institute for Music and Neurological Function which provides cognitive and physical help through music. His own occasionally idiosyncratic habits were subsumed by the enormous care he took of his patients and the help he was able to give them.

**The Menu was:**

*Baby Leeks Vinagrette* (p. 281)

*Roast Pheasants, Bread Sauce and Fried Breadcrumbs*

*Game Chips, Little Brussels Sprouts and Chestnuts*

*Cheese*

*Oranges and Lemons (Orange Sorbet in Oranges and Lemon Sorbet in Lemons)* (pp. 256–7)

And the wine was Savigny-Lés-Beaune, 1960.

CHAPTER SIX

# THURLOE SQUARE
# AND TOSTOCK, 1968

## JANUARY 5th, 1968 – TOSTOCK

**DINNER:** *Paul and Annette Reilly*
*Terence and Caroline Conran*
*David and Angela Caccia*
*Anthony Green*
*Sarah Porter*
*Jane Porter*
*Billy McCarty*

This was a post-New Year dinner party pre the Ickworth Ball. Ickworth, built in 1795 by the eccentric 4th Marquess of Bristol, was the home of the Hervey family, and consisted of a splendid rotunda with two side wings (although I read in a lively memoir of a visit to Suffolk, by a young Duc de la Rochfoucauld soon after it was built, that it was 'a far from distinguished house'). The rotunda had a curving corridor for the display of paintings and a series of formal reception rooms, so seldom used – except for occasions like this – that the furniture and objects had been outstandingly well- preserved. The family actually lived in the east wing, to one side of the rotunda and the west wing, which balanced it, was just left empty. The surrounding park with its huge ancient trees and nibbling sheep was, and still is, the model of what such a grand country house park should be and the gardens, at that time, were immaculate. In fact, many of the Marquesses of Bristol were either eccentric or just plain bad. I read in the same de la Rochfoucauld memoir, that the Eighteenth Century French writer and philosopher, Voltaire, on a visit to Britain had written: 'There are three sorts of people in England: Men, Women and Herveys.'

Victor Hervey, the 6th and then current holder of the title, had been the ringleader in his youth of the notorious 'Mayfair Playboys', a gang of loutish ex-public school boys, and was often called (quite kindly I thought, in the circumstances) 'The Pink Panther' of his day. He went bankrupt in 1937 at the age of 21 when he was selling arms to both sides in the Spanish Civil War and a deal went wrong, leaving him with debts of almost £124,000 (about £10 million in current currency). His 'Mayfair Playboys' gang assaulted a jeweller for Cartier during a massive jewellery heist, and he was sentenced to three years in prison while some others of the gang, were sentenced to the 'cat-'o-nine-tails' (a particularly unpleasant whipping). In spite of his early financial hiccups and criminal record, Victor Hervey went on to amass a fortune of some £50 million from various sources, then moved to Monte Carlo for tax reasons, with his very much younger third wife, his former secretary, by whom he had three more children (the 8th Marquess and the 'It' girls, the Ladies Victoria and Isabella Hervey). But almost all the fortune he had tried to save in Monaco was subsequently lost or spent on drugs by his eldest son and heir, the 7th Marquess, born to his first wife.

The house had already been sold to the National Trust, although the family retained a substantial lease on the east wing which remained the family seat. Unfortunately for the 8th Marquess, his elder half-brother sold back this lease to the National Trust, and went on to sell almost all the fabulous contents of the house, all to support his drug habit. A hotel bought the lease back again from the National Trust without any of the contents, as far as I could see on a recent visit, though all of the families staying with their children for half-term seemed to be having a very fun time. But that was later. We only knew the Bristols because the second wife, Juliet – Countess Fitzwilliam in her own right – was a friend, of our friend Jan Burt, from Oxford. Juliet seemed as nice as Victor didn't: she later divorced him anyway. They had one son together who died in his thirties. I can remember going to a dinner party with the Bristols and being riveted by the fact that Victor went around carrying his own personal bottle of Champagne from which he regularly refilled his glass. I'm not sure if he didn't actually have it in the pocket of his dinner jacket. Everyone else had sherry or white wine which we sipped while a butler went around asking house guests what they wanted on their breakfast trays.

Anyway, Juliet had invited us to bring a party to the Ball and it was interesting to see the inside of the rotunda in all its glory and to dance in those surroundings to a rythmic and quite unexpected steel band. According to my sister-in-law Sarah, she still remembers that I was Sambaing away with a rose stem in my mouth. I have no recollection of that, though I did like to Samba. The Vosne-Romanée that we drank with our dinner before must have been particularly alcoholic!

# Thurloe Square and Tostock, 1968

The Reillys and Billy McCarty were staying with us, and the others all lived comparatively near, including the Caccias, who now had a house about 30 miles away in Hertfordshire. Sarah Porter was then my brother's fiancée (now his sweet and most supportive wife of many years). Their elder son, Jonathan Green, lives in the US and has become a fearless journalist, travelling to every international trouble spot and a deserving winner of many journalistic awards on both sides of the Atlantic. Jane Porter was Sarah's equally attractive twin sister.

**The Menu was:**

Smoked Salmon Mousse (p. 257)

Provençale Daube (p. 281)

Baked Potatoes

Salad of Curly Endive

Cheese

Preserved Ginger Creams (p. 282)

And the wine was Vosne-Romanée, 1964.

## FEBRUARY 3rd, 1968 – THURLOE SQUARE

**DINNER in the kitchen:** Paddy Milligan
Paul Reilly
Victoria Reilly
Billy McCarty

Annette was in hospital and we had Paul and Victoria – who were staying with him – every night that week. This night Paddy Milligan joined us as well, as Spike was away, as did another of our frequent visitors, Billy McCarty who enjoyed coming to see his godson, Tom.

**The Menu was:**

Tonno e Fagioli (p. 283)

Paupiettes of Veal on a Purée of Potatoes and Celeriac (p. 283)

Braised Endives

Cheese

Omelettes Normandes (p. 285)

And the wine was Rioja Crianza, 1963.

# Mary Gilliatt's Fabulous Food and Friends

## FEBRUARY 17th, 1968 – THURLOE SQUARE

**DINNER:** *Tom and Rusty Guinzberg*
*John and Sheelagh Metcalfe*
*Francis Hope*
*Vera Russell*
*Max and Joan Reinhardt*

Tom Guinzberg, my American publisher was in London again, this time with his wife Rusty. He must have been one of the last generation of purely family publishers before they were almost all swallowed up by much less personal conglomerates and the whole feeling of publishing changed. I was fortunate (or unfortunate since one can't help but make comparisons) to have known that old era and lucky in that Tom, the son of one of the founders of Viking in 1925, took great personal care of his authors, as Max did, although Max who had had his own eponymous imprint, had not taken on Bodley Head until the late 1950s. I was always interested in how publishers started. Bodley Head had originally been set up in 1887 by two partners to sell antiquarian books and took its name from the bust of Sir Thomas Bodley over their shop door. (Bodley, in his turn had founded the renowned Bodleian Library in Oxford.) The partnership then segued into doing their own publishing and became a private company in 1921 and continued until 1936, when it was supported by a group of other publishers including the marvellous old Sir Stanley Unwin of Allen & Unwin (who still played tennis in his 90s) and Allen Lane who founded Penguin Books.

Viking was taken over by Penguin Books in 1975 and became Viking Penguin. Bodley Head was later bought by the Jonathan Cape/Chatto & Windus Group and sold in 1987 to Random House, itself owned by the huge German media company, Bertelsmann. It is all a very tangled web, more deceptive than deceiving, but now a few independent publishers are coming out of the interstices, so to speak, including Pen & Sword who are publishing these reminiscences. They belong to the Barnsley Group who publish the last of the independent British weekly newspapers. And the group is currently celebrating its 150th year.

The Metcalfes had recently had us to one of their always very pleasant parties. Francis Hope was a young writer and critic who wrote a lot for *The New Statesman* and a friend of an old boyfriend of mine, George Gunary. He was also the son of Michael Hope who later married the widowed Helen Cohen. Sadly, Francis was killed in the Turkish Airlines crash one foggy night in the 1970s, on its last leg en route from Paris to London.

Vera Russell, then the rather tempestuous wife of John Russell, the art critic, was, I believe, the daughter of Serge Poliakoff, the Russian-born abstract painter who was a leading member of the *École de Paris* and was a passionate and generous patron of painters herself. She and John were dedicated entertainers and she later started the Artist's Market, after her split with John, to show the works of both well-known and lesser known painters. However, Roger and I got struck off her guest-list quite soon after this particular dinner because Sophia, our elder daughter, then aged four, said she had swallowed a penny. We were due at the Russells for dinner in an hour but had to rush her off for an X-ray. I called Vera to say that we might be a little late but then we were kept much longer than we expected in the hospital. So I had to recall Vera and cancel at the very last minute. She was very, very cross because she was giving quite a small dinner and not just a party. Furthermore, no penny was found in the X-rays. The whole thing was a bummer, as they say. And we were never forgiven.

**The Menu was:**

*Individual Cheese Soufflés* (p. 301)

*Poulet à l'Ail*

*Endive and Olive Salad* (p. 286)

*Cheese*

*Chocolate Meringue Mousse* (p. 287)

And the wine was Gevrey-Chambertin, 1962.

**FEBRUARY 20th, 1968 – THURLOE SQUARE**

**LUNCH:** *Constance Green*
*Marion, Lady Harewood*
*Mrs Reginald Maudling*
*Vera Russell*
*Mrs Joy Horlock*
*Mrs Doreen Croxton*

Here was yet another lunch for my mother and her charity though I see I had brought in Vera Russell and she, or my mother, perhaps Mrs Maudling or Lady Harewood, had brought in some other people whom I did not know. At that time, Reginald Maudling, who had been a Chancellor of the Exchequer in the last Conservative Government, and had fought Edward Heath for the leadership of the party, but failed, was still the Deputy Leader of the Opposition. Later, when Heath became Prime Minister in 1970, Maudling became Home Secretary but there were some scandals about his business dealings and he felt he had to resign. In the 1970s, when his political future appeared to be in ruins, both he and his wife took rather too wholeheartedly to drink as a panacea. Reginald died of cirrhosis of the liver and kidney failure – the dismal end of such promise.

**The Menu was:**

*Al Dente Vegetables with a Thick Vinaigrette Sauce* (p. 288)

*Veal Escalopes with a Cream and Cucumber Sauce with Feuilletés* (p. 269)

*Broccoli*

*Sweet Orange Salad* (p. 288)

And the wine was Rothschild St. Emilion, 1959.

### APRIL 15th, 1968 – TOSTOCK

**DINNER:** *Margot Walmsley*
*Bob Hjorth*
*Peregrine and Claudie Worsthorne*
*Angus Wilson and Tony Garrett*
*Jean-Louis de Narbonne*

I do not remember much about Bob Hjorth, an American Neurologist who had stayed with us in London and now the country, except that he was a good friend and colleague of Roger's and had produced the memorable phrase; 'I'm afraid I blundered my bulk' when he had accidentally broken a cup. Margot was staying for the weekend as well, and the Worsthornes came over from a village on the coast where they were renting a cottage. They were near the painter Francis Bacon and his boyfriend and had taken us over, with the gregarious George Melly and his then wife, Victoria, who were staying with them, to have a pre-lunch drink late one Sunday morning. But the place was in absolute chaos. Curtains were torn down, furniture upturned, broken glass and crockery were everywhere. The two had had an obviously ferocious row the night before and had not gotten around to clearing up.

In the years I knew Angus Wilson and Tony Garrett I do not think I ever heard them pass a cross word. They were very caring towards each other. I cannot now recollect Jean-Louis de Narbonne. He had been brought along by Angus and Tony.

**The Menu was:**

*A Ring of Fish Mousse with a Centre of Chopped Cucumber and Dill*

*Roast Duck Breasts with Wine, Orange and Honey Sauce* (p. 232)

*Sautéed New Potatoes*

*Timbales of Lettuce puréed with Shallots and Cream* (p. 289)

*Cheese*

*Pommes en Crème Meringuees*

And the wine was Macon Villages, 1965 and Château Batailley, 1959.

### MAY 14th, 1968 – THURLOE SQUARE

**DINNER:** *Professor and Mrs Derek Denny-Brown*
*Dr and Mrs Brinton*
*Dr and Mrs Kelly*

Professor Denny Brown from Harvard was, if not idealised, at least put on a very tall pedestal by a great many of the neurologists that I knew and almost all of them had made a point of working with him for a short period. When he died in the early 1980s, more or less half the heads of all the neurological departments in America had been trained by him at the City Hospital in Boston. He had only retired from that hospital the year before and had become the James Jackson Putnam Professor Emeritus at Harvard Medical School. Like Ian McDonald, he was originally from New Zealand which, for a small country, seems to have produced a great many distinguished doctors and Nobel prize winners over the years.

Roger and I had had dinner that year with Denny, as he was known, and his English wife, Sylvia, at their home in Cambridge, Massachusetts, the day Dr Spock (the enormously popular baby and child care author, whom so many of us followed then), had been arrested for protesting very vigorously about the draft for the Vietnam War. Guests at their dinner were of opposed politics, to say the least, and the evening got very heated over the issue of whether Dr Spock should or should not have been arrested. (In the end, I am happy to say, all charges were dropped and he did not go to prison). One ardent Republican, the Professor of Veterinary Medicine at Harvard, was going on vociferously about the absolute need for the US to be at war in Vietnam, and that all retaliation against the Viet-Cong was justified, whatever it was, when Sylvia Denny-Brown, with her sweet Queen Mum voice and smile, interrupted saying, quite calmly: 'You mean you really don't *mind* us dropping Napalm? You don't *mind* us burning all those little children?' She could not have stopped the ranting guy more effectively if she'd gagged him.

Anyway, here they were with us and some senior colleagues from Queen Square. Dr Kelly had taken over from James Bull as the new Dean of the Institute of Neurology.

**The Menu was:**

*Smoked Salmon Mousse* (p. 257)

*Poulet Antiboise* (p. 290)

*Tiny New Potatoes*

*Little Green Beans*

*Cheese*

*Strawberries and Cream*

And the wines were Gewurztraminer, 1963, Château Rauzan-Gassies, 1959 and Château Suduiraut, Sauternes, 1959.

**MAY 23rd, 1968 – THURLOE SQUARE**

**LUNCH:** *Tony Snowdon*
*Terence Conran*
*James Mitchell*

This was really a lunch to discuss the possibility of what became Terence Conran's first *The House Book*. Tony Snowdon was all set to photograph it, James (who later became Mitchell Beazley but I had originally known him through Max Reinhardt and Bodley Head) was hoping to publish it, and I was prepared to write it since it had been my idea. It did not get off to a terribly good start because Tony arrived in his little Mini with the blacked out windows and decided to nip into a parking space which four youths in a bigger car were rather leisurely preparing to back into. When the youths were thwarted of their space – and of course not able to identify the driver – they indignantly leapt out of their car as one, each picked up a corner of Tony's Mini (with him in it) and dumped it in the middle of the road before finally reversing into the space successfully. Unsurprisingly, Tony was furious and rang the doorbell, scarlet with the huge indignity of it all. I do not know what the youths thought, or even if they recognised him, when he finally emerged from his hoisted car.

Other than that the lunch was, of course, interesting for the conversation and I was pleased with a Mousseline of Hollandaise sauce that I had perfected, which made the sauce much lighter and airier. Terence thought the book idea good and was gung ho about it, and indeed it was finally published to great acclaim and huge sales (but without Tony's photographs or my text because Terence, or possibly Terence and James, were simply not willing to pay either of us our normal fees). James Mitchell, who sadly died very young, founded Mitchell Beazley and did very well out of the publication. In fact so well that Terence eventually decided that it must be worth starting his own publishing company for which he paired up with Paul Hamlyn to form Conran Octopus. I might not have written *The House Book*, which was a huge best-seller (and in the end written and photographed by a whole team which with hindsight, was much more practical) but I was the first author to write a book for the newly formed Conran Octopus *(Dream Houses)* with the estimable Alison Cathie (now head of Quadrille) as Managing Director, who had headed my former publishers, Orbis. I have written many books for them since. You win some, you lose some, as they say.

**The Menu was:**

*Cold Asparagus Mimosa with a Mustard Vinaigrette* (p. 291)

*Salmon Trout Cooked in Foil with a Mousseline of Hollandaise Sauce*

*Tiny New Jersey Potatoes and Chopped Mint*

*Fresh Petits Pois and Cucumber*

*Cheese*

*Blackcurrant Leaf Sorbet* (p. 226)

And the wine was Puligny-Montrachet, 1963.

# MARY GILLIATT'S FABULOUS FOOD AND FRIENDS

## MAY 30th, 1968 – THURLOE SQUARE

**DINNER:** *Sarah and Tom Lee*
*David Hicks*
*Max Clendinning*
*Billy McCarty*
*Mike and Annabel Popovic*

Sarah Tomerlin Lee (still the Editor of the US *House Beautiful)* and her husband, Tom Lee, whom I had met in New York early in 1967, were in London because Tom was designing the interiors for a new hotel on Hyde Park Corner. I was so pleased to be able to have them to dine. Sarah had worked in some way with David Hicks before, so asked if I could invite him. In fact, David had grown up in Suffolk as I had, and actually asked me to go to a Point to Point with him when I was about 18. He was excessively handsome so I had been pleased to be seen with this Adonis. My mother knew his parents, a Colonel and Mrs Hicks, although his mother had been a widow for quite a long time and more or less kept house for David when he first moved to London. With his unerring eye, bold colour sense, and astounding flair for the innovative, David had made a huge success as a decorator (in fact I would say that he and Terence Conran together were each, in their quite different ways, responsible for the English Design renaissance in the 1960s). But he had become very grand, the more especially after he married Pamela Mountbatten, the younger daughter of Lord Mountbatten. Roger knew the latter quite well because he sometimes rang up at awkward times and in the middle of the night about the Queen (as indeed he had to Roger's father), or his wife, Edwina, with questions that were hard to answer, the more especially as Roger was not one of the Queen's or Lady Mountbatten's regular doctors and had only been called in once as a consultant. He had been to the Hicks-Mountbatten wedding, just before I met him, which had to be entirely held in candlelight because there was a long power cut. I am afraid that Princess Margaret almost always spoke of him as Mr H-h-hicks as if she had hiccups.

I had told Sarah about Billy's great talent so, of course, I asked him: Sarah had been impressed by the photographs of Max Clendinning's house in my book *English Style* and wanted to meet him as well. I thought Max, an architect, furniture and interior designer, was one of the very best of the new breed of the avant-garde British Designers, and I still think him underestimated. Looking at pictures of his work from that period only recently, I was struck all over again by the uniqueness and originality of his designs. Mike and Annabel Popovic provided the attractive ballast on the non-designer side.

**The Menu was:**

Cold Cucumber Soup with Red Caviar

Gigot d'Agneau Provençale (p. 291)

Purée of Potatoes

Green Salad

Cheese

Iced Strawberry Soufflé


**JULY 30th, 1968 – THURLOE SQUARE**

**PARTY FOR ROGER'S BIRTHDAY:**

**(in the garden)**     Princess Margaret and Tony Snowdon
Spike and Paddy Milligan
Marston and Eden Fleming
Paul and Annette Reilly
Michael and Annabel Popovic
Helen Cohen
Roger and Svetlana Lloyd
Ivor and Jan Burt
Max Clendinning
Billy McCarty
Anthony and Annie Nutting
Perry and Claudie Worsthorne
Margot Walmsley
Osbert Lancaster and Anne Scott-James
Ken and Kathleen Tynan
Terence and Caroline Conran
Kenneth Bradshaw
Tom and Fleur Meyer
Tony and Susan Crosland
Duncan Oppenheim

Roger's birthday again and much the same guests – but not quite so many of them as the last birthday party – so I was able to serve more or less a proper dinner, but cold. The only new faces were Roger and Svetlana Lloyd who had had me to an equally big dinner in New York in honour of Kiri te Kanawa. Roger Lloyd was an investment banker but also on the board of the Metropolitan Opera House and I had met them through my New York friend, Barbara Plumb.

Princess Margaret had been very nice about *English Style* and liked the pictures of Kensington Palace but she ticked me off for writing George the Fourth in some description or other. '*King* George the Fourth,' she told me with perfect seriousness, 'would have been more polite, don't you think?' Only a few weeks before, the Snowdons had had a supper party in their garden behind Kensington Palace. I remember that I was somewhat awe-inspired to be sitting next to David Frost on one side and Lord Harlech, then Chairman of Harlech Televison, on the other. Peter Sellars, who the Princess was very keen on, and was also there, had set up one of those old-fashioned striped bathing tents at the end of the lawn. Halfway through the evening he clapped his hands for silence and announced that he was now going to perform his well-known imitation of Her Royal Highness, Princess Margaret, Countess of Snowdon. He then went behind the tent. Clothes and pieces of underwear came flying up above the canvas and suddenly Princess Margaret appeared in front of the tent's flaps. With perfect timing, she curtsied gracefully to the front, to the right and to the left to tumultuous applause and retired behind the tent. More underclothes of a feminine nature this time, went flying up in the air and after a suitable pause, out stepped Peter Sellers again. It was very, very funny – but less funny, I don't doubt, in the telling.

**The Menu was:**

*Tartelettes à la Dijonnaise* (pp. 292–3)

*Boeuf à la Mode Provençale* (pp. 293–4)

*Potato Salad*

*Avocado and Grapefruit Salad*

*Tomato and Basil Salad*

*Cheeses*

*Petits Pots de Chocolat*

*And/or Raspberries and Cream*

And the wines were Champagne, Beaujolais and an Austrian White Grüner Veltliner.

# THURLOE SQUARE AND TOSTOCK, 1968

## AUGUST 18th, 1968 – TOSTOCK

**DINNER:** *Paul and Annette Reilly*
*David and Jane Barron*

We had met the Barrons at my parents' house. David was then Chairman of Shell Oil and later of the old Midland Bank. He was dark and good-looking with an idiosyncratic taste in clothes. At one dinner with the Snowdons a few years later he turned up in a black kaftan, rather like a soutane, with a Neru shirt underneath. 'Who is that Bishop?' asked Princess Margaret, 'I thought I'd met them all.' Jane was splendidly matter of fact and casually Bohemian. They were a good Catholic family and had five or six children. They had just moved into a large old house, with quite a lot of land, a few miles away. They had got it at a bargain price because it had dry rot which many would-be buyers, quite erroneously, think is the kiss of death. The Barrons did not think so and got the place for an apparent song. The dry rot was dealt with comparatively reasonably and David sold off most of the surrounding acres, which they did not need, to a neighbouring farmer 'for a small prophet' as my daughter Sophia wrote in an essay, aged six. (I have never been able to hear the term 'small profit' since, without visualizing a little bearded man in a biblical robe).

In the end, one way and another, the house, including getting rid of the rot, cost them almost nothing. We were all very envious. The only thing was that they painted more or less the whole building, inside and out, a shade of pale pea green. I thought that Shell must have had a job lot of paint that year that they could not get rid of. They also had a house in Kensington Square and when we moved near them to Douro Place the following year, we saw a lot of them in London too. In fact we both got burgled the same night by most peculiar thieves whose signature was a trail of Tampax down both our respective staircases.

Paul and Annette were staying for the weekend.

**The Menu was:**

*Spiced Green Eggs*

*Filet de Boeuf Roti, Sauce Béarnaise*

*Pommes Pont-Neuf*

*Green Salad*

*Cheese*

*Peaches with Raspberry Purée* (p. 294)

183

# Mary Gilliatt's Fabulous Food and Friends

## SEPTEMBER 22nd, 1968 – TOSTOCK

**DINNER:** *Bill and Barbara Plumb*
*Billy McCarty*
*Paul William White*

Billy was staying the weekend as were our New York friends, the Plumbs who had been in Europe again, or perhaps Morocco, and were staying with us en route back to New York. Paul White had come over from Cambridge where he was an architectural student. Paul's father was the Agent General for Tasmania in London and I think we must have somehow met the Whites at some dinner or other. Anyway, Paul became practically a member of the family till he moved back to Australia, many years later, to work for the Aborigines.

It was unusually hot for late September.

**The Menu was:**

*Piperade* (p.295)

*Vitello Tonnato* (p. 247)

*Little New Potatoes*

*Tomato Salad*

*Cheese*

*Greek Honey Tart* (p. 296)

And the wine was a Provençale Rosé.

## OCTOBER 13th, 1968 – TOSTOCK

**DINNER:** *Angus Wilson and Tony Garrett*
*Margot Walmsley*
*Bhai Patel*
*My sister, Carmel*
*Terence and Caroline Conran*
*Spike and Paddy Milligan*

Margot, Spike and Paddy were all staying the weekend. Bhai, over from the UN, and my sister, were staying with my parents. Angus and Tony were going to India to do research for Angus' new novel (*Late Call*) about an agronomist who worked all over Asia as far as I remember. Although Bhai was actually Fijian, he had lived in India (and indeed returned there later for the UN and is still living in Delhi). Spike too had been born in India and had spent his early years there before his parents moved to Australia. All in all, Angus and Tony were going to be filled with information, suggestions and addresses of contacts. Terence and Caroline had just driven over from their cottage to join us.

**The Menu was:**

*Oeufs Mollets Provençale*

*Lamb Cutlets with Artichokes and Mushrooms*

*Sautéed Potatoes*

*Green Salad*

*Cheese*

*Tarte Normande* (p. 296)

And the wine was Savigny-lés-Beaune, 1964.

### NOVEMBER 1st, 1968 – THURLOE SQUARE

**DINNER:** *Peter and Jill Parker*
*Terence and Caroline Conran*
*Annie Nutting (Anthony was away)*
*James and Thalia Joll*
*Billy McCarty*
*Helen Cohen*

We had been to New York again and were shocked to hear there that Andrew Cohen had died suddenly. We had had Helen over several times and the usual number of very small dinners. This one was to meet the Parkers again. Both Peter and Jill had been up at Oxford with Roger (in fact both Peter and Roger had gone back to Oxford again after the lengthy interruption of the war, Roger to his old college, Magdalen; Peter, who had been at London University before, to Lincoln College, where he had become a close friend with Ken Tynan). In fact, Roger always maintained that Jill Parker was at one time engaged to Ken. Peter, was a merry, versatile, showman sort of guy in the nicest way and had been a prominent member of the Oxford Union Debating Society as well as the Oxford Union Dramatic Society (OUDS) where he had been considered the best undergraduate actor of his day (in a field that included Ken Tynan, Lindsay Anderson and John Schlesinger). At that time he was still a Director of Booker-McConnell, the large industrial company which had a small publishing division, and was close to the Chairman, Sir Jock Campbell. The year before he had been asked by Barbara Castle, then Minister of Transport, to become Chairman of British Rail, but he had refused because the salary was too low, though he did accept the job in 1976. Just this year, however, Tom Maschler, the then whiz kid of British Publishing and Chairman of Jonathan Cape, had approached him to see if the company would be willing to put by a small percentage of its profits to fund a literary prize for fiction. Peter and Sir Jock agreed and the Booker-McConnell Prize was born – now the Man Booker – the most important literary prize in the world. The prize started off being £21,000 and was changed to £50,000 in 2002.

James Joll, had been a financial and economics writer and a Fellow of All Souls, the postgraduate college at Oxford, but had just joined N.M. Rothschild & Sons. We had been on *The Sunday Telegraph* together at the same time and he was a particular friend of Angela Caccia, since they too had been at Oxford together but rather later on than the others. With great prescience – or luck – James and his wife had bought a large, run down house in Notting Hill, which was a definitely derelict area then. They – like Annabel and Michael Popovic – must have been one of the first rediscoverers of that now very far from derelict area.

**The Menu was:**

*Pain de Sole with a Velouté Sauce* (pp. 297–8)

*Leg of Lamb Jardinière*

*Little Roast Potatoes*

*Green Salad*

*Cheese*

*Iced Blackberry Soufflé*

And the wines were Puligny-Montrachet, 1964, Charmes-Chambertin, 1964 and Château Suiduraut, 1959.

# THURLOE SQUARE AND TOSTOCK, 1968

## NOVEMBER 27th, 1968 – THURLOE SQUARE

**LUNCH:** *Tony Snowdon*
*Anthony Denney*
*Billy McCarty*

Anthony Denney had been the chief photographer when I was on
*House & Garden* in the mid 1950s, and was also an inspirational
decorator himself. I had been enormously influenced by his house
with its completely black dining room (*'Darling,* I am only ever in it at
night – and black is quite wonderful in candlelight'). And I remember
that he did all sorts of unusual things with skirting or base boards, like
painting them with diagonal stripes which few people had thought
of then. He was also a very good friend of Elizabeth David. Quite
unexpectedly he had got married and moved to Spain, but he was back
in London for a visit without his wife Celia, or maybe she was doing
something else. Anyway, I really wanted Tony and Billy to meet him.

**The Menu was:**

*Pâté Maison and Toast* (p. 298)

*Escalopes of Veal with Cucumber Sauce and Feuillités* (p. 269)

*Fruit*

## DECEMBER 2nd, 1968 – THURLOE SQUARE

**DINNER:** *Paul and Annette Reilly*
*Ian and Susan Anstruther*
*Ken and Kathleen Tynan*
*Bimby and Daphne Holt*
*Mr and Mrs Keith Miller-Jones*

This was sadly one of the last dinners at Thurloe Square since we
had just sold the house to an American investment banker. We had
some of our favourite neighbours and close friends and the Chairman
of Roger's Hospital Board and his wife whom I had met occasionally,
but hardly knew.

187

# Mary Gilliatt's Fabulous Food and Friends

**The Menu was:**

*Avocados Stuffed with Shrimps in a Mild Curry Sauce*

*Roast Pheasant, Fried Breadcrumbs, Straw Potatoes,*
*Little Brussels Sprouts with Bacon*

*Cheese*

*Soufflé Omelette with Grand Marnier (p. 299)*

# CHAPTER SEVEN

# DOURO PLACE AND RATTLESDEN – 1969/70 PLUS

A T THE beginning of the year we moved from my beloved Thurloe Square in South Kensington to a small cul-de-sac off Victoria Road in Kensington, called Douro Place – in 'Far West Eight' as our old Suffolk friend, Reggie Errington, had written in a poem (jokingly regretting our departure from South Kensington). Actually, to be completely accurate, we went to stay in a rented flat in Kensington for three months until the renovation of the new house was finished in March. But we had also bought a small house in Suffolk, not far from our rented cottage and still close to Bury St. Edmunds, near where I had grown up. Our lease in Thurloe Square had been getting shorter and both my father and Roger had thought it more prudent to disregard the avowed intention of our friends and South Kensington landlords, Ian and Susan Anstruther (and our shared lawyers) to give new 99 year leases, in favour of buying two smaller freehold properties.

It was a move I bitterly regretted at least as far as London, and which I have irritatingly complained about to family and friends ever since. But to be fair, I can see how it must have seemed to Roger. We shared running expenses in that I paid what staff we had, the food and wine, childrens' clothes, and a lot of the decoration and any furniture we bought, and he paid 'the heavies', the heating and lighting bills, local taxes or rates, any structural repairs and school fees – which we were just beginning to pay and would obviously increase. The local taxes on such a big house were alarmingly high on a National Health Service salary and even keeping the stucco façade spic and span was a huge financial stretch. Very few at that time could have imagined that the burden of the upkeep would be more than balanced by the staggering leap in house prices over the next 30 years. Also, we all loved Suffolk, and the children were so happy in the country, so a more permanent home there had become a goal.

We sold Thurloe Square, astonishing as it sounds now, for £28,000 (having bought it for £14,000 but done a lot to it). Naturally, in a matter of a few months after that, the Anstruthers extended the leases to 99 years, as they had promised and because of changes in the law over the next few decades, people were eventually able to buy their own freeholds. At the time of writing this, the house last exchanged hands for many, many millions. (Real sod's law.) I have never ceased to miss that house and the square and still walk past the house with melancholy.

Still, Douro Place was a pretty little house with a charmingly-planted terrace – big enough for eating on – off the end of the ground floor, with steps down to the sheltered leafy garden with a shady tree and a large two-floored studio at its end which was excellent for guests and a children's play space – and there were many happy times. We transplanted the fig tree we had planted in Thurloe Square, and, obviously content there, it thrived and grew big enough for the children to climb on. We lined the long hall, all down one side, with floor-to-ceiling bookcases and on the other with mirrors to reflect them. What bits of wall that remained were painted a welcoming apricot. Our dear and talented friend, Billy McCarty, who when he first came to England had worked in conjunction with David Hicks (actually doing many of the Hicks' Company designs), designed a special cream and tobacco carpet for the hall, landing and stairs, and an octagonal carpet for the drawing room in green, rose pink and white. We paired this with green felt walls and books on glass shelves either side of the fireplace, lit from beneath by up-lights. I had a glass and Perspex desk at one end of the double room and we had a long glass and Perspex coffee table (which the girls used to take turns to lie under pretending to be the dead Snow White, with small Tom representing the seven dwarfs). There were neat little armchairs on casters designed by Max Clendinning, our avant-garde architect and furniture designer friend. The large and comfortable Thurloe Square sofa was recovered in a much darker raspberry and red wide-striped fabric and we used the same material for Roman blinds.

Our bedroom walls were covered in dark brown hessian, allied to a creamy carpet. The dining room downstairs had an orange-stained floor (to hide its rather battered parquet) and cream, apricot and tobacco fabric walls with the same fabric-covered shutters. The house was as much 1970s (with the colours in one area repeated on a different scale in others), as Thurloe Square had been early 1960s – before the Modern

Italian influence. I cannot imagine using those carpets now, though hessian and felt walls have come right back, as has wallpaper.

Later in the Summer, *Vogue* photographed it along with our three children jumping all over the place. There is a memorable picture of our son Tom, then aged two and a half, sitting on the drawing room mantelpiece underneath a large John Bratby painting of peonies against a brick wall and bright blue sky called 'Paean to Peonies'. Roger and I had given it to each other as a wedding present along with an Elizabeth Frink bronze 'horseman' which we had bought from Leslie Waddington.

Having moved into the new house in London in March as scheduled, we moved into the house in Suffolk at the end of April. I had been driving up and down like a yo-yo to get both houses fit to occupy and we had made quite a lot of changes in the country, including putting in a new staircase and a floor-to-ceiling glass window at the end of the hall (which gave more light and looked into one end of the kitchen and out French doors to the terrace beyond). We also took down the wall between living room and dining room but left the fireplace and chimney, which we opened on both sides (installing separate flues) in order to have a fire in both rooms. Paul White had been very helpful as had two local architects. The house was mainly Elizabethan with a Victorian façade and a late Medieval back and, like our rented cottage, was painted Suffolk pink. We used quite warm colours like a nutmeg brown in the living room and dining room, and a real 1970s orange in our bedroom. The hall was very bold with mustard yellow walls and the new open tread staircase stained red.

When we sold the house in the 1980s the new owners completely changed it. But when they, in their turn, sold it on, the new buyers changed it right back to how we had had it, faithfully following photographs they had seen in my book *A House in the Country* and in a magazine.

Although we had a long narrow kitchen in Douro Place which was impossible to eat in, the Rattlesden kitchen was good and square with a short wall behind a large old dresser separating a casual eating space from the working area. There was a large, well-treed garden to which we added roses and honeysuckle (to grow up the tree trunks) and many more flowering shrubs. At one end of the garden, the lawn dissolved into woodland which the children christened the 'Forest of the Seven Rivers'; they were intrigued one day, to find an old tramp roasting a hedgehog over a camp fire using the quills like kebab skewers. At the other end of the garden, the other side of the house, the lawn descended leisurely to what was left of the River Rat (hence Rattlesden, the name of the village) just down the road. Many centuries before, this 'river' was wide enough to take barge traffic, but now it was just a trickling stream. Outside the kitchen we created quite a large terrace with a pergola which soon became covered with sweet-smelling honeysuckle and jasmine. It was ideal for barbecues and outdoor lunches and dinners and we made full use of it. Finally, all around the house itself we made a broad, gravelled path edged with lavender bushes.

Our first proper dinner party in London was in April.

### APRIL 11th, 1969 – DOURO PLACE

**DINNER:** *Tom and Rusty Guinzberg*
*Billy McCarty*
*Peter and Celia Janson-Smith*
*Peter and Tessa Baring*
*Ken and Kathleen Tynan*

My American publisher, Tom Guinzberg obviously came across the Atlantic quite frequently. I was doing two new books on the history of the kitchen and the history of the bathroom respectively, (the former, my first US Book of the Month Club choice. I had even managed to persuade Elizabeth David to let me photograph her kitchen which she had never allowed before). Peter Janson-Smith was my then agent who miraculously managed to get me a separate American Royalty, although this was a tragic story. I had been paid an advance in US dollars, less Peter's commission, and, after I had deposited it in my UK bank and it had cleared, I exchanged it for cash to pay the builders. With this large amount of cash in my handbag I popped into the supermarket on my way home to buy something for dinner. I noticed a nun unexpectedly standing rather too close behind me at the check-out and it was not till I got home that I realised that the cash had all gone. The 'nun', must have followed me all the way from the bank. Or maybe he/she just got lucky. It was certainly in my bag just before I shopped.

Peter and Tessa Baring were yet more members of the Baring banking family – of which Peter became Chairman in 1989 and indeed, oversaw its bankruptcy in 1995. This was after Nick Leeson – who was not only the Floor Manager for Barings', trading on the Singapore Monetary Exchange, but also the Head of Settlement Operations – lost the bank millions of pounds in the Far East. In truth, Mr Leeson's two jobs should have been held by two different people since, with no overseer, he only had to report to himself about deals. At that time this was the greatest banking shock ever – though nothing to the French Société Générale debacle of many billions at the beginning of 2008. But it was a disastrous blow for Barings, Britain's oldest merchant bank and bankers to the Queen. They had financed the Napoleonic Wars, the Louisiana Purchase for President Jefferson and the Eerie Canal. Byron had included references to them in his poetry. And the Duc de Richelieu in 1817 is said to have pronounced that the six great powers in Europe were England, France, Prussia, Austria, Russia and Baring Brothers. I had met Peter and Nicholas, his brother, when I was a child on a holiday with my parents in Devon, and had not seen them again till we remet at David and Angela Caccia's one evening. David and Peter had been best friends at school. Tessa was a much respected sociologist.

**The Menu was:**

*Tartelettes Lasserre* (p. 240)

*Côtes de Veau Pannés*

*Sautée Potatoes*

*Sea Kale with Eliza Acton's Norfolk Sauce* (p. 300)

*Green Salad*

*Cheese*

*Hannah Glass' Almond Custard* (pp. 300–1)

And the wines were an Austrian Reisling and Château Mouton-Rothschild, 1961.

**MAY 9th, 1969 – DOURO PLACE**

**DINNER:** *Christopher Lawrence*
*Henry Keswick*
*Billy MCarty*
*Claire Wheldon*
*Jan Burt (Ivor was away)*
*Sonia Orwell*
*Tom and Sarah Lee*

Sarah and Tom Lee were in London again and wanted to see the new house, as did Sonia Orwell. Jan and Ivor had already been several

193

times. I had never met Mr Keswick but as far as I can remember, Billy had asked if he could bring him along, possibly to look at our carpets with a view of maybe doing something to his UK house. The Keswicks were the family who mostly ran Jardine Matheson, the huge Far Eastern trading company which was almost as old as Barings. Christopher Lawrence, later went to live and work in Rome, was then working with Billy and had also become a good friend.

Claire Wheldon, who was temporarily staying with us, was the daughter of some friends of my parents who owned the big commercial orchard next door to my parents' house.

**The Menu was:**

Little Cheese Soufflés (p.301)

Veal Escalopes with Cucumber Sauce and Feuillités (p. 269)

New Potatoes

Green Salad

Strawberries with Coeurs à la Crème

And the wine was Corton, 1961.


### MAY 20th, 1969 – DOURO PLACE

**LUNCH ON THE TERRACE:**
Joyce Wreford
Photographer from Connaissance des Arts Magazine

Joyce Wreford was a design journalist I knew who as far as I remember worked on Womens' Journal which I occasionally wrote articles for and also wrote freelance for Connaissance des Arts. The latter had sent Joyce and a photographer to look at the house.

**The Menu was:**

Quiche Lorraine

Chicken and Grape Salad (p. 303)

Salad of Lettuce Hearts

Strawberries and Cream

## MAY 25th, 1969 – RATTLESDEN

**DINNER:** *Margot Walmsley*
*Paul William White*
*Prince Richard of Gloucester*
*Gerry and Mary Cookson*
*Martin and Jean Corke*
*Terence and Caroline Conran*

This was our first big dinner party at Rattlesden where we had a very good-sized dining table and rather more room for guests to stay. Margot Walmsley had come for the weekend and Paul White had brought his fellow architectural student, the young Prince Richard of Gloucester, over from Cambridge. He was rather a quiet, shy young man though his unexpected name seemed to make an impact on our Suffolk friends, the Corkes and the Cooksons.

Gerry and Mary Cookson, whom we had met through the hospitable and gregarious Corkes, had already started to become close friends. Gerry was bespectacled, pale-faced, extremely tall, and extremely clever, with impeccable taste in everything from paintings to furniture, wine to gardens. The elder son of the Chairman of Consett Iron Company Ltd and a great many coal mines, later to become the National Coal Board, he had studied chemisty at Cambridge and invented Lurex which seemed an unlikely thing for him to do, but made him a great deal more money. He and Mary, a beautiful woman, who, until Gerry came along and swept her off her feet, had very nearly married Lord Rothermere, the last of the Press Barons and then owner of *The Daily Mail*, *The Mail on Sunday*, and *The Evening Standard*. Together, the Cooksons had built a remarkable collection of paintings, furniture and objects with which they had furnished their stunning house. They were dedicated gardeners with huge style and most of all they were generous benefactors to their village and its villagers. It seemed that no one there had a health or financial misfortune that the Cooksons did not quietly take care of.

Actually the weekend was memorable because the next day we went over to my parents for lunch and just before we left to go home I went looking for our very small son. I thought he was with Roger and Roger thought he was with me. In fact he had fallen into the pond at the back of the house which was about the third time he had fallen into someone's pond or swimming pool so he obviously had a predilection for water. Margot, who was sitting on the verandah, had seen it happen and had bravely jumped in right after him not knowing that the pond was actually very shallow. She rescued Tom who was trying to get up from the slippery bottom without success but very badly jolted her back which we both felt terrible about – on every count. They were both dripping and as white as sheets.

**The Menu (for an early, really hot Summer's night) was:**

*Artichokes, Mousseline of Hollandaise*

*Poulet Véronique* (p. 303)

*Rice salad*

*Tomato and Basil Salad*

*Cheese*

*Millefeuilles*

And the wine was Châteauneuf-du-Pape, 1964.

MAY 30th, 1969 – DOURO PLACE

**DINNER:** *Richard and Virginia Storey*
*David and Angela Caccia*
*Marston and Eden Fleming*
*Anthony and Annie Nutting*

Our new opposite neighbours, Virginia and Richard Storey had kindly had us to dinner when we first moved in and we had asked them back and taken the opportunity to invite other old friends. Richard was then the head of the Portsmouth and Sunderland group of Provincial newspapers and they were a good looking young couple, with children much the same ages as ours. I was interested that Virginia was a descendent of the distinguished Sir Kenelm Digby, the Seventeenth Century scientist and religious writer and friend of Descartes, though I cannot recollect how I discovered that, perhaps because their son was another Kenelm, or I enquired about a book on the distinguished Sir Kenelm that I saw around the house. We were lucky to have them across the road.

**The Menu was:**

*Avocado Mousse*

*Veal Escalopes en Papillotte* (p.304)

*Purée of Potatoes, Courgettes*

*Green Salad*

*Baked Apricots with Coeur à la Crème*

And the wine was Château Mouton-Rothschild, 1960.

## JUNE 5th, 1969 – DOURO PLACE

**DINNER:** *Gerry and Mary Cookson*
*Peter and Cordelia Vanneck*
*George and Joy McWatters*
*Spike and Paddy Milligan*

Here were more friends to see the new house including our Suffolk friends the Cooksons and the Vannecks. Peter Vanneck at that time was already well on course to gain his early ambition of becoming Lord Mayor of London. He had become an Alderman and a member of various Livery companies. He had been ADC to the Queen since 1963 and in his current profession of stockbroker he was already on the Stock Exchange Council. The following year he was going to become Deputy Lieutenant of the County of London. Here was one man who was not letting the grass grow under his feet. We reckoned he was going to be the best-looking and most stylish Lord Mayor for decades.

Spike and Paddy were both on really good form, and Spike, who took his wines very seriously, chatted away almost non-stop to George McWatters about his cellar, how he had managed to buy Château Latour for Harveys when he was Chairman, his Indian boyhood experiences (George too, had been born in India and had fought all those years ago in Afghanistan, apparently disguised as an Afghani Sherpa). I also heard them chatting about George's television company, then Harlech TV, of which George was Vice-Chairman, with Lord Harlech as Chairman. Later it became HTV with George as Chairman. I'd never known Spike to be so talkative or George for that matter, but I noticed that both were always more voluble with other guys than with women. Not that Joy was in any way silent.

# Mary Gilliatt's Fabulous Food and Friends

**The Menu was:**

*Tuna Fish and Red Pepper Tart* (p. 261)

*Noisettes d'Agneau with Sauce Chevreuil* (p. 304)

*Mushrooms and Artichoke Hearts*

*Olive-sized Sauté Potatoes*

*Cheese*

*Strawberry Syllabub* (p. 305)

And the wines were Rüdesheimer, 1964 and Château Beau Rivage, 1960.


## JULY 5th, 1969 – RATTLESDEN

### SUPPER ON THE TERRACE AFTER MY BROTHER'S WEDDING TO SARAH PORTER: *Eliza Gilliatt*

> *My parents, Arthur and Constance Green*
> *John and D'Arcy Howell*
> *Guy and Elizabeth Scott*
> *Shirley Cundy*
> *David Shelley*
> *Peter Wilson*
> *My sister*
> *John Jones*
> *Bill and Jane Neville Dawson*
> *Witgar and Margaret Hitchcock*

My brother had got married that afternoon with my two daughters as bridesmaids and Tom, as a very mischievous page. Some old woman at the reception said 'Mark my words,' ferociously shaking her finger, 'that child will turn into a criminal.' I am happy to say that he does not appear to have done so. My parents, my sister and her future husband, John Jones, my sister-in-law, my brother's best man (Peter Wilson) and his good schoolfriend plus various other old friends all came back for supper which I'd cooked before we went to the church.

**The Menu was:**

*Asparagus and Cheese Tart*

*Chicken with Prunes* (p. 305)

*Cheese*

*Summer Pudding* (p. 273)

And the wines were Macon Blanc, 1965 and Beaujolais, 1967.

### JULY 23rd, 1969 – DOURO PLACE

**DINNER:** *Margot Walmsley*
*Leslie Bilsby*
*Bettina McNulty (Henry was away)*
*Gordon Fischer*
*Helen Fiorati*
*Frank and Hélène Dawson*
*Anthony and Annie Nutting*

Gordon Fischer, an American investment banker had bought our old house in Thurloe Square and Helen Fiorati, a leggy, glamorous blonde in that uniquely American way, was an antiques dealer and decorator from New York and over to help him with the decoration. She and her mother owned an elegant jewel box of a shop, l'Antiquaire, selling mostly Russian antiques on 5th Avenue, across from the Plaza hotel. Leslie Bilsby headed Span Developments, a company which had won many awards for its forward-looking housing designs. He had asked me to help him with some show houses on the outskirts of London and also the outskirts of Paris and we had become rather good friends. Frank and Hélène Dawson were new friends but rapidly becoming closer. We had met them the last night in Thurloe Square when we had Gordon Fischer to dinner. He had asked if he could bring two American friends of his who were also settling in London. They turned out to be the Dawsons and much the same age as me. Frank was a lawyer who had written legal textbooks and ended up, years later, as a Professor at Cambridge. Hélène was the exotic looking and

199

talented painter and sculptor who worked under her maiden name of Hélène Fesenmaier. Unfortunately, she had felt very unwell soon after she arrived and since half the house was already dismantled I suggested that she lie down in our room. Roger got her a doctor, and she turned out to have hepatitis. They were buying a large house in Chester Square, just along from Penelope and John Osborne's old house, so that they could pull down the ceilings between the top two floors of the house and turn the space into a massive studio.

When the Dawsons moved in, much of the rest of the house was filled with their joint collection of Pre-Columbian art, Hélène's paintings and sculpture and their very early furniture mixed with modern classics. They were also serious mushroom pickers (the children always called them the 'Mushroom' Dawsons) and Hélène was a fabulous cook. When *Architectural Digest* started I was asked to be their London Correspondent for a brief time until I asked the photographer I was currently using, to take pictures of the Dawson's house. When he sent in his bill to Paige Rense (who is *still* the editor) she refused to pay saying that they had a policy only to pay writers, and even that, in those days, was modest. I said that was certainly not the case with magazines in the UK and enquired as to how were they expected to be paid. She then accused me of trying to get free pictures for my books – which was nonsense and I said so forcibly. Result: the end of being London Correspondent. But at least they started to pay photographers comparatively soon afterwards, though I fear I cannot claim any credit – much as I would like to.

I thought the Dawsons would like the Nuttings and I thought Bettina McNulty, an ex-New Yorker, might like to meet Helen Fiorati *and* the Dawsons.

**The Menu was:**

*Salmon Mousse with Cucumber Sauce* (p. 306)

*Roast Contre-Filet, Sauce Béarnaise*

*Pommes Pont-Neuf*

*Salad*

*Cheese*

*Raspberries, Strawberries and Redcurrants with Cream*

And the wines were Durkheimer Spätlese, 1963 and Château Pichon-Longueville, 1959.

# Douro Place and Rattlesden – 1969/70 Plus

## AUGUST 17th, 1969 – RATTLESDEN

**DINNER ON THE TERRACE:** *Gerry and Mary Cookson*
*Betty Murphy*
*Grania Caulfield*
*Anthony and Annie Nutting*
*Bill and Cesca Pearson-Rogers*
*Merlin Pearson-Rogers*
*Paul White*

We were spending August in the country and had a lot of friends for various weekends, dinners and lunches. One such, I noticed was for the entire McWatters family who came over to lunch from Cambridgeshire where they were then living, having sold, for a time, their much-loved West Country house, Burrington, because George had to leave Harveys when it was taken over by Showerings, the Babycham people. (I say sold for a time because later they managed to buy Burrington back). He had taken a job as Chairman of Ward White, a large shoe manufacturer in nearby Northamptonshire. Naturally, Joy being the stylish hostess that she was, had made the new house in Kimbolton just as welcoming and comfortable. During their time there George became High Sheriff of Cambridgeshire and rather admired himself in the traditional tight silk breeches and brocaded coat of the office. Anyway along came George and Joy and their son Christopher – another one of my godsons – much the same age as my elder daughter, Sophia. George's brother Micky, who had stayed on at Harveys as Managing Director, his wife Wendy, and Micky's two daughters by his first marriage, Sarah and Dinah McWatters, and Joy's mother were also present. But Rattlesden was a nice elastic house for entertaining with the big outdoor table, the bright red lacquered kitchen table and the long refectory table in the dining room.

Now, some other friends from Tostock days, the Pearson-Rogers, came over for dinner with their son, rejoicing in the rather Iris Murdoch-ian name of Merlin – who was a writer. Paul White, now graduated from Cambridge was staying for the weekend as were Anthony and Annie Nutting, and the Cooksons came with Mary's daughter, Grania (by her first husband) and her mother, Betty Murphy, whose husband had been Governor of the Bahamas after the Duke of Windsor. Betty was still beautiful, though well into her 80s, and so was Grania. When you saw all three women together you could see how the Murphy beauty had spread down three generations. The following year, Grania married Hugh Cavendish (our son Tom, a veteran by then, was asked to be one of the pages) who inherited Holker Hall, an enormous house in Lancashire which had been a favourite place to stay for Queen Victoria. There are still some charming little drawings by the old Queen (who was genuinely skilled at sketching) which she had added to her various signatures in the Holker visitors' books.

**The Menu was:**

Pain de Sole with a Mousseline of Hollandaise (p. 297)

Barbecued Shoulder of Lamb with Garlic and Rosemary

Puffy Potatoes (p. 307)

Tomato and Basil Salad

Green Salad

Cheese

Blackcurrant Leaf Sorbet Ice (p. 226)

And the wines were Sancerre, 1964 and St Julian, Château Lagrange, 1959.


## AUGUST 30th, 1969 – RATTLESDEN

**DINNER:** Geoffrey and Bill Clarke
Paul and Annette Reilly
Margot Walmsley
Ian McDonald
Gerry and Mary Cookson

Geoffrey and Bill Clarke had stayed in my old flat in Flood Street when Geoffrey was working on the stained glass windows for Coventry cathedral (which had been laid out one by one on my living room floor). He also sculpted the cross on top of the cathedral which had to be lowered precariously by helicopter. They had been away a lot on various commissions and I had not seen them very much except when I photographed their early-Ninteenth Century house for my book English Style. They had made the interiors very avant-garde and Geoffrey, who loved technology and used every possible new industrial invention to its best advantage, had turned the room off their kitchen into a fitting place to house his new Mercedes (which he loved with a passion). He lined the walls with immaculate tongue and grooved wood, and added discreet recessed lighting and an early polished concrete floor which was very unusual then. I was quite surprised that he had not carpeted it.

**The Menu was:**

*Artichokes, Sauce Hollandaise*

*Veal and Tomato Casserole* (p. 307)

*Buttered Rice*

*Green Salad*

*Cheese*

*Rose Petal Water Ice* (pp. 245–6)


### SEPTEMBER 5th, 1969 – DOURO PLACE

**LUNCH ON THE TERRACE:** *Norman Parkinson*
*Liz Lambert*
*Derek, Norman Parkinson's Assistant*
*Aunt Sophia*

Liz Lambert, an American, then on *Vogue*, had come with Norman Parkinson, to photograph the house. She was married to Jack Lambert, an American architect working at that time with the Greater London Council, and the two of them were good friends of Hélène Fesenmaier and Frank Dawson. In fact Liz had great style, both in herself and their house, and took over as the *Architectural Digest* Editor in London, a job she fulfilled very well – and still does. We got to know Jack and Liz quite well and I loved their house in Islington, with a tiny tributary of the Thames welling into their beautifully-tended garden. Norman Parkinson was then the great *Vogue* photographer and I was flattered that it was he who had come to take the pictures. Aunt Sophia, who was staying with us again, was wryly amused by the whole set up. The children (who were being called upon to jump up and down on the drawing room sofa and on our bed, and, for that matter, sit on the mantelpiece, none of which they were ever normally allowed to do) were more, I would say, bemused.

# Mary Gilliatt's Fabulous Food and Friends

**The Menu was:**

*Tuna Fish, Green Bean and Red Pepper Tart* (p. 261)

*Cheese Soufflé*

*Tomato and Basil Salad*

*Blackberry Sorbet* (p. 279)

And the wine was Schloss Graffenburg, 1964.


## OCTOBER 16th, 1969 – DOURO PLACE

**DINNER:** *Sir Francis and Lady Chichester*
*Roger and Moira Bannister*
*Anthony Nutting*
*Michael and Helen Hope*
*Margot Walmsley*

The Chichesters were good friends of Joy McWatters and I had met them when I was working for her, as Joy Matthews, on *The Daily Express*. Since then I had met them several times and they had asked Roger and I to dinner in their home off St James', over their shop called 'The Map House'. Francis, a New Zealander, had always been an intrepid sailor and indeed airplane pilot. After a chequered career in New Zealand and the UK and doing a sterling job during World War Two, teaching his wealth of navigational skills, he had had the brainwave to buy up 15,000 surplus Air Ministry maps, which he then pasted on cardboard and sold, very successfully, as jigsaw puzzles. This led him to the map-making business. In 1960 he had won, in Gipsy Moth III, the first single-handed Trans-Atlantic Yacht Race (which he co-founded). In 1967, despite being diagnosed with lung cancer (which was supposed to have been put on remission by the strict macrobiotic diet that Sheila put him on) he had been the first to sail single-handedly around the world by the old clipper route. He had set sail from Plymouth, England, on August 27th 1966 in his ketch Gipsy Moth IV and returned nine months and one day later, on May 28th, 1967 having stopped just once, in Sydney. For this tremendous feat he had been appropriately knighted by the Queen, ceremoniously using the sword with which her namesake, Queen Elizabeth I, had knighted Sir Francis

Drake, the very first Englishman to circumnavigate the globe – but not by himself.

Francis was very skinny, with a lined and weather-beaten face and seemed very mild and modest in spite of his determined achievements. Sheila was rather large and rather forceful. I thought they looked just like Jack Sprat who would eat no fat and his wife who would eat no lean. I liked the fact that I could introduce Francis to Roger Bannister since both had achieved such momentuous 'firsts'. Annie Nutting was spending a couple of months in America so Anthony came on his own. Helen Cohen was happily re-married to Michael Hope of Hope's Glass and father of Francis Hope, our writer friend. Not so very long after this, Michael Hope had given Helen a horse for Christmas. She took the horse out riding one afternoon near their country house and was not home by evening. Michael sent out a search party by torchlight and they finally found her some miles from home – she and the horse had both fallen: the horse, badly injured, on top of her. Helen, badly injured too and unable to free herself, had lain exposed to the cold for hours and added a very bad case of pneumonia to her many broken bones. It was a tragic accident from which she did not ever really fully recover.

**The Menu was:**

*Courgette Soufflé*

*Sautéed Chicken Breasts with a Sauce of Fines Herbes* (p. 308)

*Pommes Pont-Neuf*

*Little Green Beans with Pine Nuts*

*Green Salad*

*Cheese*

*Apricot Tart and Cream*

And the wines were Schloss Graffenburg, 1964 and Château Calon-Ségur, 1953.

**NOVEMBER 16th, 1969 – RATTLESDEN**

**DINNER:** *Tom Lee*
*Ladislas Tarnowski*
*Penelope Gilliatt*

# Mary Gilliatt's Fabulous Food and Friends

Tom Lee was over in London from NY for his hotel business. Ladislas was over from Paris for his annual visit to his tailor. Penelope was over from NY to see her English publishers and they were all three staying the weekend.

**The Menu was:**

Smoked Salmon with Aquavit

Boiled Ham and Cumberland Sauce (p. 308)

Baked Potatoes and Sour Cream

Leaf Spinach

Cheese

Fruit

And the wine was Beaujolais, 1968.

## DECEMBER 13th, 1969 – DOURO PLACE

**DINNER:** Anthony Nutting
Claudie Worsthorne (Perry was away)
Paul White
Eileen O'Casey
Frank and Hélène and Dawson
Kenneth Bradshaw
Annabel Popovic (Michael was away)

Eileen O'Casey (who was then living a lot in New York to be near her daughter, Shivaun) was having a short time in London, so it was nice to have her in the now not-so-new house, as well as some other friends for a pre-Christmas dinner.

**The Menu was:**

Crevettes Roses with Mayonnaise.

Fricassée of Veal (p. 309)

Rice

Green Salad

206

*Cheese*

*Caramelised Oranges* (p. 255)

And the wines were Bernkasteler Riesling, 1965 and Pommard, 1964.


## JANUARY 26th, 1970 – DOURO PLACE

**DINNER:** *Ken and Kathleen Tynan*
*Katherine Whitehorn and Gavin Lyall*
*Paul and Annette Reilly*
*Tom and Sarah Lee*

We had been very sociable in the country over Christmas and the New Year and beyond and it was quite a relief to get back to quieter London. Tom and Sarah Lee were in London again, and Sarah, never shy of saying who she'd like to meet, really wanted to meet Katherine Whitehorn. At that time – and for years and years come to that – Katherine Whitehorn was my favourite columnist and a great many other people had the same opinion. Her Sunday columns in *The Observer* about the life of a contemporary woman (which she wrote from 1960 to 1996, a staggeringly long time) were always full of witty observations and included such listed gems as: 'Why do born-again Christians so often make you wish they'd never been born in the first place?'; 'The easiest way for children to learn about money is for you not to have any'; 'No nice men are good at getting taxis' and 'Americans ... often seem to be so overwhelmed by their children that they will do anything for them except stay married to the co-producer'. Her column was the first of its kind but became much emulated over the other side of the Atlantic and the Pacific. I had first met the Lyalls with Jean Robertson years before, but I had done so again recently with my friend and colleague Virginia Bredin, who worked with me in Douro Place and later. Virginia was an old friend of Kath and of Bernard Levin who had written admiringly in his column in *The Times* that 'Katherine Whitehorn was as clever as she was nice, and as nice as she was beautiful and as kind as she was all three.' It was clearly a deeply felt tribute.

She was married to Gavin Lyall, a rather silent man compared to his unusually deep-voiced and animated wife, but he was one of the leading thriller writers of the time. During his National Service – obligatory for 'healthy men' in the UK from 1949 to 1960 – he served as a Pilot Officer in the Royal Air Force which left him with an enduring love of small planes in particular and all planes in general. All his early books were based on hard-bitten, very tough pilot heroes. He and Kath had met at Cambridge and Gavin worked on the old *Picture Post* before joining *The Sunday Times* as Aviation Correspondent and eventually giving up regular journalism in favour of full-time authorship. Kath stood out as a particularly loyal and loving wife.

**The Menu was:**

Leek Tart

Culotte du Boeuf au Four (p. 309)

Mashed Potatoes with Olive Oil, Grilled Tomatoes

Salad

Cheese

Crème Brûlée

And the wine was Nuits St. Georges, 1967.

### JUNE 2nd, 1970 – DOURO PLACE

**BUFFET DINNER:** *Princess Margaret and Tony Snowdon*
*Lord and Lady Windlesham*
*Lord and Lady Davidson*
*Frank and Hélène Dawson*
*Bea Miller*
*Hugh and Grania Cavendish*
*Sir Duncan Oppenheim*
*Sir David and Lady Barron*
*Marston and Eden Fleming*
*Peter and Cordelia Vanneck*
*Gerry and Mary Cookson*
*Tony Stubbings*
*Dr Kit and Morna Wynn-Parry*
*Lord and Lady Limerick*
*Margot Walmsley*

I cannot remember what this dinner was all about except that we'd been to the Snowdon's 10th wedding anniversary party the month before and they had not yet seen the new house. HRH always liked meeting new people. And that night she insisted on going all the way up to the top floor, not only to see the rest of the house but also to say goodnight to the children. They had been to one or two birthday parties at Kensington Palace which invariably had me with my heart in my mouth as they and other kids casually picked up the fabulous Fabergé pieces from tables in the drawing room, happily putting them down again without mishap.

I had gone to my old friend, the antique dealer Stephen Long, to look for a wedding anniversary present since the christening gift I had bought at his shop for the small Sarah Armstrong-Jones had been such a success. No sooner had I walked into the shop, than I saw an old board game pinned to the wall. It was called *The Royal Game of Love* and was a kind of snakes and ladders with the goal being – after many vicissitudes – the first to reach a painting of the old Kensington Palace in the middle. What a metaphor. I could hardly believe my luck.

At that time a few wider cracks were showing in the Snowdon's often stormy marriage. They were really much too alike for easiness. We had been to dinner with them at Kensington Palace during the spring with the Osbert Lancasters and the Heinzes as fellow guests and were all going on to a party given by Norman St John-Stevas, the Conservative politican. It was a somewhat interupted dinner because HRH could not find the bell to summon the footman for the next course and Tony did not want to get up and just go and get him. In the end he clapped his hands very loudly and this guy came flouncing in, had the situation explained to him, found the bell under the table, and handed it to Princess Margaret with the comment, 'There now. It wasn't so *very* difficult was it, Ma'am?'

Tony had lost his driving licence for speeding and asked us if we could take him in our car. I think HRH went with the Heinzes. The party was fun and John Betjeman, the writer and poet, had been sitting holding forth on the stairs. About 1.30am Tony came up to us and asked if we could take him home as he had to catch a plane early the next morning. Of course we said yes and asked about HRH. 'Oh no, she's fine,' said Tony. 'She does not want to leave yet.' We took him back home and chatting about Betjman in the car he suddenly asked us if we'd like to come in and see a short movie he had just made of him – despite the early plane. We went into his study and were in the middle of watching it (although it was extremely late), when the double doors to the room were flung open and there was a tearful and very cross Princess Margaret. I went up to her and without thinking I just put my arms round her and she said, sobbing into my shoulder, 'How would you like it if Roger just left you at a party the other side of London? I actually had to take a taxi home.'

*Lèse-majestée* again. But it was the first time I had seen her vulnerability although we saw it quite a lot later. After Tony moved out she occasionally used to call us to go round late in the evening if she felt particularly lonely and miserable. Once she called after 1am when we were both in bed and we had to get dressed again to go over to Kensington Palace, where her only company was an almost empty bottle of whisky. The thing was that in spite of her occasional high-handedness and her sudden disconcerting use of her position when it suited her, she was both a generous and loyal friend. I did not really see her much after the beginning of the 1980s when I started to spend so much more time in New York and Roger had the position of Visiting Scientist at the National Institute of Health in Washington. The last time I spoke with her was just after Roger died of cancer in 1991.

Ken Tynan told me that HRH had had a dinner with them when Penelope Gilliatt was also there to whom, apparently, HRH did not address a single word. After dinner Ken told me that he went up to her and said Penelope was rather hurt that she had been ignored. HRH, he said, told me that she hadn't talked to her because she thought it would be 'disloyal to Mary'. I was astonished. I could not have cared less if she talked to Penelope or not, and I could not imagine why she wouldn't. But it was very touching – however unnecessary. I believe she and Tony were excellent and involved parents and after the divorce (and for the rest of her life) they were in regular touch with each other. I think they had just been much too much alike in many ways.

Prue Windlesham, later divorced from her academic husband, then in the Cabinet, was the then Woman's Page Editor of *The Times* and wrote under her maiden name of Prudence Glyn. The Davidsons were more neighbours from Suffolk, Bea Miller, was then the Editor of *Vogue* – and the young girl who had saved me, at age five or six, from the roof of the bus when it had turned over. Tony Stubbings was a painter and a friend of the Dawsons, who had become a good friend of ours. Dr Kit Wynn-Parry was a very nice medical colleague of Roger's with an equally nice wife. The Limericks lived just down the road. Our small sons had become friends at school and through them, so had we.

HRH rarely liked to leave a party early. David Barron had to be in Holland first thing the next morning and kept standing up hopefully every time she stood up. 'Oh dear, yet another false dawn' he said tiredly. Certainly, you could never hope to go early to bed when she was around. And no one could leave before her.

**The Menu was:**

*Avocado, Tomato and Mozzarella with Basil*

*Scaloppini di Vitello* (p. 309)

*Little Squares of Sautéed Potatoes*

*Green Salad*

*Cheese*

*Caramelised Grapes*

And the wines were Hugel Muscat, 1969, and Côtes-de-Beaune-Villages, 1967.


### JUNE 8th, 1970 – DOURO PLACE

**DINNER:** *Jim and Judy Lance*
*Dr and Mrs Newsome-Davies*
*Edith Bull (James had died)*
*Dr Anthony Hopkins*

This was a uniquely – but not unique – medical dinner. I happened to like almost all of Roger's colleagues – neurologists are necessarily pretty bright – and we entertained them quite a lot, as they generously entertained us. But I mention this dinner particularly, because the Lances were over from Sydney, and this was the first time I had met Jude, who became not only one of my dearest life long friends, but the mother-in-law to my son. Jim Lance had asked Roger if he would come to Sydney the following autumn for three weeks as Visiting Professor and that he was welcome to bring me. Roger nobly split his first class ticket and bought two tourist ones. I got to know Jude really well and, on this first Sydney visit, met my future daughter-in-law, aged three. (I also got to follow the progress of the building of the Sydney Opera House and was sent to Sydney almost every year after that, till the iconic Opera House opened, and wrote *The Times* special supplement on its tumultuous building history, as well as quite a long piece for *Vogue*) Not many great friends are privileged enough to have their children marry each other or to have known their son's wives so young, and I have dearly loved my beautiful, feisty daughter-in-law (and her older siblings) for almost all of her life. I think she is the best possible mother for my grandchildren and the best possible wife for my son. I also think she is a particularly talented writer – although it seems she would rather not do it at all than face deadlines. Curiously, she worked for a time with with *The Daily Express* in London, and there were still people in the office who had known me in my brief time there. I did not know that any newspaper kept staff so long.

**The Menu was:**

*Spinach Soufflé with Anchovy Sauce* (p. 220)

*Boeuf à l'Italienne* (p. 310)

*Green Salad*

*Cheese*

*Iced Orange Soufflé*

And the wines were Pouilly Blanc Fumé and Corton, 1964.

### JULY 14th, 1970

**DINNER:** *Lieutenant-General Sir Brian and Lady Horrocks*
*Sir Robin and Lady Darwin*
*Anthony and Susan Crosland (Susan Barnes)*
*Spike and Paddy Milligan*

In June I had been asked by a magazine to interview General Sir Brian and Lady Horrocks and to photograph their house. (In peacetime, Sir Brian also held the ceremonial title of 'The Gentleman Usher of the Black Rod', which briefly meant that at each annual opening of Parliament, he went ahead of the Queen's elaborate procession and knocked three times on the door of the House of Commons with his long black rod. He knocked because the door, for some odd reason, was traditionally deliberately slammed in his face. Weird.) Anyway, I went with the photographer with pleasure. The Horrocks' kindly asked the photographer and I to lunch and by the end of the day we had become quite friendly. They remarked that it would be nice to meet again so I said to let me know when they were next coming to London and perhaps they could come to dinner. I did not imagine for one moment that they would even remember the invitation. But a couple of weeks later to my surprise, they called and said they would be in London for a few days in mid-July and was there still a possibility of dinner? We decided on the 14th and that evening, when Roger came back from the hospital, I casually mentioned that I had asked the Horrocks' to dine. 'You WHAT?' he spluttered over his whisky, 'How did you *dare* to do that?' His reaction put military 'shock and awe' in a whole new context. I was astonished.

It turned out that volunteer soldiers from that era rarely got over any awe that they had had for their generals if, that is, they respected them. And Brian Horrocks had apparently inspired just such respect in Roger. As he had also been our friends, Robin Darwin's and Anthony Crosland's General during the Allied Invasion and the push through Belgium on their way to Germany, and Spike's General in North Africa, we asked them all to dinner as well. Men in such different spheres: the neurologist (Roger); the painter and Rector of the Royal College of Art (Robin Darwin); the Government Minister, later Foreign Secretary (Tony Crosland) and the comedian and writer (Spike Milligan) who all literally sat at his feet. It was a touching sight.

Robin Darwin was one of the sixth generation of distinguished Darwins following on from Charles Darwin. He was a painter and collector as well as being much painted himself and the Rector of the Royal College of Art. He was married to the vivacious and witty ex-Director of Dior and fashion expert Ginette Spanier. Anthony Crosland was one of the so-called Hugh Gaitskell protégées and at that time Minister for the Environment and Local Planning in the Wilson Government, though in 1977 James Callaghan appointed him Foreign Secretary. He was certainly one of the most forward Socialist thinkers of the time, obviously brilliant – and, like a lot of very clever people, many thought him arrogant – but charming and highly popular in his own circle and obviously deeply loved by his wife Susan Barnes, a very well thought-of journalist and later novelist. When, in 1979 he had an untimely and fatal stroke at the early age of 58 Susan apparently climbed into the hospital bed with him and did not leave his side unless it was imperative.

Spike – as he made sure everybody knew in his writings like *Hitler – My Role in His Downfall* and in the scripts of various shows – had *not* had 'a good war' as they said then, and often (I believe erroneously considering the bipolar disease) ascribed his subsequent depressive illness to that period. Moreover, he had certainly not shown any great respect for military authority with the exception of Brian Horrocks. Nevertheless, he sat on the floor at the Horrocks feet like an awe-struck schoolboy. One way and another, it was one of those bibulous,

213

talkative, satisfying evenings when you thought people were going rather early although it turned out to be nearly 2am.

**The Menu was:**

*Cassoulettes Lasserre* (p. 240)

*Paupiettes de Veau Clémentine* (p. 311)

*Salad*

*Cheeses*

*Summer Pudding* (p. 273)

And the wines were Puligny-Montrachet, 1959, Château Haut-Batailley, 1959 and Château Suduiraut (Sauternes), 1964.

I have to say that, after the usual August in Rattlesden and our time in Australia, we went on entertaining very regularly in London and Suffolk all through the 1970s and early-1980s – enough dinners to fill several more books. But I must just mention an almost happenstance dinner in the garden, the summer of 1972.

**JUNE 22, 1972**

**DINNER:** *Princess Margaret*
*Rudolf Nureyev*
*Dame Margot Fonteyn and other members of the Royal Ballet*
*Ken and Kathleen Tynan*
*Lord Rothschild*
*Margot Walmsley*
*Kenneth Bradshaw*
*Anthony and Annie Nutting*
*Spike and Paddy Milligan*
*Angus Wilson*
*Tony Garrett*
*Tony and Susan Crosland*

This really was an accidental party. A couple of weeks before, Princess Margaret, who was Patron of the Royal Ballet Company, had asked me if I would like to accompany her to the final year performance of the Royal Ballet School. I said that would be lovely but would she like to come back home and have supper afterwards. She said yes, that would

214

be kind. A few days later she called again and asked if I minded if she brought Nureyev and Margot Fonteyn back with her as well. I did not mind at all. A few days later again she called and asked if she could add further names from the Royal Ballet and bring Lord Rothshchild with her. I thought to balance the party by asking some other friends. And in the end the guest list was so large that I suggested that if she had Lord Rothschild to accompany her anyway, would she mind if I did not come to the performance but stayed home and cooked the dinner? It was – luckily – a particularly beautiful and barmy June evening. I filled the garden with small tables and gilt chairs that I had hired, and made a cold supper because I had no idea when they would actually all turn up. The garden smelt delicious with the entwined jasmine and honeysuckle and the planted night-scented stocks and Nicotinana in tubs, and it looked, in the candlelight (and the Christmas lights that I had entwined in the trees), a great deal more glamorous than it actually was. The children were very excited, could not sleep and were all up and hanging over the bannisters as soon as they heard the doorbell start ringing.

I so much enjoyed meeting Nureyev who was a stunningly beautiful man – not that anyone needs to be reminded – and Dame Margot, who was as charming as I had heard. Nureyev who happened to live in a nearby road, subsequently asked us to a dinner at his house because he wanted some advice about Australia which we knew quite well by that time. (After I had accompanied Roger as Visiting Professor of Neurology in Sydney, I had been asked back several times to write various articles. Quite unexpectedly, Nuryev also asked us as his guests to the première of his film: *I am a Dancer*. Roger and I sat with him in his reserved row and were first startled, and then amused, by the fact that he kept leaping up and furiously shouting things at the top of his voice like 'No – that is all wrong' and 'That should have been cut' and generally barracking his own movie.

In the scented garden that night I sat with Lord Rothschild, Nureyev, Ken Tynan, Susan Crosland, Margot Walmsley, Angus Wilson and Paddy Milligan. Angus was holding forth as mellifluously as usual to Nureyev – he was not Public Orator at the University of East Anglia for nothing – while Ken and Lord Rothschild were having a discussion on the relative merits of different burgundies. Ken was saying that he had never actually drunk a Richbourg. As it happened, I had a few bottles in the cellar which I had bought when the well-known Dr Baroulet collection had been auctioned and I got up on some pretence or other and put one aside for him to take home. 'You are mad, mad', he said, as I gave it to him when he and Kathleen left, 'Mad – but I absolutely cannot resist'. It actually was a bit mad. What I'd do to possess a bottle or two of Richebourg 1955 right now. But it was sort of a mad night anyway. When we finally stumbled up to bed after the last of the guests had left it was 4.30am.

**The Menu was:**

*Eggs in Aspic with Tarragon* (p. 312)

*Vitello Tonnato* (p. 247)

*Rice and Pimento Salad*

*Tomato Salad*

*Cucumber Sambal*

*Cheeses*

*Sliced Peaches with Raspberry Purée*

And the wines were Taittinger Champagne, 1970 with crudités and tiny asparagus and cheese tarts, Pouilly-Fumé, 1969, Vin Rosé, Bandol, 1970, Beaujolais Villages, 1970 and Muscat Hugel, 1969.

CHAPTER EIGHT

# AFTERWORD

THAT was all then. This is now. I moved to France in the winter of 2001 and the times are totally different in every possible way. But I still like to cook and I still like to entertain. I have some good friends in the area and other friends come and stay.

I would like to describe a pre-Christmas dinner that I gave for everyone in the small street where I live in a village in the Luberon. It is a very *small* street, and the residents can hardly be more different than most of my guests in London and Suffolk. One is a plumber, one was a cleaning lady – who has now moved to a different village and who I think of as a friend, one is a hairdresser, one is a man who taught disadvantaged children how to work on a farm, two were students and the last is the elderly daughter of brave parents, now dead, who hid members of the Marquis from the occupying Germans and spies for the Vichy government. They all came bearing flowers or wine and were all rather wary of English cooking which they still thought of as frightful, even if they had hardly left the village.

The conversation was terrific – like almost all the French, they were well educated; they obviously kept up with the news and they argued ferociously about politics. They drank a lot and actually – despite their worst fears – ate a lot – and did not leave till after midnight.

### DECEMBER 23rd, 2003

**DINNER:** *Frederique Flory*
       *Etienne Arnaud*
       *Charlotte Flory*
       *Gilles Arnaud*
       *Yannick and Audrey Flemati*
       *Miraille Dumond*

# MARY GILLIATT'S FABULOUS FOOD AND FRIENDS

**The Menu was:**

*Large Crevettes and Basil Mayonnaise*

*Slow Cooked Leg of Lamb Boulangère*

*Haricot Beans*

*Salad of Endives, Blue Cheese, Pear and Walnuts*

*Cheese*

*Bombe Surprise*

And the wines were Château Neuf-du-Pape Blanc, Château Beaumont, 1995 and Château Suduiraut, 1990.

Just as a postscript to that now absurd but still clinging French belief that the English know nothing about food (though rereading some of my menus I have to concede that I can see their point) I must add that my daughter Sophia Gilliatt and our dear friend William Ledward got together some other investors to open a restaurant together in the spring of 2009 – the Restaurant du Lac – overlooking the Etang de la Bonde, just outside the village of La Motte d'Aigues. The talented and eclectic chef will be a local friend, Philippe Sublet, who worked with the gifted Roux brothers at Le Gavroche, at *No. 1, the Aldwych* in London and the internationally famous *Fat Duck* at Bray, before working at the popular *La Rotonde* at Aix and finally alighting beside the lake at *La Bonde*. Aside from its food, and the fact that unlike most local restaurants it stays open most of the winter, it will be the only good restaurant with a lake view in the Luberon, and there are even three en suite bedrooms for those who have had too good a meal to drive home or simply want to stay anyway.

# RECIPES

NOTE: In the 1960s I adopted or adapted a great many recipes from the late Jean Robertson's *The Sunday Telegraph Cookery Book (Collins)* which was published in 1963. I also used Elizabeth David a great deal, and a little of Arabella Boxer and Claudia Roden. Over the years, although I bought many cook books as they came out, I often just adapted the recipes a little and then rarely looked at the books again, unless I was looking for inspiration – cooking by memory and by trial and error more often than not. Most recipes are for four unless otherwise stated, and can of course, be doubled, trebled or quadrupled for larger numbers.

### JERUSALEM ARTICHOKE SOUP (JANUARY 16th, 1964)

*450g/1lb of Jerusalem Artichokes*

*1 tbsp butter*

*300ml/½ pt milk and the same of chicken stock*
*600ml/1pt milk*

*50ml/2 tbsp of cream (unless all milk is used)*

*Salt and pepper, optional sprinkling of curry powder or chilli*

*Croutons*

Scrub or well wash the nobbly artichokes, then peel and roughly chop. Melt the butter in a saucepan and toss in the chopped artichokes. Leave them to simmer gently till soft enough to press through a sieve or food mill or purée in a food processor. Return the purée to the pan, work in your choice of liquid (I personally like the half milk, half stock mixture). Season to taste and simmer for 15 minutes and stir in the cream just before serving. If you want to zip it up a little, add the curry or chilli powder at the last minute. Serve with a separate dish of croutons.

MARY GILLIATT'S FABULOUS FOOD AND FRIENDS

## INDIVIDUAL SPINACH SOUFFLÉS WITH ANCHOVY SAUCE
### (FEBRUARY 23rd, 1964)

(This was a great favourite at Langan's Brasserie in Piccadilly.)
I like making soufflés for around eight people. If half that number, halve the quantities.

*Heat the oven to 200 °C/400 °F/gas mark 6*

*Two packets of frozen spinach (a reliable quantity which fresh spinach is not)*

*2 tbsp unsalted butter*

*2 tbsp flour*

*300ml/½ pt hot milk*

*Salt, pepper, nutmeg to taste*

*1 tbsp anchovy essence or paste and 55g/2oz grated Gruyèré*

*4 egg yolks*

*6 egg whites*

*A pinch of cream of tartar*

**For the Sauce**

*1 tbsp of lemon juice or white wine vinegar*

*3 yolks of egg*

*150–175 gms/6 tbsp of butter, cut into small pieces*

*Anchovy essence or paste to taste*

Butter 8 small cocotte dishes, and tie baking paper or foil around each one so that the paper is some 2 inches higher than the rim of the dishes. If you would rather do one large soufflé use exactly the same measures but butter a regular soufflé dish and do the same thing with the paper. (**Note:** This helps the soufflé or soufflés to rise so you can do the same for all soufflé recipes.)

Cook the spinach and drain till it is quite dry. Melt the butter and gradually stir in the flour. When it is well amalgamated start stirring in the pre-heated milk a bit at a time so that the sauce does not get lumpy. Season very well. Add the spinach a bit at a time till it is well mixed. Taste the seasoning again and augment if necessary. I then add some anchovy essence or paste and the cheese. Take the saucepan off the heat and carefully add the yolks one at a time till they are well mixed. Add the cream of tartar and stir. Just before you want to cook the soufflés, beat up the whites of the egg till they hold their shape, season and gently fold into the egg and spinach mixture. Pour carefully into each cocotte dish (or the larger soufflé dish) run your finger round the top of the mixture to clear the rim and place in a baking tin or on a baking sheet in the middle of the hot oven. Open the oven door carefully and test after 20 minutes. If not quite risen as spectacularly as you'd like, leave for another 5–10 minutes. Serve immediately with the sauce.

You can make this just before or while the soufflés are cooking. Using a bain Marie add the lemon juice or vinegar to the top saucepan and reduce a little. Gradually add the yolks, one at a time, stirring gently. Now start adding the butter piece by piece till the sauce starts to thicken well. Watch carefully to make sure that the water does not get beyond a gentle simmering state. Season to taste and add more anchovy essence or paste to taste. Turn off the heat and rest the top saucepan askew over the hot water (not touching it) to keep warm. Pour into a jug and serve separately with the soufflés.

## CARBONNADE DE BOEUF (FEBRUARY 13th, 1964)

I like this Flemish version topped with crispy bread spread with Dijon mustard.

*700g/1lb 9oz of chuck steak*

*85g/3oz/½ cup of chopped gammon*

*3 tbsp oil*

*2 onions, thinly sliced*

*600 mls/2 cups of 2 parts light ale to 1 part brown ale or all Guinness if you like really dark gravy*

*2 crushed cloves of garlic, crushed with salt*

*1 tsp dark brown sugar*

*A bouquet garni of 4 bay leaves, a spring of thyme and a small bunch of parsley*

*Salt and pepper, to taste*

*Medium slices of stale baguette or French loaf, spread each side with Dijon mustard*

*1 tbsp red wine vinegar*

Cut the meat into 5cm/2 inches squares and the ham into large dice. Heat the oil in a frying pan and gently brown both the meat and the ham. Keep them both hot while you then brown the sliced onions in the same hot oil. When they are done, arrange the meat and onions in layers in a casserole. Pour the mixed beer or Guiness into the frying pan and heat it slowly, scraping the edges of the pan with a wooden spoon or spatula to remove any bits stuck to the sides. When it is very hot, pour it over the meat and onions and add the garlic, brown sugar, bouquet garni and seasoning. Cover tightly and cook for two and a half hours in a low pre-heated oven. Arrange the mustard spread slices of bread over the top, dunking them down into the gravy. Remove the lid and cook till the bread is crisp, turning up the temperature if necessary. At the last moment, stir in the vinegar without disturbing the bread too much.

## SYLLABUB (FEBRUARY 13th, 1964)
### Serves 4–6 people

This is one of the oldest of English puddings. The word was an amalgamation of the words Sillery (a district in Champagne, France) and Bub, the Elizabethan word for a sparkly drink. In fact it was originally made by milking a cow directly into a bowl of cider or sparkling wine and skimming off the resulting foam. But that was really too ephemeral quite apart from the difficulties of keeping a convenient cow at the ready. This nicely alcoholic version, enough for 4–6 people, is best made a day or two before and can last two or three days.

*150ml/¼ pt/½ cup of Sherry, Madeira or Port*

*2–3 tbsp Brandy*

*Juice and zest of 1 lemon*

*3 tbsp sugar*

*300ml/½ pt good double cream*

*A little nutmeg and tiny sprigs of rosemary or twists of lemon peel for each glass*

Mix the wine and brandy in a good-sized bowl and add the juice and zest of the lemon. Leave overnight. Next day, strain the alcohol and lemon mixture. Add the sugar and stir until dissolved. Pour in the cream, stirring all the time. Using a wire or rotary whisk, but not an electric beater, gently whip the wine and cream until it thickens enough to stand in soft peaks and be sure not to over-beat. Spoon the mixture into the chosen wine glasses and leave in a cool place – not the refrigerator. (Serve in little custard glasses or very small wine glasses with a tiny sprig of rosemary or twist of lemon in the middle.) Interestingly, some time in the mid-Nineteenth Century the syllabub seems to have merged with another ancient British dish, the trifle.

### SHRIMP COCKTAIL (FEBRUARY 23rd, 1964)
### Serves 8 people

I have produced two versions of this dish. One, more or less the classic kind I used to prepare then and the other one I invented a couple of years ago. It would have been almost impossible to buy coriander in the shops during the 1960s and early 1970s. In the U.S., of course, it is hard to get small shrimps (unless you can get the small Norwegian or North Sea shrimps either frozen or in jars) – shrimp cocktail in the U.S. is four large shrimps in a spicy tomato cocktail sauce. But when there, I have successfully peeled and cut up the three or four shrimps per person to use in both the following recipes.

### FOR THE CLASSIC VERSION

*4 tbsp of double cream or crème fraîche or sour cream*
*and the same amount of mayonnaise*

*50ml/3 tbsp of Heinz Tomato Sauce*

*1 tsp sherry*

*A good dash of Lee & Perrins Worcester Sauce*

*A few good lettuce leaves from the heart, shredded*

*¼ chopped cucumber, salted and well drained*

*600g/1lb 5oz/2 cups unpeeled small shrimps or*
*2 packets small frozen shrimps*

*Some chopped parsley for garnish*

Mix all the liquid ingredients together, preferably the night before, and chill thoroughly.

Just before the meal put equal proportions of shredded lettuce and cucumber in a large wine glass or a grapefruit glass, add equal amounts of shrimps and pour over sauce. Garnish with the chopped parsley.

## CORIANDER, PICKLED GINGER AND SHRIMP COCKTAIL

*600g/1lb 5oz/2 cups small shrimps or crayfish tails*

*2 tbsp pickled ginger*

*1 chopped fennel bulb or avocado (optional)*

*½ a peeled and chopped cucumber*

*1 dsp white wine or cider vinegar*

*4 dsps virgin olive oil*

*1 dsp pickled ginger juice from the jar*

*Salt and freshly ground black pepper*

*1 small bunch of coriander*

Divide up the shrimps or crayfish tails between eight large wine glasses or grapefruit bowls. Chop up the pickled ginger slices and divide equally. Peel and chop the avocado and chop the fennel, if either or both are used, and add, with the cucumber to the shrimp and ginger mixture.

Make a dressing with the oil, vinegar, ginger juice from the jar, salt and pepper and pour over the shrimp mixure, mixing well. Reserve eight small sprigs of coriander for garnish, chop the rest and mix well with the shrimps etc. Top each glass with a sprig of the coriander and serve.

## MONT BLANC EN SURPRISE (FEBRUARY 23rd, 1964)

*600ml/1 pt/2 cups cold heavy cream*

*1½ tsp vanilla essence*

*100g/3½oz icing or confectioner's sugar*

*3 egg whites*

*A pinch of salt*

*150ml/¼ pt/½ cup of cold water*

*125g/4½oz/¾ cup granulated sugar*

*Ice cubes*

*A good-sized Charlotte mould or bowl and two smaller bowls*

**For the 'Surprise':**

*115g/4oz/½ cup of walnuts, roughly chopped*

*250g/9oz/½ cup granulated sugar*

*3 tbsp water*

*1½ tbsp powdered instant coffee*

*Some marrons glacés or other candied fruit for decoration*

*Have ready a well oiled or greased pan*

This is not the usual chestnut purée Mont Blanc but a white frozen mousse, a literal 'snow' mousse, which is easy to make in advance.

Pour the cold cream into a chilled bowl and set it into a bowl of ice cubes and beat until it is almost firm. Then fold in the vanilla essence and icing or confectioner's sugar. Set aside.

Beat the egg whites with a pinch of salt until they form peaks and are stiff but not dry.

Put the cold water into an enameled saucepan, add the granulated sugar and boil to form a thick syrup. Pour immediately, a little at a time, into the beaten egg whites, beating well until the mixture is smooth and meringue-like. Set the bowl into ice cubes and continue to beat till the mixture is thick and cool. Lightly fold it into the whipped cream. Spoon the mixture into the serving mould or bowl and freeze for two or three hours. Put the two smaller bowls into the freezer so that they are really cold for later.

While the cream and meringue mixture is freezing, make the 'Surprise' nougatine.

Put the walnuts into a moderate oven (180 °C / 350 °F / gas mark 4) to warm but do not let them brown. Put the sugar and three tablespoons of water into an enameled saucepan and boil to form a light caramel syrup. As soon as this is achieved, add the warmed walnuts, stir well for a few seconds so that all the nuts are covered in caramel and, taking due care, pour the mixture into an oiled pan, spreading it into one layer with a spatula. Let it cool and harden, then chop into small pieces.

When the mousse has set around the edges, take it out of the freezer along with the two bowls. Scoop out one cup of the unset mixture from the middle and pour it into one of the chilled bowls. Return to the freezer. Then scoop out all but an inch of the remaining unset cream into the other cold bowl. Beat the powdered coffee and the nougatine into this mixture. Pour it back into the middle of the mould, then pour the reserved cupful of mousse from the fridge on top and smooth off. Return to the freezer for another two or three hours. The centre should stay a little softer and creamier than the edges.

When ready to serve, run a knife dipped in hot water around the edge of the iced mousse, dip the bottom in some more hot water for a second only and turn out onto a serving dish. Decorate with some chopped marrons glacés or candied chestnuts or other candied fruit.

### HARD BOILED EGGS STUFFED WITH TUNA (MARCH 13th, 1964)

Hard boiled eggs can be stuffed in a variety of ways for a first course and are easy to do.

*Hard boil as many eggs as there are diners*
*(a good rule of thumb is 8 minutes in boiling water, 8 in cold)*

*1 small tin of tuna fish*

*Salt and pepper*

*A bunch of spring onions or scallions finely chopped (optional)*

*About 2–3 tbsp mayonnaise to taste*

*Chopped parsley and/or chives*

*1 lettuce, shredded*

Shell the eggs carefully, cut them in half and remove yolks. Set aside. Mash the egg yolks. Mash the tuna, season well, add the mashed egg yolks and chopped spring onions or scallions if preferred. Mix well, then add mayonnaise to get the right consistency – not too stiff, not too runny. Add some chopped parsley or chives, reserving some for garnish.

Carefully pile the mixture back into the egg whites doming each one. Sprinkle some chopped parsley or chives on top and put on a bed of shredded lettuce on a serving plate. Garnish with more sprigs of parsley or chopped chives.

### BLACKCURRANT LEAF SORBET (MARCH 13th, 1964)

Blackcurrant leaves can be picked from a vegetable garden all the year round or you could ask an obliging greengrocer or nursery in advance. Give several days notice. They will keep well in a plastic zip bag in the fridge. The sorbet has a most delicate taste of blackcurrants and is a pleasing pale green.

# RECIPES

*12 blackcurrant leaves and extra for serving, if liked*

*1 cup of water*

*6 juicy lemons and two juicy limes*

*175g/6oz/¾ cup of castor sugar*

*Some green colouring (optional)*

*1 egg white, beaten*

Rinse blackcurrant leaves and place in a wide flat bowl. Boil the water, add the lemon juice from six of the lemons and all the zest and pour over leaves. Cover and leave to steep for two hours or so.

Pour steeping juice and leaves through a fine sieve, pressing leaves well to extract every bit of juice.

Throw leaves away. Pour steeping water into a saucepan and add the sugar. Let the sugar dissolve gently in the hot water before bringing the liquid to boiling point. Boil for a few minutes or so then turn off the heat and let cool. When quite cool add the juice and zest of the two juicy limes. The mixture should be a pale green but if you like it a little greener add a drop or so of green vegetable coloring and mix well. Turn into an ice tray (or trays) and freeze for two or three hours. Take mixture out of freezer, mix well with a fork, beat the egg white stiffly and add gently to the frozen juice. Stir lightly to mix. Put back into the freezer till ready to serve. Turn into a glass dish or individual serving dishes. You can make a pretty presentation by lining the serving bowl or bowls with blackcurrant leaves.

## OEUFS MOLLETS ON A BED OF BUTTERED SPINACH (MARCH 15th, 1964)

These are halfway between a soft and hardboiled egg and lend themselves as a good substitute for poached eggs as well as a vehicle for various sauces and beds (including buttered spinach). The spinach can be made just with the butter and seasoning or mixed with a cheesy Béchamel.

As many eggs as there are people or, for a more substantial dish, allow two eggs per person and, say, four spares. Plunge into boiling water for five minutes. Remove immediately and plunge into cold water for another five minutes. Tap them very gently all over on a hard surface and then peel with care to avoid splitting the eggs. (As a precaution against this I usually boil more eggs than I need. Left-overs or ones that get split can be used for family later).

**For the Buttered Spinach:**

*900g/2lb young spinach*
*(older leaves will need to be ripped from the stems and the stringy spines)*

*115g/4oz/½ cup butter*
*(spinach absorbs butter like a sponge or like aubergines or eggplants absorb oil)*

*Plenty of salt, freshly ground black pepper and nutmeg*

*Paprika for dusting*

Rinse the spinach well. Put it in a heavy covered saucepan without any water or salt and cook for five-six minutes over a gentle flame. When the spinach is cooked, drain it in a colander, pressing the leaves until they are quite dry. While you are doing this, melt the butter in the same saucepan taking care not to burn it. When the spinach is as dry as possible add it to the melted butter, season well and mix thoroughly before serving it in individual cocotte dishes – or one large dish – with the eggs on top dusted with a little paprika.

Variations are made by mixing the buttered spinach with half a cupful of a cheesy Béchamel sauce. Or you can make **Spinach a la Crème** cooking young spinach as above, but after you have drained it well, put it through a sieve before adding it to half the amount of butter suggested for buttered spinach. To this add four tablespoons boiling double cream, season well as before and mix thoroughly together. You can use this *over* rather than under eggs in a cocotte dish or oval vegetable dish.

Nowadays I might toss the well-dried spinach in a little hot olive oil and a clove (or two) of gently sautéed, chopped garlic before seasoning it, rather than using all that butter or butter and cream.

### TOURTE BOURGUIGNONNE (MARCH 15th, 1964)
### Serves 4 people

I usually make a shortcut by using bought packets of puff or short crust pastry rather than making it myself. Though my skilled and patient daughter-in-law always makes it herself and I do admit that the results are meltingly good.

# RECIPES

*225g/½lb pie or stewing veal*

*115g/4oz gammon and of pork fat*

*1 chopped onion, 1 clove of garlic mashed with a little salt, salt, pepper, nutmeg, cinnamon, mace*

*3 tbsp cooking brandy*

*2 eggs*

*1 tbsp of water*

*1 packet of short crust pastry*

Mince all the meat together and work in all the other ingredients and one of the eggs, beaten. Leave for an hour or two in a cool place for the various tastes to mature.

Butter a 20cm/8in flan ring or tart tin. Roll out the pastry thinly. Lay the pastry over the top of the ring or tin and push down to line it, cutting away the overlap. Roll this overlap out again. Brush the inside of the flan ring with the white of the other egg, reserving the yolk and fill it with the meat mixture formed into small thumb-shaped sausages. Cover with the rest of the pastry, trim and pinch down the sides with a fork. Paint the top with the egg yolk mixed with an equal quantity of water. Make four escape holes for the steam and bake for 45–50 minutes in the centre of a pre-heated oven at 190 °C/375 °F/gas mark 5. This can be eaten hot or cold.

## SALAD OF LETTUCE HEARTS WITH A WARM BUTTER AND TARRAGON DRESSING (MARCH 15th, 1964)

This was an old Elizabeth David Recipe with slight variations and is good served with the pastry, rather than after.

*Allow half a tender fresh gem lettuce heart per person, cut into quarters*

*A handful of finely chopped tarragon leaves*

*A pinch of sugar*

*Sea salt or Fleur du Sel, freshly ground black pepper*

*3 tbsp slightly salted butter, freshly melted*

Place the quartered lettuce hearts in a salad bowl. Season them gently and scatter well with the chopped tarragon.

Have ready the hot melted butter and, at the very last moment, pour it over the lettuce, toss and serve. It must be eaten immediately or the butter will congeal.

## GLACÉ AU MELON DE I'LE ST. JACQUES (MARCH 15th, 1964)

Again, this is based on an old Elizabeth David recipe with an ethereal, almost other-worldly taste.

*1 good large melon*
*(whatever is in season and available at the time, whether, cantaloup*
*Charentais, honeydew or rock, as long as it is sweet and juicy)*

*125–175g/4½–6oz/½ cup–¾ cup castor sugar depending on size of melon*

*The yolks of 4 eggs*

*A small liqueur glass of Kirsch or Poire*

*The juice of half a lemon*

*300ml/½ pt/1 cup softly whipped cream*

Cut a neat slice off the stalk end of the melon and set it aside. Carefully scoop out the seeds and fibrous part from the middle of the melon and discard. Then, just as carefully, scoop out all the melon flesh without damaging the skin. Put the melon flesh into a saucepan over a very low heat and add the sugar. Cook gently for two or three minutes or till it is soft enough to sieve, or purée in a food processor, then set it aside. (If you are frightened of curdling the eggs in the next part of the recipe, use a bain Marie but, if the eggs are really well beaten first, and you are careful about keeping a low heat under the saucepan, you should be fine).

Mix the very well beaten egg yolks in with the puréed melon and cook over a very low heat until the mixture starts to thicken to the consistency of a thin custard. Take the mixture off the stove and leave to get quite cold. When it is cold, add the small glass of Kirsch or Poire and the juice of half a lemon. Stir thoroughly and fold in the whipped cream. Leave in a covered bowl in the refrigerator. Three hours before you want to eat the glacé, transfer the melon mixture into ice trays, cover them well with foil and put in the freezer. Stir well after the first hour and then again after the second to avoid ice crystals forming.

Just before you want to serve the glacé, fill the melon shell with the cream, cover it with the reserved stalk end. Bring it to the table on a glass compôtier with a stem, lined with vine or other large green leaves, or on a flat round dish, similarly decorated.

# RECIPES

## TARAMOSALATA (MARCH 29th, 1964)

It is perfectly easy now to buy little pots of very good Taramosalata, but it was difficult to find it in the 1960s. I made my own well pounded version and although not particularly authentic, it tastes good. Nowadays I would make it in a food processor, in a fraction of the time. Nowadays too, I might serve it with a good neat Vodka like Chopin or Belvedere or the French Wild Goose. If there is any left over it keeps for several days in the fridge and is good served with drinks before a meal.

*225g/½lb smoked cod's roe*

*1–2 lemons*

*A small pot of crème fraîche or sour cream*

*Freshly ground black pepper*

Scoop out the smoked cod's roe and put into a food processor with the juice of a lemon and a couple of tablespoons of the crème fraîche or sour cream. Whizz to a thickish consistency adding more lemon juice and crème fraîche, or sour cream, as desired. Season to taste. It is unlikely you will need salt, but you can add a little if you think it needs it.

## POMMES ANNA (MARCH 29th, 1964)

I often do Pommes Anna with crushed or minced garlic sprinkled on each layer of potatoes as well. But this is entirely optional. The classic way is with butter alone.

*40g/1½oz butter*

*900g/2lb potatoes*

*2 cloves garlic, optional*

*Salt and freshly ground pepper*

Make sure the butter is soft and spread some of it on the bottom and sides of a round or oval pottery or pyrex dish. Peel the potatoes, dry them and slice them evenly, the thickness of a coin, on a Mandoline slicer if you have one, or else by hand. Dry the potatoes and arrange them in overlapping layers, interspersing each layer with dabs of butter, garlic if you are using it, and salt and pepper. Cover tightly with foil and bake in the centre of a warm oven 190 °C/345 °F/gas mark 5 for about 45 minutes, but take the cover off after 30 minutes so the top will get crunchy and brown.

## ROAST YOUNG DUCK WITH WINE, ORANGE AND HONEY SAUCE (MAY 3rd, 1964)

Choose a young, plump-breasted duck – or ducks – weighing at least 1.3kg (3lb), since they are creatures with a high ratio of bone to flesh it is not worth buying a duck weighing less.

**For each duck use:**

*2 small peeled oranges*

*A stick of celery*

*Salt and freshly ground pepper*

*100ml/3½ fl oz/¼ cup fresh orange juice*

*100ml/3½ fl oz/¼ cup white wine*

*3 tbsp melted or runny honey*

Stuff the duck (or ducks) with the two small peeled oranges and the celery and season with salt and pepper. Prick the bird(s) all over, rub with salt and put on a roasting rack in a hot oven, 220°C/425°F/gas mark 7 for 10–15 minutes. Then reduce the heat to 190°C/375°F/gas mark 5.

After half an hour at this heat, spoon off most of the fat in the roasting pan and pour 50ml/ (2 fl oz) tablespoons orange juice and the same of white wine over the duck(s). Baste the bird or birds regularly with this mixture.

After another quarter of an hour, spoon over two tablespoons of the melted honey. Repeat after another quarter of an hour with one more tablespoon of honey. After a final 15 minutes, the duck(s) should be a lacquered golden brown and ready to serve. To make the sauce, skim off any excess fat. Add the rest of the wine and orange juice, boil briskly for a couple of minutes, then serve separately in a sauce boat.

## PEARS POACHED IN RED WINE, HONEY AND CLOVES (MAY 3rd, 1964)

This dinner must have been a paeon to wine and honey and clearly not very well thought out. The dish is equally good done with quinces when they are in season.

# RECIPES

*Take a fairly hard pear, 2 cloves and a tbsp of runny honey*
*for each person*

*300ml/½ pt red wine*

*The zest of one orange; 2 cinnamon sticks*

*Crème fraîche or whipped cream*

Peel the pears but do not core them and stand upright in a casserole containing the wine and cinnamon sticks. Pour one tablespoon of honey over each piece of fruit, cover tightly and cook in a very low oven (110 °C/225 °F/gas mark ¼) for two hours. Test with a slim skewer to see if they are cooked through. They should have become a deep mahogany red. When they are quite cooked, chill and serve with the wine, cinnamon removed, and some crème fraîche or whipped cream into which you have stirred the zest of an orange. If the wine is not much reduced you can always chill the pears and boil the sauce down a little, chilling it after you judge it sufficiently reduced.

## VEAL GOULASH (MAY 9th, 1964)

I have made numerous versions of veal goulash, but my mother used to have a good Hungarian friend and her excellent recipe was much like this. At least, it approximates the taste.

*1.3kg/3lb stewing veal, cut into 4cm/1½ inch squares*

*Seasoned flour to dip*

*2 tbsp butter*

*2 tbsp olive oil*

*2 chopped onions*

*4 peeled and sliced medium carrots*

*450g/1lb skinned and sliced tomatoes*

*2 cloves of chopped garlic*

*Salt and pepper*

233

*600ml/ 1 pt/2 cups white wine*

*1 tsp caraway seeds*

*2 tsp good Hungarian paprika*

*300ml/½ pt/1 cup sour cream*

Put veal squares in a plastic bag with a couple of tablespoons seasoned flour and shake thoroughly.

Melt half the butter and olive oil in a frying pan and when hot add the veal, a couple of handfuls at a time and brown gently on all sides. Transfer into a casserole. If necessary, add the rest of the butter and oil and fry the sliced onions, garlic, carrots and tomatoes. Add to veal in casserole, season well and stir. Heat the white wine in the frying pan and add to meat and vegetables together with the caraway seeds and the paprika. Stir well again, put on the casserole lid and place in the middle of a medium oven at 180 °C/350 °F/gas mark 4 for half an hour and then lower to 170 °C/325 °F/gas mark 3 for another two hours. Test to see if done, if not keep at the same temperature for another half hour or so. Stir in some sour cream and sprinkle on some more paprika before serving.

## ICED CUCUMBER SOUP (MAY 22nd, 1964)

*2 tbsp olive oil*

*1 peeled and sliced cucumber – with a little extra to shred for garnish*

*Onion sliced and cooked in 300ml/½ pt/1 cup milk with a sprig of parsley and 4 peppercorns*

*300ml/½ pt/1 cup good vegetable or chicken stock*

*4 tbsp single cream*

*Chopped chives for garnish*

Heat the oil in a heavy saucepan and very gently sauté the peeled and sliced cucumber for 10 minutes or until soft. It must not be allowed to brown. While the cucumber is simmering add the onion to the milk in another pan and let that simmer too. When the cucumber is soft add the stock to it, stir well, cover and let the mixture go on simmering for another 10 minutes before putting it through a food mill and sieving or whisking it up in a food processor.

Strain the milk, add to the cucumber and stock and season to taste. Let the soup cool before putting it in the refrigerator to chill. Just before serving, stir in the single cream and garnish with the chopped chives and shredded cucumber.

## COLD CHICKEN WITH A CREAMY CURRY SAUCE
### (MAY 31st, 1964)

This is a version of a recipe from the old fuschia pink Constance Spry tome which she called 'Coronation Chicken' because, as far as I remember, she cooked it for the Queen's Coronation in 1953. Coronation or not, it is a nice elastic dish and does as well for a summer lunch or dinner, as for the large buffet for which it was created.

*Poach a nice chicken by covering the bird with water – or water with a couple of chicken stock cubes – to which you have added a bouquet garni of 4 bay leaves, 3–4 peppercorns, 1 halved onion and 1 sliced carrot.*

Bring to the boil gently, the turn down the heat and simmer for 40 minutes. Turn off the heat and allow the bird to cool in the liquid while you make the sauce.

**For this you will need:**

*1 tbsp of olive oil*

*1 finely chopped onion*

*1 tbsp of good curry powder*

*1 heaped tsp tomato purée*

*3 tbsp red wine vinegar*

*150ml/5 fl oz/½ cup, water*

*A bay leaf, salt, pepper and sugar*

*A slice or two of lemon and the juice of the rest, plus extra to taste*

*450ml/16 fl oz/1½ cups, mayonnaise*

*1–2 tbsp apricot purée*

*2–3 tbsp lightly whipped cream, plus a little extra*

*A good sprinkling of paprika*

Heat the oil, add finely chopped onion, cook gently for two or three minutes, then sprinkle with the curry powder and cook for another couple of minutes. Add the tomato purée, vinegar, water and bay leaf. Bring to the boil then add salt, pepper and a pinch of sugar, the lemon slices and lemon juice to taste. Simmer with the pan uncovered for 5–10 minutes. Strain the sauce and cool. Add the sauce by degrees to the mayonnaise together with the apricot purée. Adjust the seasoning to taste adding a little extra lemon juice if needed. Finish by folding in the whipped cream.

When the chicken is quite cold, remove from the stock and carefully skin, joint and neatly slice, making sure there are no bones left amongst the flesh. Arrange the chicken on a serving dish and cover with enough of the creamy curry sauce to coat all the slices without drowning it. Sprinkle with paprika and serve with the rest of the sauce in a sauce boat, mixed with a little extra cream and seasoning to taste.

## RICE SALAD (MAY 31st, 1964)

This is very good served with the cold chicken in its creamy curried sauce or with any cold buffet.

*Cook as much basmati rice as you need for the number of people you are serving*

*Drain. While it is still hot, add half a cupful (or a cup if you are using a lot of rice) of strongly flavoured French dressing. You can make this by combining two cloves of minced garlic with 1 tbsp wine or Balsamic vinegar: 3 tbsp virgin olive oil with some French mustard, rock salt and masses of black pepper. You will need strong seasoning because the rice absorbs flavour like litmus paper.*

*Add as many as you like of the following: finely chopped red and yellow peppers, cucumber, sultanas, fennel, seeded and skinned tomatoes and little peas*

## STRAWBERRIES WITH BALSAMIC VINEGAR
## (MAY 31st, 1964)

To a bowl of freshly hulled strawberries sprinkled with sugar, add two-three tablespoons of good Balsamic vinegar. Mix well. Serve with thick cream or crème fraîche to taste.

# RECIPES

## EGGS STUFFED WITH TUNA WITH TOMATOES AND BASIL
## (JUNE 11th, 1964)

Make the recipe of March 13th (p. 226) 1964 and serve the eggs on a dish surrounded by slices of the best-tasting tomatoes you can find, well seasoned, sprinkled with good virgin olive oil and edged with nicely matched basil leaves.

## ICED COFFEE MOUSSE (JUNE 11th, 1964)

Iced mousses and soufflés are not only light and appropriate for summer eating – though they are just as good in any season – but have the virtue of being able to be made the day before or well before anyway, thus cutting out last minute hassle.

*1 and a half sheets or 1 tbsp powdered gelatine*

*55g/4 tbsp good instant coffee*

*1 tbsp of cognac or rum*

*1 level tbsp Barbados or soft dark brown sugar*

*Zest of an orange, 3 cloves, 2 allspice berries and small stick of cinnamon*

*300ml/½ pt/1 cup boiling water*

*300ml/½ pt/1 cup whipped double cream*

*2 egg whites*

If you are using sheet gelatine cut it into strips and leave it to soften in cold water to cover.

Put the coffee powder, alcohol, sugar, orange zest, and spices into a jug, cover with the boiling water and leave in a warm place to infuse for half an hour.

Strain the coffee mixture through a fine sieve into a pan, heat and bring to just below boiling point. Add the drained sheet gelatine (or the powdered variety) to the coffee and stir till it is completely dissolved in the liquid. Leave to cool.

As soon as it is cold enough put it in the fridge until it starts to set, at which point stir it into the whipped cream. Beat the egg whites to a snow and fold them into the coffee cream. Put the dish back in the fridge and leave it to set for at least one hour before serving.

## LAMB CUTLETS FARCIES IN PUFF PASTRY WITH A TOMATO COULIS (JULY 6th, 1964)

This is an elegant little dish that is actually comparatively quick and easy to make. Any leftovers can either be eaten cold the next day or gently reheated in a 150 °C/300 °F/gas mark 2, oven. I evolved this version myself. Serve it with the tomato coulis – with the mustard if you like the sauce to have a bit of a bite, without it if you don't.

*Allow 2 small lamb cutlets a person, trimmed of any excess fat*

*1 or 2 tbsp olive oil*

*15g/1 tbsp butter*

*225g/8oz finely chopped mushrooms*

*1 finely chopped clove of garlic*

*A few chopped leaves of fresh rosemary*

*Salt and pepper*

*1 packet of good puff pastry*

*A beaten egg yolk*

Heat the oil in a large pan and quickly brown the cutlets on both sides. Season and set aside. Wipe the pan, melt the butter and gently cook the mushrooms, rosemary and garlic until all the moisture has evaporated. Season to taste.

Roll out the pastry thinly and cut out a hand-sized piece for each cutlet. Thinly spread both sides of the cutlets with the mushroom farci and wrap neatly in the pastry pieces leaving the bone exposed. Brush the pastry covered cutlets with the beaten egg and cook in a moderately hot oven (190 °C/375 °F/gas mark 5) for 25 minutes or until the pastry is crisp and golden. Serve with separate sauce boat of tomato coulis.

**For the Tomato Coulis:**

*2 tbsp olive oil*

*A small chopped onion*

*1 carrot, sliced*

*A small piece from the top of a celery stick, including the leaves*

*6 sprigs of parsley*

# RECIPES

*900g/2lb tomatoes*

*A clove of garlic*

*6 torn basil leaves or tsp dried basil*

*1 dsp of salt*

*Freshly ground pepper, a pinch of sugar (optional)*

*4 tsp Dijon mustard (optional)*

Heat the oil in a deepish frying pan or a wide shallow pan and add the chopped onion, sliced carrot, chopped celery and sprigs of parsley. After two or three minutes add the sliced tomatoes, garlic, basil and salt. Cook gently, uncovered for about half an hour, stirring from time to time until the tomatoes have become a pulp and most of the moisture has evaporated. Sieve through a food mill or whizz well in a food processor and taste for seasoning. If you think sugar is needed add a pinch to taste and if you like the sauce to have a bit of a kick stir the mustard in, a little at a time.

## APPLE SNOW (JULY 6th, 1964)

This is a light, fruity and refreshing way to finish any lunch or dinner.

*Peel, core and chop 900g/2lb apples*

*4 tbsp castor sugar*

*6 cloves, optional*

*A tbsp finely chopped lemon zest*

*Whites of two eggs, extra sugar to taste*

*Pinch of cream of tartar*

Place all the ingredients, except the egg whites and cream of tartar, in a heavy saucepan and just barely cover with water. Bring to the boil, turn down the heat and simmer till the apples are pulped and the moisture has evaporated. Drain to get rid of any excess moisture and remove any cloves. If necessary make a smoother purée with a potato masher. Let this cool and, when the purée is cold, fold in the egg whites beaten to a snow with a pinch of cream of tartar and, if preferred another dessertspoon of castor sugar. Pile up on a dish to serve. This can be

239

made just before dinner rather than at the last minute. But don't make it too early on or it will get grainy.

## CASSOULETTES LASSERRE (JUNE 3rd, 1964 DERBY DAY)

I had this in the Restaurant Lasserre in Paris in the early 1960s and it was so good I tried to repeat it myself at home. I do not know if I figured out the ingredients exactly but this version tastes very good too. However, the Lasserre version came with smart little pastry handles that I was not skilled enough to emulate. Of course you can make your own short pastry but I am not a particularly skilled pastry cook myself and the bought version is easy to use. One packet will easily cater for four people.

Use those large individual tart or patty tins with four or eight moulds to a tin. If you lack experience, you might want to make some extras and choose the best-looking to serve. It is not a hardship to eat the rest on your own the next day.

Grease the moulds lightly but thoroughly with butter and cut out rounds of greaseproof paper that are one and a half times the circumference of the mould. Use the pieces to line each mould smoothly. Roll out the pastry as thinly as you can and cut circles out with a pastry cutter that is again larger than the circumference of the moulds but fractionally smaller than the rounds of greaseproof paper (this way you have some paper to pull on when you want to take the little cassoulettes from the moulds without breaking them).

Gently press the rounds of pastry into the moulds so that the pastry comes almost up to the top of the moulds – leaving the edge of paper, then prick the bottom and the sides. At this stage, put the uncooked moulds into the fridge for half an hour or so – this prevents the pastry from rising when it meets the heat of the oven.

**For the Filling:**

*1 fillet of sole for 4 people*

*150ml/5 fl oz/½ cup of white wine or vermouth*

*8 medium stalks of asparagus, all woody stem removed and cooked al dente*

*Or 8 large white mushrooms chopped finely and melted in a little hot butter then seasoned, or both*

*2 tbsp butter*

# RECIPES

*1 tbsp flour, sieved*

*150ml/½ cup of single cream*

*Salt and freshly ground pepper*

*Optional, well beaten yolk of 1 egg*

*Small bunch of chives or tarragon, plus extra for garnish*

*Some very fresh parsley for garnish*

Gently poach the fillets of sole in the white wine or vermouth and as soon as they are done, drain, being careful to reserve the wine and keep it warm.

Cut the fish in pieces and divide between the pastry cases in the baking tin. Chop the asparagus into small pieces and place on top of the fish or use the Duxelles of mushrooms, or both if you prefer.

Melt the butter in a heavy saucepan, and stir in the flour to make a roux. Cook slowly, stirring well and add the hot wine bit by bit, still stirring. Thin a little with the cream, taste and season well. The sauce should be the consistency of thick cream. If you want it to look shiny when served, you can gently stir in the well-beaten egg but on no account boil or the sauce will curdle. Stir in some chopped tarragon or chives.

About 20 minutes before serving, cover the cassoulettes with foil and reheat in a low oven (150 °C/300 °F/gas mark 2).

At the last minute garnish each one with a small sprig of tarragon or two crossed chives and surround with sprigs of fresh parsley. They can be served individually or from a large dish with a spatula.

## OGEN MELONS STUFFED WITH RASPBERRIES WITH KIRSCH (JUNE 24th, 1964)

*Take ½ small ogen (or Charentais) melon for each person*

*2 tbsp of raspberries per person*

*1 dsp castor sugar per person*

*A sprinkling of Kirsch per person*

*4 vine leaves or other large decorative leaves per person*

241

Cut each melon in half and carefully slice a slither off each end so that the melons will not tip on a dish. Just as carefully scoop out the pips and fibrous matter from each centre. Tip the raspberries into a bowl with the sugar and mix together gently. Pile two tablespoons of the fruit into each melon and sprinkle the raspberries with a teaspoon or so of the Kirsch. Arrange the leaves on each serving plate and put half a melon on each arrangement.

## VEAU MARSALA (JULY 18th, 1964)

This is a quick and easy dish that takes a brief five minutes to cook and needs to be done at the last moment and served immediately. You can prepare the veal in advance up to the cooking point except for the dusting of flour. You will need about three or four small, thin squares of veal per person. The Italians call them *Scaloppine* or *Piccate*. A good butcher will cut them for you or you can buy escalopes of veal in a supermarket and cut them yourselves allowing, in this case, one escalope per person and cutting each one into three or four pieces. Put your pieces of veal, a few at a time, between two sheets of greaseproof paper on top of a cutting board and beat them as thin as possible.

**You will need:**

*Salt and pepper*
*The juice of one lemon*
*1 tbsp flour*
*2 tbsp butter*
*2 tbsp of Marsala per person*
*1 tbsp chicken or beef or veal stock*
*Some parsley for garnishing*

Season the escalopes well on each side with salt, pepper and a little lemon juice. Dust each one lightly with flour while you melt the butter in a heavy frying pan. When the butter is ready, brown the *scaloppine* quickly on each side, add the relevant amount of Marsala, let it bubble and then add the little bit of stock and stir well so that the butter, Marsala and stock are well mixed. Turn down the heat and simmer a couple of minutes until the sauce turns syrupy. Turn onto a heated dish, garnish with parsley and serve right away.

# RECIPES

## STRAWBERRIES WITH A RASPBERRY PURÉE (JULY 18th, 1964)

This is an excellent dish when the summer moves on and strawberries or raspberries and cream have become a cliché. It is very simple. Allow about half a small punnet per person of both strawberries and raspberries, or about three tablespoons of each fruit per person plus a tablespoon of sugar per person.

Hull and slice the strawberries and put them either into one dish or share them out into individual dishes. Add the sugar to the raspberries and purée in a food processor. You may or may not want to then put the purée through a sieve to get rid of the pips. You can also add a little Kirsch to the purée if you want. Simply pour the purée over the raspberries and serve. The dish can be made well before dinner.

## SOME CRUDITÉS (JULY 30th, 1964)

These make the ideal light, fresh starter to a rich main course, just as the rose petal sorbet (see p. 245) makes a good ending.

### Here are some suggestions:

*Thinly sliced cucumber dressed with salt, pepper, virgin olive oil and a little wine vinegar, garnished with a tiny bit of chopped mint*

*Black olives*

*Baby carrots grated into acidulated water, drained and blanched in boiling water for just two minutes, drained again and dressed with chopped spring onions or scallions or chopped chives, salt, a touch of sugar and a little virgin olive oil, garnished with finely chopped chives*

*Radishes sprinkled with a little sea salt*

*Celeriac peeled, grated into acidulated water, drained and blanched in boiling water for two minutes, drained again and folded into a mustardy mayonnaise, garnished with a little chopped parsley*

*Very thinly sliced fennel, seasoned with sea salt, black pepper, a little lemon juice and virgin olive oil and sprinkled with very thin small slices of Parmesan cheese and chopped fennel leaves*

You can serve these on their own or with crusty French bread and butter or a little good virgin olive oil. Alternatively add dishes of thinly sliced salami, Parma or St. Daniele ham, and fresh little shrimps.

### BEEF WELLINGTON (JULY 30th, 1964)

This was a very popular luxury dish in the 1960s and 1970s and seems to be making a reappearance. It is only worth doing it with an expensive tender cut of beef like rolled contre-filet (the eye of the sirloin), or a piece of whole fillet tied into shape. Allow about 115–140g/4–5oz per person. To be really luxurious you will need a small tin or jar of pâté de foie gras, but you can get away with a Duxelles of mushrooms, moistened with tomato sauce (or you can use both). There are many variations on the theme.

**You will also need:**

*450g/1lb finely chopped mushrooms*
*(or 675g/1 ½lb if you are aiming to stuff some tomatoes as garnish)*

*1 clove of garlic crushed with a little salt*

*3 tbsp butter*

*Salt and pepper*

*A small amount of tomato purée to moisten the mushrooms*

*A small tin or medium size tin or jar of pâté de foie gras depending on how lavish you intend to be (optional) or how many people you need to feed*

*1 ½ stuffed tomato per person for garnish*

*At least one packet of puff pastry rolled thin*

*The beaten yolk of an egg*

Chop the mushrooms finely and cook them gently with the crushed garlic in half the butter until the liquid has evaporated. Season to taste and moisten with a little tomato purée. Melt the rest of the butter in a heavy frying pan and, when it is really hot, sear the beef all over, remove from the pan and season well. Cool a little then spread the seared beef with the pâté and Duxelles of mushrooms, or just the mushrooms (reserving enough to stuff the garnishing tomatoes). Place the beef in the middle of the rolled out pastry, bring the sides up and pinch the top together so it is well-sealed. Trim away any excess pastry. If you like you can roll the trimmings out again and cut out leaves to decorate the top of the roll. Brush the pastry all over with the beaten egg.

# RECIPES

Allowing 12 minutes cooking time for every pound of beef – so that 1.3kg/3lb piece of beef will take 45 minutes. Cook in the centre of a pre-heated oven 230°C/450°F/gas mark 8 for 10 minutes, making sure the pastry does not burn. If it looks as if it is going to catch, cover it with foil. After 10 minutes reduce the heat to 190°C/375°F/gas mark 5. About 10 minutes before the beef is cooked remove any foil covering so that the pastry becomes golden. Serve on a long dish, garnished with halved tomatoes (seeds scooped out) stuffed with some of the mushroom Duxelles. A nice addition is a sauceboat full of Sauce Madère.

## SAUCE MADÈRE

*55g/2oz butter*

*1 medium onion, finely chopped*

*1 small carrot, finely chopped*

*125g/4½oz mushrooms, thinly sliced*

*150ml/½ cup of Madeira*

*1 tsp flour*

*Salt and pepper*

Melt 40g/1½oz butter in a heavy pan and gently soften the finely chopped onion and carrot until they turn pale gold but no more. Add the mushrooms and cook for another five minutes, then add the Madeira. Bubble quickly for a minute, then turn down the heat and simmer for 15 minutes or until it has reduced somewhat. To thicken the sauce lightly work in the teaspoon of flour to the rest of the softened butter and drop into the pan, half a teaspoon at a time, stirring it in well and simmer for a minute or two more. Season to taste.

## ROSE PETAL WATER ICE (JULY 30th, 1964)

This sounds wonderfully esoteric and indeed it is a delicious and refreshing end to a fairly elaborate dinner. All you must have for this is a jar of rose petal jam which is not nearly so difficult to find as you might imagine. Still if you like the sorbet and want to repeat it it is a good idea to buy a few jars at a time to keep on hand. This recipe is for six, though four people will probably finish it easily.

*175g/6oz/½ cup granulated sugar*

*150ml/5 fl oz/½ cup of water*

*½ jar of rose petal jam*

*Juice of ½ orange*

*2 tsp lemon juice*

*1 beaten white of egg*

Bring the sugar and water to the boil then turn the heat down and simmer for about eight minutes. Leave to cool then press the rose petal jam through a sieve. Stir the jam into the syrup with the orange and lemon juice and pour the mixture into an ice freezing tray and put in the freezer. Cover with foil and, after about two hours or so, remove from the freezer and fold in the egg white, beaten to a snow. Refreeze. Serve in individual glasses on plates scattered, if you like, with rose petals or with crystallised rose petals scattered on the sorbet itself.

## COLD ORANGE AND TOMATO SOUP (AUGUST 12th, 1964)

*900g/2lb ripe tomatoes or 2 tins of Italian tomatoes*

*4 spring onions or scallions*

*Salt, pepper and a handful of fresh basil leaves*

*1 orange*

*1 tsp each white wine vinegar and white sugar*

*1 glass of white wine*

*150ml/5 fl oz/½ cup of cream*

Whizz the tomatoes in a food processor and simmer the resulting purée for 10 minutes with the chopped spring onions or scallions, six basil leaves and several small thin slices of orange zest (the peel only with no pith). Strain, add all the other ingredients, leaving the cream until last. Stir well and leave to chill in the fridge till needed.

Stir in a few more torn basil leaves and float a decorative sprig on top of each bowl.


## VITELLO TONNATO (AUGUST 12th, 1964)

This is my version of the classic vitello tonnato and was (and is) one of my favourite summer dishes. It can be made properly by roasting a boned leg of veal previously incised and stuffed with small pieces of anchovy. Reserve the juices, let it get cold and slice it thinly before marinating it in the tuna sauce for several hours or a day. A short cut can be made with thin slices of bought chicken or turkey breast.

Whatever meat you use, you will need the following for the sauce and garnish for four–six people:

*1 tin of tuna fish, drained of oil*

*300ml/1 cup of good mayonnaise*

*The reserved juices from the roasted veal (if using it), plus a little veal stock*

*A jar of capers, drained*

*A little salt, 2 lemons*

*A tin of anchovy fillets, optional*

The classic tonnata mayonnaise suggests sieving the tuna but I find that sometimes the sauce gets rather grainy that way. I prefer the sauce to be a little coarser and less smooth. It is a question of choice. Pound or purée the tuna fish and incorporate it gradually into the mayonnaise.If you have used proper roast veal, add the juices from the roast meat thinned with a small amount of veal stock, a little at a time. Add a tablespoon or more of drained capers and some salt and lemon juice to taste. Pour enough over the sliced meat to cover it, reserving the rest and leave to marinate. When you want to serve it arrange the meat in overlapping slices on a large dish. Pour over the rest of the reserved sauce. The classic vitello tonnato is usually left ungarnished but sometimes I criss-cross the dish with anchovy fillets and scatter some more capers in each resulting diamond shape. Also, I either surround the dish with slices of lemon or quarters of lemon so that guests can squeeze more juice over the dish if liked. Or I serve lemon quarters separately and surround the dish with tiny halves of well-seasoned tomatoes and basil leaves.

## TEA ICE CREAM (AUGUST 12th, 1964)

*300ml/½ pt/1 cup single cream*

*175g/6oz/½ cup sugar*

*2 very well beaten egg yolks*

*300ml/½ pt/1 cup double cream*

*300ml/½ pt/1 cup very strong Indian tea (without milk) left to cool*

Scald the single cream with the sugar and when it is hot, but not near boiling point, gradually stir in the egg yolks, a little at a time, making sure that they do not curdle. When the mixture has thickened to the texture of thin custard, leave to cool. When cold, add the double cream and tea, stirring well to amalgamate. Pour into an ice tray (or trays) and freeze. After a couple of hours, take the ice cream out and give it a good stir then put it back in the freezer.

## SWEDISH COCKTAIL (OCTOBER 3rd, 1964)

This was something my father used to make, but I am not at all sure where he got the recipe (although he did a lot of business in Sweden and was fond of the country). In any event, it's a nice, refreshing and savoury starter.

**For four people you will need one individual glass or china serving dish for each person:**

*Any sort of good-tasting melon*

*1 cucumber*

*1 avocado (optional)*

*A jar of pickled cucumber or gherkins*

*Some finely chopped smoked ham*

*Some good vinaigrette made with 1 clove of garlic crushed with a little sea salt, plenty of freshly ground black pepper, 1 tsp of Dijon mustard, 1 tbsp of wine or Balsamic vinegar, 3–4 tbsp virgin olive oil*

*1 tsp of dill or caraway seed pounded in a mortar, scalded in 150ml/5 fl oz/ ½ cup of boiling water, together with 2 tsp sugar, left to cool and strained, reserving the liquid*

*The juice of half a lemon, some chopped dill or chopped fennel leaves*

# Recipes

Cut the melon in half, remove all the fibrous parts and pips, then make as many melon balls as you can with the small end of a potato baller.

Peel and deseed the cucumber, cut into small chunks, sprinkle with salt and leave to drain.

Cut the avocado in half, skin, remove the stone, and cut into the same size chunks as the cucumber.

When the cucumber is drained, divide it, the avocado (if used) and the melon between each serving dish. Distribute some finely chopped pickled cucumber or gherkins and the chopped ham between each dish and spoon over an equal amount of vinaigrette – to which you have added two tablespoons of the dill or caraway seed extract. Squeeze lemon juice over and stir. Garnish with some chopped dill or fennel leaves.

## BLACKBERRIES WITH SWEET GERANIUM CREAM

Sweet geranium leaves (regular geranium leaves are not at all the same thing) have the same sort of affinity with blackberries as basil does with tomatoes, tarragon with chicken. They are easy to grow or to obtain from a local plant nursery. This dessert is simplicity itself. For four people you will need 300ml/½ pt/1 cup single cream and six sweet geranium leaves. Pour the cream into a heavy saucepan, add the sweet geranium leaves (bring the cream to a boil). Turn off the heat, cover and leave to marinate and cool for at least an hour or two. Have ready a bowl of well-sugared blackberries and, just before you serve them, strain the cream into a bowl or sauceboat, pushing against the leaves with a wooden spoon to extract every last bit of flavour.

## BORSCH WITH SOUR CREAM (NOVEMBER 13th, 1964)

This beetroot and sour cream soup can be served hot or cold, but in this winter season, obviously hot.

*2 onions*

*2 cooked beets and 2 raw beets*

*25–30g/2 tbsp salted butter*

*600ml/1 pt/2 cups good beef stock*

*A bouquet garni*

*Salt, celery salt and black pepper*

*150ml/5 fl oz/1 cup sour cream or yoghourt*

Grate one of the onions – being careful to reserve the juices – and both the raw beets – again reserving the juice (it is good to wear rubber or plastic gloves for this operation, or wash your hands immediately afterwards). Sweat the beets gently in the butter for 15–20 minutes. Then add the stock, the bouquet garni and the seasoning to taste and simmer gently for around one and a half hours. Do not allow to boil. Strain and leave to cool. When the soup is cold, skim off the fat from the top with a tablespoon dipped in boiling water and add half of one of the cooked beets finely grated (again reserving the juice). Then add the juice of both the onions (to extract the juice from the second onion, mince it and press the pulp through a sieve), and the juice from the rest of the beets (made by mincing them and squeezing the juice through a piece of butter muslin). Check the seasoning and reheat – again on no account letting the soup boil (if it does the beautiful clear red will turn to an unappetising brown and all the point of the borsch will be lost). Serve in separate soup bowls with one dessertspoon of sour cream or yoghourt floated on top of each serving. Pass the rest of sour cream or yoghourt separately.

## OEUFS MOLLETS EN SOUFFLÉ (NOVEMBER 15th, 1964)

This is best served in individual earthenware ramekin or soufflé dishes so that everyone can be sure of getting an egg and it makes an impressive starter.

Prepare four oeufs mollets (by carefully spooning the eggs into boiling salted water for no more than five minutes and then into cold for the same amount of time. When cool tap the eggs gently all over and peel very gently. It is easy to crack the eggs by mistake, either in the water or when peeling, so it is a fail safe idea to do two or three spares. Do not use very freshly laid eggs either, because their shells are much more difficult to remove). When they are ready place one in the bottom of each buttered ramekin or individual soufflé dish.

*3 tbsp butter*

*1½ tbsp flour, sifted*

*350ml/12 fl oz/1¼ cups heated milk*

*2 tbsp finely grated Gruyère*

250

# RECIPES

*1 tbsp finely grated Parmesan*

*3 tsp Dijon mustard*

*Salt, pepper and grated nutmeg*

*6 well beaten egg yolks and 8 lightly salted well beaten egg whites*

Using a good-sized heavy saucepan melt the butter and off the heat add the sifted flour, stir well with a wooden spoon, put it back over the heat and let it bubble without browning for a couple of minutes before gradually stirring in the heated milk, bit by bit and stirring all the time. When smooth let it simmer gently on the lowest heat for about 10 minutes, stirring regularly before adding the cheeses, the egg yolks and the mustard. Mix well then season generously.

30 minutes before you want to serve them, pre-heat the oven to (200 °C/425 °F/gas mark 7). Make sure the top shelf is in the middle and place a baking sheet on it to heat up well. Whip the egg whites until they stand in peaks. Work the resulting froth into the soufflé mixture, half at a time, with a spatula, using a gentle stirring movement – if the little bubbles trapped in the egg whites are burst by too vigorous mixing the soufflé will not rise as it should. The blend should be fairly even but do not try to smooth out every last bit of the beaten whites. When the whites are reasonably absorbed, tip the mixture over the oeufs mollets so that it comes some three quarters of the way up each dish. Place the dishes on the hot baking sheet in the centre of the oven and bake at once for 10–12 minutes until hopefully well risen and golden. Serve at once.

## SMOKED HADDOCK SOUFFLÉ (JANUARY 4th, 1965)

Use the same basic soufflé mixture as that suggested for the oeufs mollets en soufflé (above) but without the cheese and nutmeg and substituting 450g/1lb smoked haddock fillet poached in a little white wine and flaked, being careful to search for any stray bones. Mix these small pieces of fish in with the egg mixture before you add the well-beaten whites. The soufflé can also be served in ramekins or individual soufflé dishes. If it is served in a larger soufflé dish it will probably need cooking for 15–20 minutes at the same temperature. After quarter of an hour check surreptitiously to see if it has risen and is golden enough.

## GRAPES UNDER THE GRILL (JANUARY 4th, 1965)

*450g/1lb sweet, seedless grapes*

*2–3 tbsp soft Barbados or other dark brown sugar*

*200ml/7 fl oz/¾ cup heavy cream*

Chill the grapes and cream in the refrigerator until they are ice cold. Pull the grapes from the vine and put them in a shallow ovenproof dish. Whip the cream and spread it carefully over the fruit and put the casserole back into the fridge until you are ready to serve it. At the last moment sprinkle all over with the sugar and put the casserole under a very hot pre-heated grill just long enough for the sugar to melt and bubble. Or use a salamander.

## OEUFS MAYONNAISE SAUCE VERTE (JANUARY 24th, 1965)

Allow one and a half hard boiled eggs per person. Arrange in segments on individual dishes and cover them with a sauce verte made by amalgamating a purée of herbs and leaves into a good mayonnaise made as follows.

For 300ml/1 cup of mayonnaise allow about 55g/2oz herbs and leaves – spinach, watercress, parsley, chives, tarragon, chervil, basil, mint, whatever you can lay your hands on at the time. Add these to two parts of spinach and watercress, to one part of mixed herbs. Blanch the spinach, watercress and herbs in boiling water for three minutes, then drain well, pound and push through a sieve or whizz in a food processor. Just before serving mix this purée into the mayonnaise.

## CHICKEN PIE (JANUARY 24th, 1964)

I vary this recipe all the time depending on the season, what vegetables are available, my mood, my time, or whether I decide to make it with a short crust or puff pastry. Sometimes I poach a chicken specially. Sometimes if I have some good chicken stock available and enough left over chicken, I simply use that. Purists might not agree but whether you take short cuts or not, it is always comforting food. My daughter-in-law, for example, makes a delicious chicken and celeriac variation with short crust pastry. I like using plenty of tarragon in this version.

# RECIPES

*1 chicken*

*2 sliced onions, 4 bay leaves, 1 cleaned and chopped leek,*
*bouquet garni for poaching chicken*

*2 peeled cloves of garlic, chopped*

*Water to cover, 2 good chicken stock cubes (optional)*

*Salt and freshly ground black pepper*

*2 leeks*

*Half a packet frozen petis pois*

*225 grams/half a pound of haricots verts*

*12 sliced asparagus stalks (optional)*

*12 small sliced mushrooms (optional)*

*3 tbsp butter*

*2 tbsp sieved flour*

*150ml/5 fl oz/½ cup white wine or Vermouth*

*600ml/1 pt/2 cups well-flavoured chicken stock*

*Good bunch of tarragon*

*150ml/5 fl oz/½ cup double cream or crème fraîche*

*1 beaten egg yolk*

Place the chicken in a large saucepan with the onions and leek, half the garlic, bay leaves and bouquet garni. Pour over the water, season and slowly bring to the boil. As soon as it bubbles, skim any scum off the top and add, if you like, the chicken stock cubes. Dissolve, cover the pot and simmer for 45–60 minutes. Let the chicken get cold in the resulting stock before skimming off the fat from the top of the liquid and straining it. Reserve and remove the bones and skin from the chicken. Cut into small neat pieces and arrange in a pie dish.

In the meantime, cook the various vegetables separately and fairly al dente, and sauté the chopped mushrooms, if used, with a couple of cloves of chopped garlic. Season well. If you do not use mushrooms, chop the garlic anyway and use in the sauce. Scatter the various vegetables over the chicken in the pie dish and mix well together.

Melt the butter in a separate heavy saucepan, and gently add the flour, stirring well, cook for several minutes then slowly add the white wine or vermouth followed by some hot chicken stock a little at a time till you get a sauce the consistency of heavy cream. Chop most of the bunch of tarragon and add it to the sauce, stirring well. Add the cream or crème fraîche and season really well. Pour over the chicken and vegetables in the pie dish, amalgamating them well together. Check seasoning again. (The chicken and vegetables absorb a lot.)

Roll out the pastry as thinly as possible and cover the pie. Crimp the edges with a fork, roll out any trimmings and form into leaves or rosettes and decorate the pie. Make a steam hole in the middle and brush with the beaten egg yolk. Three quarters of an hour or so before dinner, put the pie in the centre of an oven pre-heated to 200°C/400°F/ gas mark 7. After 15 minutes reduce the heat to 180°C/350°F/gas mark 4 and cook for another 15–20 minutes checking to see that the pastry is not burning. If it appears to be browning too much cover with a piece of foil. When the pastry looks crisp and golden, turn the heat down and keep warm till ready to serve.

## OEUFS ESPAGNOLÉS (FEBRUARY 1st, 1965)

This makes a good winter starter, or, with two eggs a light lunch or supper dish. It is best served in individual flame-proof brown gratin dishes. These quantities are for one.

*1 medium onion, finely sliced*

*1 tsp butter, melted*

*1 tomato, skinned, seeded and sliced*

*½ clove of minced or chopped garlic*

*1 egg per person*

*Salt and pepper*

*1 tbsp finely grated parmesan cheese*

*2–3 tbsp double cream*

Cook the finely chopped onion in the hot butter and add the tomato. Cook gently together for a few minutes until they have melded together nicely. Add the chopped garlic, stir well and break in the egg. Season well, sprinkle with the cheese and cover with the cream. Cook for a few minutes on top of the stove and then finish off under a hot grill for another minute or so. The whites should be set but not solid.

## CARAMELISED ORANGES (FEBRUARY 1st, 1965)

Use one seedless orange for each person plus the juice of one extra. Peel the zest from each piece of fruit using a very sharp knife or a zester and cut each strip into match-stick size strips. Blanch the strips in boiling water for eight minutes and then transfer them to a syrup made by boiling 175g/6oz/1 cup of sugar in 300ml/ ½ pt/1 cup of water for 15 minutes. Simmer the syrup and strips of peel for another 15 minutes until the strips are soft and translucent, rather like a marmalade.

Scoop out the peel and reserve while you continue to boil the syrup for another five minutes, then add the orange juice. Pour this over the stripped oranges already arranged in a white or glass dish, and leave them, if you can, to marinade for 24 hours or overnight. Serve very cold, with a little bunch of the 'marmalade' on top of each orange, surrounded by the syrup.

## CHICKEN DIJONNAISE (MARCH 10th, 1965)

*Allow a quarter of a chicken for each guest,*
*or you can use a mixture of chicken thighs and pieces of breast*
*(with the skin still on) if you prefer white meat.*

**You will also need:**

*100ml/3½ fl oz/⅓ cup Dijon mustard,*
*or a mixture of Dijon and Pommery coarse grained mustard*

*Salt and freshly ground black pepper*

*100ml/3½ fl oz/⅓ cup white wine or vermouth*

*150ml/5 fl oz/½ cup crème fraîche*

Spread the mustard over the chicken pieces, then put them in a bowl and leave to marinate for two hours or so.

Pre-heat the oven to 180°C/350°F/gas mark 4 and arrange the chicken in a flameproof dish, or oven pan, skin side up. If there is any mustard left in the bowl, scrape it out and spread it evenly over the chicken pieces. If they look a bit patchy, mustard-wise, you can always add a bit extra from the jar. Season with salt and pepper and pour the white wine or vermouth all around the chicken.

Set the dish on the centre rack of the oven and bake, basting regularly, for 30–40 minutes or until it is done. Dark meat takes longer than light. Now scrape the mustard *off* the chicken and back into the baking dish and transfer the chicken pieces to the serving platter, cover and keep warm.

Skim as much fat as you can from the cooking juices and set the baking tin over a medium heat. Bring to the boil, scraping the pan as you go, whisk in the crème fraîche and lower the heat. Simmer this sauce for between 5–10 minutes or until it is reduced to a coating consistency. Season lightly to taste, spoon the sauce over the chicken pieces and serve with a green salad or rice or both.

## DUBLIN BAY PRAWNS WITH AIOLI (APRIL 26th, 1965)

To make 300ml/ ½ pt/1 cup sauce: take two, three or four cloves of garlic, according to how garlicky you want to make it (in the case of the Dublin Bay prawns – or any good sized prawns or shrimps – I only wanted it faintly so, so used two). Normally, in the case of a Grand Aioli for example with salt cod, hard boiled eggs and many accompanying vegetables – I would use at least four cloves. Reduce the cloves to a paste. Mix them with the yolks of two eggs, half a teaspoon of Dijon mustard, salt, pepper and half a teaspoon of lemon juice. Slowly drip in about 300ml/ ½ pt/1 cup of good quality virgin olive oil, stirring with a wooden spoon till the mixture starts to emulsify, add a little more lemon juice, then, still stirring, add the oil in a steady stream. Finish off with a bit more lemon juice to taste and adjust the seasoning if necessary.

## ORANGE SORBET IN ORANGE SKINS (APRIL 26th, 1965)

You can often find a place to buy these, but homemade ones do taste so very good.

**This recipe is for six people:**

*1 lemon*

*6 Jaffa oranges and one extra*

*175g/6oz/1 cup sugar*

# RECIPES

*300ml/½ pt/1 cup water*

*The juice extracted from the orange pulp*

*1 dsp of stiffly whipped egg white*

*6 dsps Cointreau*

Using a potato peeler, a very sharp small knife, or a zester, peel the zest from the lemon and extra orange. Put this and the sugar in a heavy saucepan, cover with the water, and heat slowly till the sugar dissolves completely, then cool.

Meanwhile cut a slice off the tops of the 6 oranges, put the slices aside, and carefully scoop out the pulp without harming the skin. Crush the orange pulp through a sieve (including the pulp from the extra orange) to extract as much juice as you can, and squeeze the juice from the lemon.

When the syrup is quite cool, mix it with the orange and lemon juice and put it in an ice tray in the freezer. Freeze until the mixture gets mushy. Before it actually freezes stir it around with a fork and amalgamate the stiffly whipped egg white. Put the container back in the freezer and continue the freezing process.

While this is going on put one dessertspoon of Cointreau in each orange skin and swill it around. Leave the oranges in the fridge until the sorbet is stiff then fill each orange with it, smooth the top, replace the lids and stand them in the freezer until it is time to serve.

## SMOKED SALMON MOUSSE (JULY 30th, 1965)

**This is for four-six people:**

*2½ sheets of gelatine or one small envelope of gelatine crystals*

*2 tbsp water and a little bit extra if necessary*

*2 egg yolks and 3 whites*

*200ml/7 fl oz/½ cup of fresh double cream*

*225g/8oz smoked salmon, whizzed in a food processor*

*3 tbsp sour cream or crème fraîche*

*1 dsp of tomato purée*

*Tabasco, salt and pepper*

*The juice of half a lemon, plus lemon slices to garnish*

If you are using leaf gelatine, break it up, cover with cold water and leave to soften for around 20 minutes. Drain it, heat the two tablespoons of water in a small pan, add the leaf gelatine and stir till dissolved. If you are using crystals, there is no need to soak them first, but again they should be dissolved in two tablespoons of hot water.

Beat the egg yolks with two tablespoons of cream, add the gelatine and then the mashed smoked salmon thoroughly mixed with the sour cream or crème fraîche. Beat until smooth. Whip the rest of the cream and fold it in. I add a little tomato purée just to colour the mixture a realistic smoked salmon pink without giving a tomato taste. Season well with salt, pepper, Tabasco and lemon juice. Put the mixture in the fridge to chill for quarter of an hour or so before whipping up the whites stiffly and gently folding them into the salmon mixture.

Turn into a soufflé dish and put in the fridge to set. Garnish with some chopped chives or thin slices of lemon.

### CLASSIC COQUILLES ST. JACQUES (MARCH 3rd, 1967)

Fishmongers – who are a very rare breed nowadays – always used to sell scallops in their shells and if you can get them so much the better because this dish was always meant to be served in the shells. It tastes just as good however, eaten from little buttered ramekins.

**For eight people:**

*24–36 scallops depending on their size,*
*well-washed and kept in cold water till needed*

*Salt and freshly grated black pepper*

*8 shallots (or spring onions or scallions) chopped very fine*

*200g/7oz/¾ cup butter plus a little butter for greasing the shells*
*– or ramekins – if used*

*⅔ cup of stale breadcrumbs*

*3 tbsp chopped parsley*

Dry the scallops on paper towels and cut into three or four pieces if large, in half if they are small. Season them with salt and pepper and put them in the buttered shells or ramekins. Set the oven to 190°C/375°F/gas mark 5.

Cook the chopped shallots or spring onions (or scallions) in two tablespoons of the butter until they are soft and, in the meantime, melt the remaining butter in a separate pan. Share the onion around each scallop receptacle and sprinkle them with the melted butter and the breadcrumbs. Arrange the shells or ramekins on a roasting pan and put them in the pre-heated oven for 10–12 minutes at 190 °C/375 °F/ gas mark 5, or until the scallops feel tender when pierced with a sharp knife. Serve them immediately scattered with some of the chopped parsley.

## LEMON CHICKEN (MARCH 3rd, 1967)

This is very fresh tasting and as good cold as it is hot.

**For six–eight people:**

*2 chickens just under 1kg/2lb 4oz each cut into quarters, or just 8 good-sized quarters*

*600ml/½ pt fresh lemon juice*

*400g/14oz/2 cups flour*

*Salt and freshly ground black pepper*

*2 tsp paprika*

*150ml/½ cup vegetable corn or Arachide oil*

*3 tbsp grated lemon zest or 2 tbsp and 1 tsp lemon extract or oil*

*50g/1¾oz/¼ cup brown sugar*

*150ml/¼ cup good chicken stock*

*2 lemons cut in wafer slin slices*

*Some chopped parsley to garnish*

*Quarters of lemon to garnish*

The day before, put the chicken pieces in a bowl just large enough to contain them and pour over the lemon juice. Cover and put in the fridge to marinade turning occasionally

The next day drain the chicken well and pat dry with paper towels. Fill a large plastic bag with the flour, salt, black pepper and paprika, shake well to mix it all up, then put two chicken pieces in the bag at a time and shake very well again in order to coat the chicken all over.

Pre-heat the oven to 180 °C/350 °F/gas mark 4, and heat the oil in a large heavy frying pan. When it is very hot, fry a few chicken pieces at a time until they are crisp and golden. As they are cooked (each batch will take about 10 minutes) arrange them in a large shallow baking pan. When they are all done sprinkle two tablespoons of lemon zest over them and do the same with the brown sugar. Mix the chicken stock with the extra zest or lemon extract or lemon oil and pour around the chicken. Put a thin lemon slice on top of each piece and bake for 35–40 minutes or until tender.

Serve on a clean dish, garnished with the parsley and lemon quarters. Serve the jus separately.

## POULET A L'ÉSTRAGON (MAY 2nd, 1967)

Chicken with tarragon sauce has been one of my summer favourites for years. It was actually quite hard to get tarragon, basil and so forth then unless you grew your own, which I always did.

**For four people:**

1 good roasting chicken

4 tbsp softened butter

A large bunch of tarragon, half of it finely chopped

½ lemon

1 ½ tbsp of flour

Salt and freshly ground black pepper

150ml/½ pt/½ cup of Vermouth or white wine

150ml/½ pt/½ cup of single cream or crème fraîche

Pre-heat the oven to 230 °C/450 °F/gas mark 8. Clean the chicken, pat dry and put half the butter, half the bunch of tarragon and half a lemon inside the bird. Lightly dust the outside of the bird with a tablespoon of flour, rub it in, season with salt and pepper and rub the remaining butter all over the outside flesh. Put into a baking tin and place in the centre of the hot oven for 10–15 minutes. Baste and turn the oven down to 200 °C/400 °F/gas mark 6. Keep basting every quarter of an hour or so and if the bird looks as if it is burning, turn the oven down to 180 °C/350 °F/gas mark 4 and put a piece of foil over the top.

After an hour test the bird for clear juices, it might take another quarter of an hour. Remove the chicken which should be beautifully crisp and golden, cover with foil and let it rest while you make the sauce. Pour about two tablespoons of the buttery juices in the roasting pan into a heavy saucepan and add the remaining flour off the heat. Stir to a smooth roux, put back on the heat and, still stirring, add the vermouth or white wine bit by bit. When it is amalgamated, add the cream or crème fraîche and again stir well. Season and add the chopped tarragon. Serve the sauce separately.

## LITTLE TUNA FISH, GREEN BEAN AND RED PEPPER TARTS (MAY 26th, 1967)

Again these made a nice little summer dish and I see that I often served them. It was hard to get fresh red peppers or capsicums then so I used small tins, but now they are so plentiful you can certainly use the fresh which are, of course, much crisper.

**For 6 people:**

*1 packet short crust pastry*

*1 tin tuna fish in oil*

*2 tbsp mayonnaise*

*150g/5½oz/½ cup little French beans chopped small and cooked al dente*

*1 small tin of red peppers or half a fresh red pepper also chopped small*

*Salt and freshly ground pepper*

*Chopped chives*

Roll out the pastry thinly and fill some medium-sized tart tins (or one large tart tin or dish if you prefer). Put in the fridge for half an hour or so, then scatter some pastry beans on the bottom and bake for 15–20 minutes or until a pale gold in a moderate oven 180 °C/350 °F/gas mark 4. Take out, remove the beans and cool on a wire rack.

In the meantime drain well and chop the tuna, mix with the mayonnaise and then the finely chopped cooked beans and the peppers. Season well. Pile into the cooled tarts and serve sprinkled with the chopped chives

## PAPRIKA CHICKEN (MAY 26th, 1967)

You don't need a particularly special chicken for this good-tasting dish.

**For four people:**

*1 chicken weighing about 1½kg/3lb 5oz, jointed, or the same weight of assorted chicken pieces*

*2 tbsp flour*

*Salt and freshly ground pepper*

*1 tbsp butter and 1 of olive oil*

*1 chopped onion*

*4 tbsp Vermouth*

*4 tbsp white wine*

*300ml/½ pt/1 cup hot good chicken stock*

*1 chopped red pepper*

*1 clove of garlic, creamed with a little salt*

*1 tin of tomatoes, drained*

*2 tsp paprika*

*Bouquet garni*

*4 tbsp chopped walnuts*

Roll the pieces of chicken in some seasoned flour and brown in a heavy pan in the hot olive oil and butter. Add the onion and let it colour a little before adding the vermouth and the wine. Bubble altogether for a few minutes, then add the hot stock, the chopped pepper, the garlic, tomatoes, paprika, salt, pepper and the bouquet garni. Cover and simmer for 20 minutes then add the walnuts. Continue cooking for another half an hour. Taste for further seasoning. Serve with rice or noodles.

# RECIPES

## SALAD NIÇOISE (MAY 29th, 1967)

I have always enjoyed making salad Niçoise and this is my own version.

**For four people:**

*First make a dressing with 2 cloves of garlic pounded with a little salt,*
*freshly ground black pepper, a pinch of sea salt, 1 tsp Dijon mustard.*
*2 tbsp white wine vinegar, 6 tbsp virgin olive oil and whisk well together*

*300g/10½oz/1 cup little French beans, topped and tailed*

*Sea salt or Fleur du Sel and freshly ground black pepper*

*12 little new potatoes*

*1 finely sliced red onion*

*2–3 tbsp virgin olive oil*

*2 medium sized tins of tuna or one large one*

*1 tbsp mayonnaise*

*½ lemon*

*2 divided lettuce hearts*

*6 chopped spring onions or scallions*

*6 sliced radishes (optional, but they added a nice crispness)*

*1 sliced red pepper*

*1 sliced yellow pepper (optional, but they make the salad more colourful)*

*4 hard boiled eggs, sliced*

*8 really good medium sized tomatoes*

*A handful of black Niçoises olives*

*A handful of basil leaves and a nice looking spring onion or two*

Cook the beans al dente, drain well, refresh in cold water to maintain their greenness, drain again and put in a bowl with two tablespoons of the dressing and a sprinkling of sea salt.

Cook the new potatoes and as soon as they are done, drain, slice and put in a bowl with the sliced red onion, the two–three tablespoons of virgin olive oil, plenty or sea salt or Fleur du Sel and black pepper, mix gently.

Drain the tuna fish well, mix with the tablespoon of mayonnaise and squeeze in the lemon juice.

Put the pieces of lettuce hearts in a large salad bowl, leaving a hole in the middle into which you pile the tuna. Scatter the sliced potatoes and onions over the top of the lettuce, then the beans with the chopped spring onions or scallions and the sliced radishes. On top of these put the sliced red and yellow peppers if used, followed by sliced hard boiled eggs alternated with slices or quarters of already well-seasoned tomatoes. Pour the rest of the dressing over and around, scatter with a handful of little black olives, tuck some basil leaves all round the sides of the bowl and tear a few more to sprinkle all over the top of the salad. You can finish with a nice sprig or two and a couple of spring onions.

Bring to the table like this and then each person can toss their own.

### BOLLITO WITH SALSA VERDE (MAY 29th, 1967)

My father always loved a good dish of boiled meats and the different accompaniments (*bollito*, or the French and much less elaborate version, *pot au feu*, sound a whole lot more appetizing), so did my husband and I think a great many men. You need quite a lot of people to eat it or to know that you can have it again the next day either in the same way or with variations. The left-over broth is delicious and can easily be frozen for excellent stock. In fact you can always make variations to the ingredients according to what is available and the state of your purse at the time.

**This can easily feed 10–12 with lots over. Take any or all of the following, but there must be a good mixture:**

*1kg/2lb 4oz salted silverside of beef (soaked for an hour or two first) or a small fillet of veal or both*

*1kg/2lb 4oz gammon or boiling ham*

*2 leeks quartered, 2 onions stuck with cloves and 2 more onions halved, 4 carrots quartered, 4 bay leaves, a few sprigs of thyme and parsley, a stick of celery, mace and peppercorns, a bouquet garni, salt*

*1 chicken*

*A small ox tongue*

*A cotechino Italian sausage*
*(The Italians invariably start the bollito off with a calf's or pig's head or a calf's foot because they take the longest to cook and by all means use any of these too if you can get them)*

# RECIPES

You will need a huge saucepan or two very large ones. Keep one for the meats that cook the quickest. If you are using two pans – and I am presuming that that is what most people will do – divide the vegetables, herbs and seasonings between the two.

Bring a large pan of water to the boil and drop in the silverside and/or the veal and the ham. When the water comes back to the boil reduce the heat until the pan is just at simmering point. Skim off any scum that has risen to the top before adding all the vegetables, herbs and seasonings, or half of them if you are using two pans. Cover the pan and simmer for about two hours. After about an hour you can add the chicken, the tongue and the *cotechino* sausage but turn the heat up under the pan so that the stock reaches boiling point again just before you add them. Bring the pan back to the boil and, again, skim off any scum before you lower the high heat to simmering point.

If you are using two pans, bring the second one to the boil about an hour after you have put the first one on and repeat the exact procedure of the first.

Test every now and again to see how the various meats are doing. If they cook before you are ready do not worry, you can bring the pan right down to its lowest temperature and the meats and chicken will keep warm very happily.

While the meats are cooking you can make the traditional sauces that accompany the dish.

### For the Salsa Verde:

*A teaspoon to a dessertspoon each of finely chopped onion and capers, a large bunch of parsley, chopped finely, a clove of garlic and a fillet of anchovy, mashed. Pound them together in a mortar. Add the juice of half a small lemon and add about two tablespoons of olive oil gradually, drop by drop until the sauce is rather thick – you may need a little more olive oil.*

### For the Spicy Tomato Sauce:

*Chop 900g/2lb tomatoes. Put them in a heavy saucepan with a small finely chopped onion, a finely chopped carrot, a piece of finely chopped celery and a little chopped parsley. Season well and add a pinch of sugar. Simmer till the tomatoes have turned pretty much into a purée and then put through a sieve. If the purée is still a little watery, put it back into the saucepan until the excess moisture has reduced. Add a dessertspoon of wine vinegar and a dessertspoon of Dijon mustard and stir well.*

**For the Creamy Horseradish Sauce:**

*Take 2 tbsp bought Horseradish sauce and stir well into 4 tbsp sour cream or crème fraîche. The Italians sometimes add 1 tbsp or so of finely chopped walnuts.*

When you are ready to serve, remove the various meats from their pan or pans, carve as much as you want of each, arrange on a large dish, moisten with a little of the stock and serve with the Salsa Verde, the Spicy Tomato Sauce and the Horseradish Sauce as well as a selection of mustards. I also serve it with white haricots beans and sweet-sour cabbage (see below). It always seems to me to be quite enough without potatoes but many people serve them as well.

You can keep the meats warm in the hot stock in case anyone wants any seconds, but when they are cold you should wrap them all, put them in the fridge, drain the stock and reserve for the next day. You can eventually freeze what is left of the broth – if anything.

## SWEET-SOUR CABBAGE (MAY 29th, 1967)

*1 large green cabbage, with the hard stalk removed and cut into strips*

*2 tbsp olive oil or a little bacon fat if available, or a bit of both*

*1 small onion chopped*

*2 or 3 large ripe peeled tomatoes – or 1 dsp of tomato purée diluted with a little water*

*1 tbsp soft white sugar*

*Salt and pepper*

*1 tbsp white wine vinegar*

Sauté the onion in the hot fat, or oil, in a large pan till golden, add the tomatoes or the purée and when the tomatoes are soft or the purée amalgamated, add the shredded cabbage. Stir it around well, add salt and pepper and a large tablespoon of wine vinegar. Let it simmer for 20 minutes, stirring frequently with a wooden spoon and five minutes before serving stir in the tablespoon of soft white sugar.

Another cabbage dish I sometimes serve with a Bollito (or a Shepherd's or Cottage Pie) is with Moutarde de Meaux, the very grainy French mustard. Simply cook the shredded cabbage in boiling water till tender.

Drain well. In the meantime, melt a couple of tablespoons butter in the pan into which you have added a couple of tablespoons of Moutarde de Meaux. Heat it, put the cabbage back for a couple of minutes until it is is hot and the grainy, mustardy butter is well amalgamated.

## STRAWBERRY ICE CREAM WITH RASPBERRY PURÉE
### (JUNE 10th, 1967)

Let me say at once that since you are serving the ice cream with a delicious fresh raspberry purée you could easily get away with some good bought strawberry ice cream – especially on a hot summer's day.

The raspberry purée is very simple. Depending upon the number of people buy one or two punnets of raspberries. Whizz them in a food processor with about four tablespoons of sugar and either sieve or don't sieve to get rid of the pips. Add, if you like, a tablespoon of Kirsch and mix well. Serve either poured over the ice cream or some on the ice cream and some in a sauce-boat, to be passed around separately.

## STUFFED COURGETTES WITH AVGOLEMONO SAUCE
### (JUNE 23rd, 1967)

I don't know how I came to make up this dish: maybe the coincidence of a job lot of courgettes and some excess minced meat in the fridge. Anyway, I still make it, with variations.

You can have it for a starter allowing one courgette for each person, or for a main course allowing two or three. I am not very specific about quantities because, having made it up, I have always just made it, but it is a very economical dish.

**For a starter for four–six people you will need:**

*1 medium sized courgettes or zucchini for each person*

*2 tbsp of olive oil*

*1 onion, chopped*

*1 clove of garlic, mashed with a little salt*

*225g/8oz minced meat*

*1 tbsp tomato purée*

*1 tbsp pine nuts*

*Salt and pepper*

*The chopped leaves from 3 stems of fresh rosemary*

**For the Avgolemono Sauce:**

*2 or 3 egg yolks beaten together*

*The juice of a lemon*

*A little good stock (chicken, vegetable or beef)*

*Salt and pepper*

Cut a slim slice down the length of each courgette. Carefully scoop out the flesh from each and chop (I usually slip the blade of a small, sharp knife as close to the skin as I can, criss-cross the flesh and then scoop out with a teaspoon). Have ready a pan of salted boiling water, throw in the courgette shells and tops and, when the water comes to the boil again, take them off the stove and drain them well, first in a colander and then upside down on paper towels.

Heat the oil in a frying pan and gently fry the chopped onion, when it starts to get pale gold add the garlic, then the meat. When the meat starts to colour add the tomato purée, the chopped courgette flesh and the pine nuts. Stir well and cook till browned. Season well adding a little more tomato purée if the meat seems at all dry. Stuff the courgette shells with this mixture, doming it slightly, put back the tops and put in a small ovenproof dish. Cover with foil and put in the middle of a low to moderate oven (180 °C/350 °F/gas mark 4) for about 15 minutes.

While they are heating make the sauce. Pour the beaten eggs, the lemon juice and say three tablespoons of stock into a bain Marie set over simmering water. Beat together well with a whisk until the sauce starts to thicken. Taste for seasoning. If you want the sauce to taste more lemony add a bit of extra juice and, if it looks as if it is getting too thick, add a little extra stock.

When you are ready to serve them, take the courgettes out of the oven and, for a starter, place one on each guest's plate, pour over a little of the sauce and serve the rest separately. You can add a sprig or two of rosemary to each plate as a garnish. If the dish is for a main course, I usually serve it in the dish straight from the oven, again with some of the sauce poured over and more served separately on the side. Also, if I am serving it as a main course, I often make the sauce adding four tablespoons of butter cut in little bits and added gradually rather like an Hollandaise. This not only makes a richer, more substantial sauce but also means I can make it a little beforehand and keep it off the stove (but over warm water).

## VEAL ESCALLOPES IN A CUCUMBER SAUCE (JULY 13th, 1967)

This is a very easy standby summery dish. I often make a whole lot of little pastry crescents, as a crunchy garnish for this sort of dish, by rolling out a packet of puff pastry, stamping out rounds with the rim of a small wine glass, cutting them in half, crimping the edges slightly with a small fork, painting them with a beaten egg and baking in a well greased baking tin in a fairly hot oven (200 °C/400 °F/gas mark 6) for 10 minutes or so or until they are risen and golden. They keep well for several weeks in a tin or plastic box.

On this particular occasion I may not have used them since we had pastry first anyway.

*1–2 cucumbers depending on the number of people*

*Salt and plenty of black pepper*

*You will need 1 escalope of veal for each person with perhaps 1–2 over for seconds.*

*A little flour seasoned for dusting the escalopes*

*2 tbsp butter*

*300ml/½ pt/1 cup sour cream or crème fraîche*

*Some chopped parsley or chives for garnish*

Peel the cucumber(s), chop into small squares, sprinkle with salt and put in a sieve over a bowl to get rid of excess moisture

Just before you are ready to eat the escalopes dry each one on a paper towel and dust with the seasoned flour. Melt the butter in a large frying pan and when it is sizzling add the meat, brown lightly on each side and then add as much of the cream as you need to make a nice bubbly sauce. Add the cucumber and cook for a few seconds. Season well and ladle each escalope onto a big serving dish, distribute a spoonful or two of cucumber on each piece of veal and pour the sauce over the dish. If you are using the pastry crescents arrange them around the outside of the dish allowing two or three for each person. Sprinkle with the chopped parsley or chives and serve.

## TOMATES À LA CRÈME (AUGUST 4th)

Elizabeth David had written in a *Sunday Times Colour Supplement* in January that year, that any restaurateur who put this recipe of de Pomiane's on his menu would, in all probability, soon find it listed in the guide books as a regional speciality. It was, she said, so startlingly unlike any other dish of cooked tomatoes – de Pomiane himself said the recipe came from his Polish mother.

'Take six tomatoes' he wrote. 'Cut them in halves. In your frying pan melt a lump of butter. Put in the tomatoes, cut side downwards, with a sharply pointed knife puncturing here and there the rounded sides of the tomatoes. Let them heat for five minutes. Turn them over. Cook them again for another ten minutes. Turn them again. The juices run out and spread around the pan. Once more turn the tomatoes cut side upwards. Around them add 80g (3oz or six tablespoons near enough) of thick cream. Mix it with the juices. As soon as it bubbles, slip the tomatoes and all their sauces on to a hot dish. Serve instantly, very hot.'

## CRISPY FRIED AUBERGINES AND GARLICKY YOGHOURT (AUGUST 5th, 1967)

I am always surprised how very far one clove of garlic goes in permeating yoghourt, so make sure your guests are garlic lovers. This was a showy little hors d'oeuvre from my friend and colleague, Jean Robertson.

**For four–six people (double the quantities for more):**

I would allow half an aubergine or eggplant per person.

*Salt, pepper and paprika*

*115g/4oz/¼ cup flour*

*1 egg*

*75ml/2½ fl oz/¼ cup water*

*1 creamed clove of garlic*

*150ml/5 fl oz/½ cup yoghourt*

*Olive oil for frying*

Slice the aubergines thinly, sprinkle with salt, drain for quarter to half an hour on kitchen paper to release excess moisture, dab dry.

In the meantime, make the batter. Sift the flour into a basin and season with salt, freshly ground pepper and paprika. Make a well in the centre and drop in an egg. Stir the egg in gradually and, bit by bit, stir in the water.

While the batter is curing, make the yoghourt sauce by stirring the creamed garlic into the yoghourt and season to taste.

Have ready a pan of very hot oil deep enough to cover the battered slices of aubergine. Dip the aubergine in the batter and deep fry for three–four minutes. Drain well on kitchen paper and serve at once with the yoghourt sauce. If you are put off by the term 'deep frying' or hate the fumes and the bother, you can cook the aubergine slices in just enough very hot oil for them to absorb and crispen, but they are actually lighter, dryer and crisper with the quick deep frying method.

## APRICOT SOUFFLÉ (AUGUST 5th, 1967)

This is very light and flourless and can be made with fresh or dried apricots.

### For six–eight people:

*450g/1lb dried apricots or 900g/2lb fresh*

*1 tbsp vanilla flavoured sugar*

*2 tbsp castor sugar*

*3 tbsp Kirsch*

*300ml/½ pt/1 cup double cream*

*8 beaten egg whites, 2 reserved separately*

*Butter, for rubbing*

First make a purée. If you are using dried apricots soak 450g/1lb apricots in water for several hours or overnight in a casserole and then, without changing the water, bake them covered in a moderate oven (180 °C/350 °F/gas mark 4) for half to three quarters of an hour. Drain, then purée in a blender or through a sieve. Sweeten the purée with a tablespoon of vanilla-flavoured sugar (pre-bought or sugar stored with a stick of vanilla in the middle) or with half a teaspoon of vanilla essence). Add three tablespoons of Kirsch.

If you use fresh apricots, omit the soaking and cooking, instead peel, purée and add the sugar and Kirsch. Whip two of the egg whites and fold them into a cup of whipped cream. Carefully blend the purée into the cream. Just before it is time to cook the soufflé, pre-heat the oven to 200 °C/400 °F/gas mark 6, butter a soufflé dish and sprinkle it all over with castor sugar. Whip up the whites of the other six eggs to a snow peak, adding a little more castor sugar. Using a spatula gently fold half the egg whites into the apricot purée. When they are perfectly blended add the other half. Turn the mixture into the soufflé dish and bake in the centre of the oven for 15–20 minutes. Serve right away.

## TOMATOES STUFFED WITH TUNA (AUGUST 26th, 1967)

Allow one or two good, large tomatoes per person. Simply cut them in half, scoop out the middles (which you can reserve for what you want or chuck) and stuff with some well-drained and pounded tinned tuna. Then sprinkle with the juice of half a lemon and gradually incorporate some well-seasoned mayonnaise. If it is very thick you could always add a little of the discarded tomato pulp, well-seasoned.

## STUFFED GREEK TOMATOES (AUGUST 26th, 1967)

Cut the tops off some good-sized tomatoes, allowing one or two per person, scoop out the flesh and reserve.

*300g/10½oz/2 cups cooked rice*

*2 tbsp chopped onion*

*2 tbsp currants*

*2 cloves of finely chopped garlic*

*Salt and freshly ground pepper*

*A few basil leaves torn into little pieces or 1 tbsp chopped oregano*

*Any left over cooked minced beef or lamb (optional)*

Mix all these ingredients together. Stuff the tomatoes with it and bake them in a covered dish in a moderate oven (180 °C/350 °F/gas mark 4) sprinkled with olive oil for about half to three-quarters of an hour. If they look as if they are burning, cover with foil.

# RECIPES

## CHERRY AND WALNUT SALAD (AUGUST 26th, 1967)

I often used this Constance Spry salad in the summer when cherries are plentiful. Make a two-to-one mixture of dark stoned cherries and shelled walnuts. Mix this into a dressing made with a pot of lightly whipped crème fraîche (in those days I used double cream mixed with the juice of half a lemon) seasoned with freshly ground black pepper and a tablespoon of tarragon vinegar. Sprinkle with chopped tarragon.

## SUMMER PUDDING (AUGUST 26th, 1967)

This should be made the day before to allow the juices of the fruit to seep into the bread. It can be made with a mixture of strawberries, raspberries, redcurrants, blackcurrants, whitecurrants, blackberries, mulberries, loganberries, blueberries, whatever, in fact, happens to be available the day you want to make it. I also sometimes add a bit of peeled and cored, chopped apple. There are many different ways of making it but this is what I do.

Line a pudding basin with thin slices of a sandwich loaf, crusts removed. You will need to cut some of the bread into triangular-shaped pieces to make them all fit like a jigsaw. The side pieces can protrude over the top of the dish because you will be folding them over later.

Hull and cut up the strawberries if you are using them and de-stalk the currants. Throw the mixed fruit into a heavy bottomed saucepan and add about four tablespoons of sugar. Cook, stirring the fruit over a very gentle heat until the juices start to run. Take off the stove and drain, making sure to reserve the juice.

Pour the fruit into the bread-lined bowl. Fold over the slices of bread protruding over the edge of the bowl and, if there is still a gap, seal it with another piece or two of crustless bread, making sure that the fruit is completely covered. Cover with a small plate or saucer that fits easily into the bowl and weigh it down with weights or anything heavy that comes to hand. Put the bowl and the separate reserved juice into the fridge.

If you feel brave enough the next day, you can turn it out onto a good-sized plate or shallow bowl (but it really does not matter). Serve with the reserved juice and some cream for those that want it.

# Mary Gilliatt's Fabulous Food and Friends

## CIRCASSIAN CHICKEN (SEPTEMBER 11th, 1967)

This is a Turkish dish, also called *Sherkasiya* and is much eaten in the Middle East. I used to amalgamate an Elizabeth David recipe from her *Mediterranean Food* and one from an Arabella Boxer book with the same title.

**For one roasting chicken you will need:**

*3 medium onions, one halved*

*3 stalks parsley*

*Paprika, cayenne and sea salt*

*4 slices of dry white bread, crust removed*

*85g/3oz/¼ cup each of shelled walnuts, almonds and hazel nuts*

*1 clove of garlic*

*2 tbsp butter*

Put the chicken in a heavy pan with one onion halved and the parsley. Just cover with water, add a teaspoon of sea salt, bring to the boil, skimming off any scum that rises to the surface. Then turn down the heat, cover and simmer for an hour or till tender. Leave in the stock till cool enough to handle, then lift the chicken out and strain and reserve the stock. Remove all skin and bones from the chicken and cut into neat slices. Keep warm.

In the meantime, whizz the bread in a food processor till reduced to small crumbs, then add the nuts together with the garlic, a large pinch of sea salt, paprika and cayenne pepper. Process again till the nuts are quite small. Finely chop the remaining two onions and fry them in the butter. When golden, add the nut and bread mixture and a little of the stock, taste for seasoning and cook till thick.

Arrange the chicken on a bed of saffron rice, pour the sauce over it and serve.

## CHOPSKA SALAD (SEPTEMBER 11th, 1967)

This is a Bulgarian salad, so not so far from Turkey. Chop up a lettuce or the heart of a cabbage, a peeled cucumber, three peeled and deseeded tomatoes, a red onion, a red pepper, and 2 sticks of young

274

celery with their leaves. Toss them in a good, well-seasoned vinaigrette and serve in a little mound on each plate topped with a little grated Parmesan.

## RHUBARB TART (SEPTEMBER 11th, 1967)

This tart is made in the Alsatian manner, that is to say whatever fruit is used – and you can just as easily make it with apples or pears or cherries – is set in a custard of cream, milk and eggs.

*1 packet short crust pastry*

*2 small egg yolks*

*3 tbsp vanilla sugar, or sugar and a few drops of vanilla essence*

*150ml/5 fl oz/½ cup single cream*

*75ml/2½ fl oz/¼ cup milk*

*225g/8oz young rhubarb cut into 2½cm/1in lengths*

*1 tbsp of castor sugar*

Pre-heat the oven to 220 °C/425 °F/gas mark 7. Roll out the pastry thinly and line a tart tin or an earthenware flan dish with it, crimping the edges with a fork unless the edges of the flan dish are already crimped. Put in the fridge while you make the custard mixture. Whisk the egg yolks with the sugar and the vanilla essence if used, till the mixture whitens. Then dilute with the cream and milk, stirring it in slowly. Fill the pastry with the pieces of rhubarb, pour over the custard mixture and bake for 25 minutes. Sprinkle the tart all over with a tablespoon or so of castor sugar and return to the oven for a further five minutes. Serve either just warm or cold.

## GREEN CHEESE MOUSSE (SEPTEMBER 26th, 1967)

This is called green cheese mousse because of the colourful but mainly green filling – and not because of the cheese (unless, maybe, you used a Sage Derby) and you will definitely need an oiled, flat, ring mould. It makes an elegant, but quite rich, starter or a good main course for a lunch.

**For six–eight people (you may need two flat ring moulds):**

*70g/2½oz gelatine powder or 2½ sheets*

*2 tbsp water*

*115g/4oz/½ cup creamy Gorgonzola or Dolcelatte cheese*

*3 tbsp sour cream or crème fraîche*

*2 egg yolks and 4 whites*

*100ml/3½ fl oz/⅓ cup double cream*

*Salt, pepper and Tabasco*

If you are using gelatine powder, heat up the two tablespoons of water in a small pan but do not boil and stir the gelatine till it is fully dissolved. If leaf gelatine is used, break it up, cover with cold water and leave to soften for about 20 minutes. Drain it, put it in a small pan with the two tablespoons of water and leave it to warm until dissolved.

Thoroughly mash the cheese with the sour cream or crème fraîche. Beat up the two egg yolks – reserving the whites – with two tablespoons of the cream, add the dissolved gelatine and then the cheese. Beat well until smooth. Whip up the rest of the cream and fold it, adding salt, pepper and Tabasco to taste. It should be quite highly seasoned.

Put the mixture in the fridge for 10–15 minutes before whipping the four whites till they stand in peaks and gently folding them in to the mixture. Turn this into the ring mould and put back in the fridge to set for an hour or so. Turn out onto a large serving dish by first running around both inner and outer edges with a knife dipped in boiling water and then dipping the base in very hot water for literally a moment (otherwise it will melt).

Fill the centre with a salad made of chopped cucumber, fennel, spring onions or scallions, a very little crisp eating-apple, a couple of sticks of tender celery, a couple of tomatoes, skinned and drained of juice and a few walnuts. Season gently but do not dress. If you want you can pass a vinaigrette around separately.

## PROVENÇALE CHICKEN WITH BLACK OLIVES
### (SEPTEMBER 26th, 1967)

There are so many way of using chicken breasts and now that you can so easily get chicken fillets, it is one of the easiest dishes to prepare.

# Recipes

Allow half a chicken breast per person, with or without the crispy skin which so many people eschew nowadays. I made this with the skin in those days but have made it just as often without.

**Apart from the chicken breasts you will need:**

*Salt and freshly ground black pepper*

*Flour, for dusting*

*3 tbsp olive oil*

*2 finely chopped cloves of garlic*

*A few sprigs of chopped thyme*

*4 tbsp black olives*

*2 chopped red peppers*

*Some chopped parsley or sprigs of thyme or some leaves of basil for garnishing*

Flatten out the fillets a little with a rolling pin or a wooden mallet, season with salt and pepper and dust with a little flour. Heat three tablespoons of olive oil in a large, heavy frying pan with a lid and as soon as it heats up put in the fillets. Cook them quite fast for two or three minutes until one side is brown, turn them over, add the garlic, the thyme, the olives and the chopped red peppers, lower the heat and cover the pan. The chicken should be cooked in 15–20 minutes. Look at it after 10 minutes and stir the peppers and olives around a little. Serve the chicken on a hot dish with the red peppers and olives all around and pour over the juices from the pan. Garnish with parsley, thyme or basil.

## JAMBON PERSILLÉ (OCTOBER 26th, 1967)

I always particularly liked this homely, colourful pink and green Burgundian dish of ham and parsley, served, particularly at Easter in France, from pristine white earthenware bowls and find it rather satisfying to make. You *could* make a version with bought cooked ham and aspic jelly which will be just that, a version and a travesty of the real thing. The taste, not to mention the satisfaction you get, by cooking it the long way is a whole different thing. However it is is somewhat easier to use gammon rather than a whole joint of ham.

**You will need:**

*1–1½kg/2lb 4oz–3lb 5oz gammon*

*A cut up knuckle of veal (flesh and bone which you may have to order from a butcher)*

*1 split calf's foot (which you may also have to order)*

*1 bottle cheap dry white wine*

*1 onion*

*1 carrot*

*A few white peppercorns and a little salt*

*A stick of celery, a small bunch each of thyme and parsley*

*1 tsp tarragon vinegar*

*4–6 tbsp finely chopped parsley*

Scrub the gammon, cover it with water and leave it to soak in a big bowl overnight. Drain, put it in a large saucepan, cover it with fresh water, bring it slowly to the boil, turn down the heat and let it simmer for 50 minutes. In the meantime, in a separate heavy saucepan, cover the cut up knuckle of veal and the split calf's foot with the wine, and add the cut up onion, carrot, peppercorns, celery, the small bunches of parsley and thyme, and a very little salt. Put the lid on the pan, bring to the boil and simmer for much the same time as the gammon.

After the 50 minutes, remove the gammon from its water, rinse it, peel off the skin and cut the flesh into squares much the size of a small matchbox. Take out the knuckle of veal and the calf's foot, throw away the former and set the latter aside. Strain the wine stock through a fine sieve lined with muslin or a piece of clean napkin or a tea towel kept for the purpose. Put the ham and the calf's foot back into a clean saucepan, pour over the wine stock and leave it to simmer slowly over a low heat until the ham is so soft it can be cut with a spoon.

Remove the ham from the pot, throw away the calf's foot, and strain the stock in the same way as before. Leave to cool then skim any fat from the surface. Crush the ham into small pieces using a potato masher and if necessary complete the process with two forks, one in each hand. Put the ham into a white bowl, earthenware terrine or soufflé dish. The stock will have become jellied by this time, so, making sure there is no residue of fat, melt it gently in a clean saucepan with the tarragon vinegar, adjust seasoning if necessary, stir in the chopped parsley and pour it over the ham, stirring to make sure that the parslied stock is well distributed. Leave in the fridge to set.

## BLACKBERRY WATER ICE (OCTOBER 26th, 1967)

**This serves four but can so easily be doubled or trebled:**

*200ml/7 fl oz/⅓ cup water*

*175g/6oz/1 cup sugar*

*675g/1½lb blackberries to yield 300ml/1½ pt/1 cup juice*

Put the water and sugar together in a heavy saucepan over a moderate heat and let the sugar dissolve before bringing the syrup to boiling point, keep on a slow boil for 10–15 minutes and then cool.

Meanwhile press the berries through a fine sieve, or whizz in a food processor and then sieve. When the syrup is cold, stir in the blackberry juice. Pour into an ice tray and freeze covered with foil. The mixture will take about two to two and a half hours to set, but give it a good beating with a rotary whisk three or four times during that period.

## SMOKED SALMON QUICHE (NOVEMBER 10th, 1967)

This makes a pleasant lunch dish.

**You will need:**

*1 packet short crust pastry*

*2 tbsp butter*

*3 eggs and 1 extra egg yolk*

*300ml/½ pt/1 cup single cream*

*Salt and pepper*

*175g/6oz chopped smoked salmon*

Pre-heat the oven to 200°C/400°F/gas mark 6. Roll out the pastry thinly and line a tart tin or dish. Brush inside with the melted butter. Beat the eggs lightly, add the cream, stir well, add seasoning and stir well again. Lay the salmon over the uncooked pastry shell and pour over the cream and egg mixture. Brush the pastry with the remaining melted butter. Place in the centre of the pre-heated oven and cook for about 25 minutes.

## WINTER SALAD (NOVEMBER 10th, 1967)

This is a combination of endive, celery, avocado, Gruyère and chopped chives or celery. Cut celery and endives into slim pieces and keep in iced water till it is time to serve. Drain thoroughly, add slivers of not too ripe avocado and slivers of cheese. Toss in a good vinaigrette.

## CRÈME BRULÉE (NOVEMBER 10th, 1967)

This is one of the most luxurious of little puddings.

**You will need:**

*300ml/½ pt/1 cup double cream*

*1 vanilla pod*

*3 egg yolks*

*2 tbsp sugar*

*Some castor sugar, for sprinkling*

Pre-heat the oven to 150°C/300°F/gas mark 2. Pour the cream into a heavy, completely clean saucepan, put in the vanilla pod, bring slowly to the boil, then turn off the heat and leave to cool. Every now and again give the cream a stir to stop any skin from forming. In the meantime, whip the egg yolks and sugar together until white and frothy. Stir in the cooled cream and put the mixture in the top of a bain Marie.

Steadily stir the mixture with a wooden spoon over nearly boiling water, being very careful not to let it curdle, until it just starts to coat the spoon. Turn the creamy custard into little cocotte dishes or one shallow ovendish if you prefer. Cover the dish or dishes with foil and bake for quarter of an hour in the oven.

Take out, uncover and when cool evenly sprinkle the surface of the cocottes or dish with castor sugar so that there is no custard showing. Put the dish or cocottes in a baking pan then half fill it with cold water and put it under the hottest grill you can muster. Watch very carefully while it brulées. It will take about a minute for the sugar to turn from white crystals to a caramel-coloured syrup. Take from under the grill at once. When cool, the sugar will have set hard and clear.


## BABY LEEKS VINAIGRETTE (NOVEMBER 22nd, 1967)

Use only very young baby leeks, not much bigger than a plump asparagus stalk and allow three or four per person. Wipe carefully, remove any dirty outside leaves and cut off the stalk end. Lay in a large pan or frying pan with a lid, just cover with boiling, salted water to which a little lemon juice has been added, cover and cook quickly for five–eight minutes according to size. Drain thoroughly, processing every last bit of water out with a gentle squeeze of the fingers and leave them, green end down, in a colander to cool. Lay in a serving dish or put three or four on each plate. Make a good thick vinaigrette with salt and freshly ground black pepper, a teaspoon of Dijon mustard, a teaspoon of chopped parsley and a teaspoon of lemon juice. Add a dessertspoon each of white wine vinegar and a chopped shallot and four tablespoons of good virgin olive oil. Beat well. Garnish with a little extra chopped parsley or chives.


## PROVENÇALE DAUBE (JANUARY 5th, 1968)

There are so many versions of the French daube (braised meat) and, even if you are a small family, it is a good idea to make a large quantity because the rest can be frozen for another day.

### For 8–10 people you will need:

*2kg/4lb 8oz chuck or topside or shin of beef*

*4 finely chopped cloves of garlic*

*A small bunch of fresh marjoram chopped or 1 tbsp of dried*

*Salt and pepper*

*A marinade of 4 tbsp olive oil and 300ml/½ pt/1 cup red wine*

*225g/8 oz salt pork*

*2 tbsp oil*

*2 chopped onions*

*4 chopped carrots*

*300ml/½ pt/1 cup good stock or water*

*2 slices of orange peel*

Cut the beef into good bite-sized chunks and roll in a mixture of the chopped garlic and marjoram, salt and pepper. Put the beef in a large bowl, cover with the marinade of oil and wine and leave to marinate for at least three–four hours or better still, overnight.

Remove the meat, dry it, strain the marinade and reserve. Dice the salt pork, heat the olive oil in a large heavy fireproof casserole with a lid, put in the pork and cook gently until it is crisp then add the onions and carrots. Cook a little, then add the meat. Pre-heat the oven to 180 °C/300 °F/gas mark 2. In the meanwhile boil the strained marinade until reduced by a quarter, pour it over the meat and vegetables, add the stock or water and the slices of orange peel. Put a couple of sheets of greaseproof paper over the top of the casserole to trap the steam and put on the lid, or make a seal with a flour and water paste and cook the casserole in the low oven for about four hours. You can serve it in the casserole.

## PRESERVED GINGER CREAMS (JANUARY 5th, 1968)

This is a good Christmas/New Year dish for which those jars of preserved ginger in syrup come in useful. Quantities here serve eight.

**You will need:**

*A sprinkling of cinnamon and nutmeg*

*1 strip of lemon peel*

*600ml/1 pt/2 cups single cream*

*5–6 egg yolks*

*3 or 4 tbsp sugar*

*1 tbsp of ginger syrup*

*1–2 tbsp finely chopped ginger*

Put the cinnamon, nutmeg and lemon peel in the cream and bring it to the boil in a heavy saucepan. Beat the egg yolks very thoroughly with the sugar and slowly pour the hot cream into the mixture stirring well.

# RECIPES

Return the mixture to the rinsed saucepan and cook very gently, as for custard, until the mixture has thickened and coats the spoon. Take the pan off the stove, fish out the lemon peel and go on stirring until the cream has cooled. Then add the syrup and half the chopped ginger, distributing it well.

Leave in the fridge over night, stir well again so that the ginger does not sink to the bottom and pour into little custard or wine glasses. You can sprinkle more little bits of ginger over the top just before you serve them.

## TONNO E FAGIOLI (FEBRUARY 3rd, 1968)

This is a Tuscan *antipasto* made with white beans. White haricot beans or good butter beans will do. If they are dried soak a couple of handfuls overnight in plenty of water. Drain them, cover them with water again, bring to the boil and simmer for three hours or until tender. Add salt to taste. A short cut is to use a can or cans of haricots blancs depending on the number you are feeding.

Drain or strain the beans and arrange on a serving dish. Add a few strips of raw onions and plenty of good Tuscan virgin olive oil. Top with best quality tinned tuna (look for tuna from the *vetresca* or stomach) in squares.

*Fagiolini col Tonno* on the other hand, also makes a good starter and is made from little French beans, cooked *al dente,* drained, then, while they are still hot, pour a tablespoon or so of good virgin olive oil over them with a little lemon juice, salt and pepper. Again put squares of tinned tuna fish on top.

## PAUPIETTES OF VEAL OR PORK (FEBRUARY 3rd, 1968)

This is really a stuffed veal dish but, since veal is generally so expensive, you can just as well make it with pork fillet.

### For six people you will need:

*6 thin veal escalopes or slices cut from a pork fillet approximately 7½ × 10cm/ 3 × 4in. Beat them out with a rolling pin or the flat side of a meat chopper on a damp board till they are as thin as you can make them.*

**For the Farci:**

Salt and freshly ground black pepper

2 shallots

6 green olives

4 tbsp chopped lean ham

85g/3oz sausagemeat

4 small beaten eggs

A couple of sprigs of thyme

3 tbsp butter

450ml/16 fl oz/1½ cup good stock

Bouquet garni

Mashed potato, hot

1 good tbsp flour and 1 tsp of butter for a beurre manié

2–3 tbsp chopped parsley for garnish

**For the Mirepoix:**

Cut into dice (about ½cm/¼in square)

2 small onions

1 scraped carrot

1 parsnip

1 leek

3 Brussels sprouts

3 skinned and seeded tomatoes

150g/5½oz/½ cup tiny peas

When you have beaten out the slices of meat, season them on one side with salt and black pepper. Chop the shallots finely, stone and chop the olives and put in a basin with the chopped ham, sausage meat, beaten eggs and thyme. Season very well and mix thoroughly.

In the meantime have ready the Mirepoix of diced vegetables. Melt half the butter in a large wide pan, put in the Mirepoix and shake gently for a few minutes. Set aside.

Spread the farci thinly on the seasoned side of the meat, roll up from the wider edge and secure with cotton to form paupiettes.

Melt the rest of the butter in another pan and sauté the paupiettes gently until they turn a golden brown. Take them out and lay them on top of the Mirepoix, cover them with the stock, bring to the boil, then turn down the heat and simmer for about an hour.

Have ready a good potato purée or a purée of potato and celeriac and arrange it down the centre of a hot serving dish. Carefully remove the cotton from the paupiettes and lay on the purée. Cover with foil and keep warm while you strain the liquid from the pan and skim off any fat. Put the pan back on the stove and re-heat the liquid. Work the teaspoon of butter into the tablespoon of flour and add piece by piece to the liquid. Stir till boiling, adjust seasoning and reduce to a syrupy consistency. Spoon enough over the paupiettes and purée to coat, and serve the rest separately. Sprinkle the parsley over before serving.


### OMELETTES NORMANDE (FEBRUARY 3rd, 1968)

This is a good festive dish and, since we were a small number of good friends, I suspect I was just experimenting, the more especially as we were eating in the kitchen and I could do last minute things by the stove.

**For the apple filling (this should be made not more than two hours in advance):**

600g/1lb 5oz apples
*(or enough for about 3 cups when peeled, cored and sliced)*

*Juice of 1 lemon*

*175g/6oz/6 tbsp unsalted butter*

*175g/6oz/1 cup sugar*

*6 tbsp Calvados*

*100ml/3½ fl oz/⅓ cup double cream*

**For the omelettes:**

*8 medium eggs*

*A pinch of salt*

*4 tbsp sugar*

*175g/6oz/6 tbsp butter*

Peel, core and slice all the apples, sprinkling them with lemon juice to keep them from going brown.

Heat half the butter in a large heavy frying pan until it is chestnut coloured and foaming. Add just as many apples that will fit in one layer and sauté them over a high heat for between seven–ten minutes, stirring them every now and again to ensure that they do not burn. Remove the cooked apples, set them aside, add more butter to the pan and repeat until all the apples are done.

Return all of the apples to the pan, sprinkle them with the sugar and stir gently for a couple of minutes until the sugar caramelises. Then pour in half of the Calvados, set alight and shake the pan until the flame subsides. Remove the pan from the heat, wait till the bubbling subsides, stir in the cream and tip the apple mixture into a bowl.

The actual omelettes should be made just before serving. Put a good-sized serving platter – preferably oval – to warm in the oven.

Separate three of the eggs and beat the egg whites with a pinch of salt until they are firm. Add two tablespoons of the sugar and continue to beat until the whites are stiff. Beat the whole eggs, the egg yolks and the remaining sugar with a fork, but not too vigourously. Then fold in the beaten egg whites.

Separate the mixture into equal amounts to make two omelettes. Set an omelette pan over high heat and melt half the butter until it is brown and foaming. When the foam subsides pour in the first lot of egg mixture. Let it cook for not quite half a minute – just long enough to set the exterior and do not cook any longer. Remove the pan from the heat, put half the apple mixture in the centre of the omelette, fold, then slide down to the edge of the pan, grasping the handle of the pan from underneath. In one motion invert the pan over the middle of the serving dish so that the bottom of the omelettes will be on top. Make the next omelettes in exactly the same way and, when both are on the serving dish, sprinkle each of them with two tablespoons of sugar. Heat the rest of the Calvados and pour it over the omelettes. Set them aflame and, as the Calvados runs to the bottom of the dish, spoon it back over the omelettes to caramelise them.

### ENDIVE AND OLIVE SALAD (FEBRUARY 7th, 1968)

All you do for this is rub a peeled garlic clove all over a crust of bread until the garlic is used up. Douse the bread with a tablespoon of good virgin olive oil and cover with about 20 small black olives, stoned. Cut a thin slice from the base of a couple of endives, remove the damaged outer leaves and tear the rest into the bowl on top of the olives. Leave to stand for an hour or so before seasoning with a good squeeze of lemon juice, salt and black pepper. Mix very well before serving. Sometimes I also add some slices of very well skinned orange from which any pips and pith have been removed.

## CHOCOLATE MERINGUE MOUSSE (FEBRUARY 7th, 1968)

This is one of those always good, gooey meringue puddings and useful for using up left-over coffee.

**For six you will need:**

*5 tbsp strong coffee*

*225g/8oz sweet dark chocolate and an additional 115g/4oz all broken into small pieces*

*3 eggs, separated*

*300ml/½ pt/1 cup milk*

*½ tsp vanilla extract or essence*

*A pinch of salt*

*250g/8oz/1⅓ cup castor sugar*

*Small pieces of candied orange peel (optional)*

Put three tablespoons of the coffee and 225g/8oz broken up chocolate into a small enamelled saucepan, set over a low heat and stir until it is completely smooth. Remove the pan from the heat, stir in the egg yolks and the milk, return to the heat and cook, stirring constantly until the mixture begins to thicken. Add the vanilla extract or essence and continue to stir until it is almost simmering then immediately set aside.

Now, in another saucepan, partially melt the additional pieces of chocolate with the remaining two tablespoons of coffee. Before the chocolate has completely melted, and in very small bits, stir it into the other chocolate cream. This will result in tiny bits of hard chocolate distributed throughout the cream.

Next beat the egg whites with a pinch of salt until they turn white and frothy, then beat in a spoonful of sugar at a time until you get a firm and shiny meringue. Gently fold a quarter of the meringue into the chocolate cream and then fold the whole lot back into the rest of the meringue. Pour into a serving bowl and when quite cool put it in the fridge to set. Serve it nice and cold with, if you want, some chopped candied orange on top.

## AL DENTE VEGETABLES WITH A THICK VINAIGRETTE SAUCE (FEBRUARY 20th, 1968)

This is a good, fresh, healthy starter. Choose whatever vegetables are in season and to hand like tiny Brussels sprouts, blanched in boiling salted water for two–four minutes, rinsed in cold water to hold the greeness and well drained. Also, for example:

Spring onions or scallions, plunged for 60 seconds in boiling salted water and well-drained.

A cauliflower divided into individual flowerets, plunged for two–four minutes in boiling, salted water with a squeeze of lemon juice and well-drained.

Broccoli divided similarly into individual flowerets and also plunged for two–four minutes in boiling salted water, rinsed in cold water and well-drained.

Baby leeks cooked as the recipe for November 22, 1967.

Baby white mushrooms, washed under running water, immersed in cold, salted water, drained well and rubbed with the cut half of a lemon.

Arrange the various vegetables on a dish, sprinkle with chopped parsley or chives and serve separately with a thick vinaigrette made with three teaspoons of Dijon mustard, four tablespoons of good virgin olive oil, one dessertspoon of white wine vinegar, two finely chopped shallots, and seasoned with salt and pepper.

## SWEET ORANGE SALAD (FEBRUARY 20th, 1968)

I say sweet orange salad to distinguish it from an equally good and refreshing salad made from Seville oranges (made in the same way). However, Sevilles have a short season and are not always easy to get whereas an ordinary orange can be bought anytime and pretty well anywhere.

Allow one orange per person. Peel, remove as much of the pith as you can, cut into horizontal slices, put into a serving dish, sprinkle generously with castor sugar and one teaspoon per person of Grand Marnier or Curaçao. Leave to marinade in the fridge for several hours.

# RECIPES

## TIMBALES OF LETTUCE (APRIL 15th, 1968)

This would be particularly good in the summer if you had a vegetable garden with a whole row of lettuces looking as if they are going to run to seed unless you do something about it – and quick. However this was spring and I guess I was just experimenting in the country where there always seemed to be more time to mess around. If you have individual half-cup baking dishes use them, otherwise you can use a regular baking dish.

**For eight–ten people you will need:**

*8 tight heads of lettuce or 10–12 little gem lettuces*

*Salt, freshly ground black pepper and nutmeg*

*5 tbsp butter, plus extra to grease*

*6 tbsp minced shallots, spring onions or scallions*

*375g/13oz/3 cups of very stale breadcrumbs from good bread with an extra tbsp finer breadcrumbs*

*300ml/½ pt/1 cup cold milk*

*5 eggs*

*150ml/5 fl oz/½ cup double cream*

*115g/4oz/½ cup grated Parmesan or 175g/6oz/¾ cup grated Gruyèré*

*Finely chopped parsley, to garnish*

Trim the lettuces and separate the leaves. Throw them into a large saucepan of boiling water and add a teaspoon of salt when they come to the boil again. Go on boiling uncovered for 8–10 minutes to blanch the lettuce (the bottom part of the leaves should still be hard and the leaf part limp). Drain, refresh under running water, then squeeze a handful at a time to get rid of as much water as possible. Chop coarsely and set aside.

Now melt the butter and sauté the minced shallots, spring onions or scallions until they are soft but not coloured, then add the chopped lettuce leaves and cook gently for another 10–15 minutes or so until every last bit of moisture has evaporated. Take off the stove and pre-heat the oven to 190°C/375°F/gas mark 5.

While the lettuce is cooking, soak the breadcrumbs in the milk and mash them with a fork until all the milk has been absorbed. Beat the eggs and combine with the breadcrumbs and lettuce adding the cream, and grated cheese. Blend very well and season well with salt, pepper and nutmeg.

Grease the moulds (or mould) with butter, line the bottoms with buttered waxed paper – buttered side up – and sprinkle with the extra finer breadcrumbs. Fill with the lettuce mixture, place in a shallow pan and pour in water to come about a third of the way up the sides of the moulds or mould. Carefully put the pan on top of the stove and bring the water to a simmer, then put the pan in the oven to cook for about 15 minutes for the little moulds or 30–35 minutes for the large one – or until the mixture is firm and has shrunk a little from the sides.

Unmould gently, peel off the waxed paper, sprinkle the timbales with some finely chopped parsley and serve.

### POULET ANTIBOISE (MAY 14th, 1968)

This was based on another Elizabeth David recipe which I've adapted from her *A Book of Mediterranean Food*.

**For four–six people you will need:**

*8 tbsp olive oil plus extra if needed*

*1kg/2lb 4oz sliced onions*

*Salt, a little cayenne pepper and black pepper*

*1 good-sized chicken*

*A handful of black olives*

*12 small squares of bread, fried in olive oil till crisp*

*A little chopped parsley for garnishing*

Pre-heat the oven to 170 °C/325 °F/gas mark 3. Pour the oil into a deep casserole, pile the sliced onions on top and season with a little salt, cayenne pepper and black pepper. Put the cleaned, seasoned chicken on top of the onions, cover the casserole and cook gently in the oven for about an hour and a half. Although it is important to check the dish every now and then, the onions must not brown – turn the oven down if you see any signs of colouring – but rather almost melt into a purée. Add a little more oil if it seems necessary. When the chicken is tender, carve it into pieces and serve on a dish with the onions all around, together with some stoned black olives and the squares of freshly fried bread. Sprinkle with the parsley

## COLD ASPARAGUS MIMOSA WITH A MUSTARD VINAIGRETTE (MAY 23rd, 1968)

This is a good fresh spring and early-summer dish and the sieved hard boiled egg really does look like scattered mimosa flowers.

Allow 225g/8oz young green asparagus per person. Trim off the fibrous parts of the stalks, tie into bundles and put these tips in a large saucepan of boiling salted water. Cook for about five minutes or until nicely al dente. Drain, refresh in cold water and lay out on sheets of paper towel to dry.

In the meantime, hard boil two eggs and mix about three tablespoons of chopped parsley, chervil and chives together. Put one and a half tablespoons of Dijon mustard into a bowl with three tablepoons of white wine vinegar. Mix well, then, very gradually, add ten–twelve tablespoons of good virgin olive oil, beating it well and not allowing the sauce to separate. If it does, beat harder until it comes together again before adding more oil. Season well with salt and pepper.

Peel the hard boiled eggs and separate the yolk from the whites. Rub the yolks through a sieve to get a Mimosa like effect. Arrange the asparagus on a large dish, sprinkle with the herbs, pour some of the mustard vinaigrette over the tips and sprinkle with the 'mimosa'. Hand round the rest of the sauce separately, giving it a good stir if it looks on the verge of separating.

## GIGOT D'AGNEAU PROVENÇALE (MAY 30th, 1968)

This takes rather longer than a conventional English roast but is usually meltingly good.

You will need to allow some two hours for a 2 kilo/ just over 4lb leg of lamb.

*2kg/4lb leg of lamb*

*3 cloves of garlic*

*Several stalks of rosemary*

*Salt, pepper, finely sliced rosemary or thyme leaves, chopped and olive oil*

*3 onions*

*1 large aubergine (eggplant) sliced, sprinkled with salt, left to drain,
then dried well*

*1 red pepper*

*6 tomatoes, skinned and chopped*

*12 black olives*

Pre-heat the oven to 220 °C/425 °F/gas mark 7. Make a lot of small
incisions with a sharp pointed knife all over the joint. Cut two of the
cloves of garlic into slithers and insert one through each incision. Do
the same with the little rosemary spikes or thyme leaves. Brush the
meat with some olive oil and put it in a roasting pan in the centre of the
oven. After 10 minutes baste and reduce the heat to 180 °C/350 °F/gas
mark 4.

Chop the onions and put them under the meat to cook. After about
20 minutes baste the meat again and then spread the aubergine slices
around the meat. Let them cook for around 45 minutes turning them
over half way through. Now add the finely sliced red pepper and
season both the meat and the vegetables with salt and pepper. Let
another half an hour go by before adding the skinned and chopped
tomatoes and the third clove of garlic finely chopped. A few minutes
before serving, stir in the stoned olives and chopped rosemary or
thyme.

Carve and serve the meat on a large dish surrounded by its rich
vegetable sauce.

## TARTELETTES À LA DIJONNAISE (JULY 30th, 1968)

These tartlets make quite an easy starter for a large party.

**For 24 small tartlets you will need:**

*2 packets of short crust pastry (Reserve any left over pastry for later)*

*24 tartlet well-greased moulds or muffin tins*

*2 tbsp Dijon mustard*

*115g/4oz/½ cup grated Emmenthal or Gruyèré plus another
115g/4oz/½ cup cheese for later*

*1 tbsp olive oil*

# RECIPES

**For the Tomato filling you will need:**

*3 tbsp olive oil*

*1 small onion chopped fine*

*1.3kg/3lb ripe skinned, seeded, juiced and chopped tomatoes or two tins of whole Italian plum tomatoes drained and chopped*

*2 large finely chopped cloves of garlic*

*½ tsp each of dried thyme, oregano, marjoram and savory*

*Salt and black pepper*

Roll out the pastry thinly and line the moulds. Brush the mustard evenly over the pastry shells and sprinkle with the cheese. Prick the bottom crusts and put in the fridge to firm.

Pre-heat the oven to 180 °C/350 °F/gas mark 4 and partially bake the shells for 10–12 minutes. Remove from the oven but keep the oven heated at the same temperature if you are serving the tartlets soon.

Heat the olive oil in a pan, add the chopped onions and cook them stirring occasionally, until they are soft but not coloured. Add the tomatoes, the finely chopped garlic, half of the herbs and some salt and freshly ground pepper. Simmer fresh tomatoes for 5–10 minutes but do not allow them to become a pulp because you will want them to retain their shape. Tinned tomatoes will only take a few minutes. Fill the pastry cases with the tomato mixture, sprinkle with a tablespoon of olive oil and the remaining herbs, finishing with the grated cheese and put back in the oven for about 15 minutes or until the pastry is reheated and the cheese has formed a glazed crust mostly hiding the tomatoes. Unmould and serve.

## BOEUF À LA MODE PROVENÇALE (JULY 30th, 1968)

This is a great summer party dish because a comparatively small amount of beef goes a long way and it *has* to be cooked the day before.

These quantities are for eight people but obviously you can magnify or reduce them as needed, although you will need several fireproof casseroles for a lot of people.

293

*1.8kg/4lb round or topside of beef*

*225g/8oz bacon cut into small pieces or smoked lardons*

*3 cloves of garlic, peeled and slivered*

*3 or 4 tbsp bacon fat*

*4 sliced onions*

*3–4 tbsp butter*

*A calf's foot, cut up*

*5–6 chopped carrots*

*A piece of celery*

*A piece each of orange and lemon peel*

*2 bay leaves, a small bunch of thyme, 12 peppercorns, 6 cloves*

*1 bottle of cheap red wine*

Make incisions all over the beef and lard it with the small pieces of bacon or lardons and the slivers of garlic. Tie round with string, season with salt and pepper and brown it on all sides in very hot bacon fat.

Fry the onions in the butter till brown then put the beef in a deep casserole, cover with the onions and add the calf's foot, carrots, celery, peel, bay leaves, thyme, peppercorns and cloves, then cover with half water, half red wine. Cook extremely slowly either on top of the stove or in the oven 140°C/275°F/gas mark 1 for seven or eight hours.

Remove the meat, which should be so soft it can be cut with a spoon, remove the calf's foot, take off the string around the beef and put the meat in a serving dish. Strain the sauce over the joint and, when it is quite cold, remove the fat with a spoon constantly dipped in very hot water. The meat should now be covered with a soft, clear jelly and is ready to serve, garnished with sprigs of parsley or tomatoes or whatever you prefer.

## PEACHES WITH A RASPBERRY PURÉE (AUGUST 18th, 1968)

I seem to remember reading in one of Elizabeth David's many, many erudite articles about food that the exquisite peach should never be messed up (although I am sure that as the elegant writer she was she would never have used such careless colloquialisms). Alas, it is hard to get really exquisite peaches nowadays and this dish of peaches – or nectarines – enveloped in a raspberry purée made by whizzing the raspberries in a food processor with three or four tablespoons of sugar and perhaps a tablespoon of Kirsch, sieving it for pips, then cooling it in the fridge – is a refreshing end to a dinner.

## PIPERADE (OCTOBER 13th, 1968)

This is a very well known provençale dish of peppers, onions and tomatoes with beaten eggs but now that I live in Provençe, I curiously cannot recollect seeing it on any menus. It makes a good light lunch or supper dish with some good crusty bread and, perhaps a salad, as well as a starter before a cold main course.

**For four–six people you will need:**

*2 large red onions*

*4 tbsp olive oil*

*450g/1lb mixed red, yellow and green peppers*

*450g/1lb skinned and chopped tomatoes*

*A few leaves of basil, ripped*

*2 cloves of finely chopped garlic*

*Sea salt and black pepper*

*5 eggs*

Chop the onions and cook them gently in the oil in a heavy frying or sauté pan until they start to colour. Cut the peppers in half, deseed, cut away the pith, cut in to strips and add to the onions. Go on cooking gently for 10 minutes before you add the chopped tomatoes, basil and the finely chopped garlic. Cook for another 10 minutes and add some sea salt and black pepper. Take the vegetable mixture off the heat for a few minutes while you beat the eggs. Season them, then pour them into the pan, put the pan back on a low heat and stir constantly for a few minutes until the eggs have set and blended with the juices.

## GREEK HONEY TART (OCTOBER 13th, 1968)

This recipe, from Jean Robertson, comes from the Isle of Siphnos and is known as Siphniac honey pie. The Greeks use an unsalted Greek sheep's milk cheese called *myzithra* but fresh milk, cottage cheese or any good cream cheese can be used instead.

### For four–six people you will need:

*A packet of short crust pastry or homemade short crust*

*225g/8oz of cottage or cream cheese*

*4 tbsp clear warmed honey*

*4 tbsp castor sugar*

*2 eggs, beaten*

*Large pinch of cinnamon, plus extra for sprinkling*

Pre-heat the oven to 200 °C/400 °F/gas mark 6. Roll out the pastry thinly and line a greased tart, flan tin or flat pie dish. Soften the cream cheese with a fork and add the honey, work the cheese and honey together well then add the sugar, the beaten eggs and a good pinch of cinnamon. Mix well and pour into the pastry case. Bake for 30 minutes. Sprinkle with a little more cinnamon and leave to cool. You can serve warm or cold.

## TARTE NORMANDE (OCTOBER 13th, 1968)

This is just a simple – but delicious – apple tart and was one of my family's favourites.

### For 6–8 people you will need:

*A packet of short crust pastry or homemade short crust*

*8 medium sized apples*

*4 tbsp butter*

*4 tbsp sugar*

*A small piece or two of lemon peel*

*6 tbsp apricot jam (optional)*

*Whiped cream, crème fraîche or ice cream, to serve*

Roll out the pastry and line a tart tin or earthenware pie dish and prick the base well. Put it in the fridge to set. Pre-heat the oven to 200 °C/ 400 °F/gas mark 6.

Peel, quarter, core and slice the apples evenly. Melt the butter in a large pan and add as many of the apple slices in one layer that you can. Sprinkle with the sugar. You may need to do two lots. Add the lemon peel and toss gently with a spatula until the apple slices are soft but still hold their shape. Take out carefully with a slicer and set aside. Set aside separately the buttery-sugary juices. Sometimes I paint the base with apricot jam, sometimes I just use the apples plain and simple. Arrange the apple slices in overlapping circles around the pastry and pour over a little of the buttery juice.

Put the tart in the oven for about 20–30 minutes. Keep an eye on it and, if it looks as if it will burn, turn the oven down. You can serve it hot or warm but, just before you serve it, heat up the rest of the buttery juices and pour over the apples. The tart can be served with whipped cream, crème fraîche or ice cream.

## PAIN DE SOLE (NOVEMBER 1st, 1968)

This was another showy dish that I made in those days, which was probably more of a restaurant dish than a home one, but interesting to make on occasion. You could make it with less expensive fish than sole like hake or cod, weighed after all skin and bone is removed, but the sole is particularly delicate.

**For six people you will need:**

*300ml/½ pt/1 cup milk*

*4 tbsp butter*

*4 tbsp flour*

*Salt and black pepper*

*450g/1lb of fillet of sole whizzed in the food processor and pounded well*

*2 eggs, beaten*

*150ml/5 fl oz/½ cup double cream*

*Some sprigs of parsley, watercress or chopped chives for garnish*

Heat the milk and, in a separate saucepan, melt the butter and add the flour off the heat, stir well to make a roux, put the pan back on the heat and add the hot milk bit by bit till the mixture is smooth and bubbling. Season very well, take off the stove again and cool completely. When cold, pound in the fish, then add the eggs and the cream, mix very well together and adjust the seasoning. Pour into a buttered mould and either steam in a large steamer or cover and poach in a pan a third full of simmering water for about 40 minutes. Leave to set for a few minutes before running a sharp knife around the edges and turning out onto a dish.

**While the fish is cooking, make a velouté sauce with:**

*1½ tbsp butter*

*1½ tbsp flour*

*100ml/3½ fl oz/⅓ cup fish stock*

*100ml/3½ fl oz/⅓ cup Vermouth or white wine*

*Or if fish stock is hard to come by 200ml/7 fl oz/⅔ cup Vermouth or white wine*

*4 tbsp single cream*

*The juice of ¼ lemon*

Melt butter, add the flour off the stove to make a roux, put the pan back on a low heat, stirring all the time and gradually mix in the stock and wine or all wine. When it is amalgamated and thick, gradually add the cream, season, bring to the boil and turn down the heat so the sauce barely simmers. Add a squeeze of lemon juice and pour over the pain de sole as soon as it has been turned onto the serving dish. Garnish with a few sprigs of parsley, watercress or chopped chives and serve.

## PÂTÉ MAISON (NOVEMBER 27th, 1968)

This is an uncomplicated little pâté to serve with hot toast.

**For four–six people you will need:**

*450g/1lb cleaned chicken livers*

*85g/3oz/6 tbsp softened butter*

# RECIPES

*75ml/2½ fl oz/5 tbsp sherry*

*75ml/2½ fl oz/5 tbsp brandy*

*Salt, freshly ground black pepper, a pinch of mixed spice*

*A minced clove of garlic*

*A pinch of dried thyme, marjoram or basil*

Sauté the chicken livers in two tablespoons of the butter for just three or four minutes. Scoop out the sautéed livers and set aside while you add to the pan a small glass of sherry and another of brandy. Mash the livers to a fine paste with plenty of salt, freshly ground black pepper, the garlic, the spice, the herbs and the rest of the softened butter. Stir in the liquid from the pan. When it is all amalgamated, pack into a small earthenware terrine and put in the fridge to set.


## SOUFFLÉ OMELETTE WITH GRAND MARNIER
### (DECEMBER 2nd, 1968)

This is baked in the oven as opposed to being cooked in an omelette pan on top of the stove. It needs as much care as a soufflé.

**For six–eight people you will need:**

*85g/3oz/6 tbsp sugar, plus 1 tbsp*

*4 well beaten egg yolks*

*3–4 tbsp Grand Marnier or, if you prefer, rum*

*6 egg whites*

*A little icing sugar to sprinkle*

Pre-heat the oven to 180°C/350°F/gas mark 4. Pour the sugar into a bowl, make a hole in the centre, add the beaten yolks and mix with a wooden spoon. Beat until the mixture runs from the spoon in a long, shining ribbon. Add a tablespoon of the Grand Marnier (or rum) then beat the whites till stiff, add a tablespoon to the egg and sugar mixture, fold in gently, then gently fold that mixture into the rest of the stiffly beaten whites. Butter a fireproof dish and pile the mixture in, piling it

299

up to form an oval about 8–10cm/3¼–4 inches high. Smooth with a palette knife then, with a flat blade, make a depression the whole length of the omelette with small slashes either side. Set the dish on a medium hot plate for just one or two minutes to set it, then put in the centre of the pre-heated oven for about five–six minutes. Turn the dish for another five–six minutes and, if you are worried about it burning, cover loosely with a sheet of greaseproof paper or foil. In the meantime, turn the grill to high. When it is very hot, take the soufflé omelette out of the oven, sprinkle with the icing sugar and put under the very hot grill for a few minutes until the sugar turns golden.

While the omelette is under the grill, quickly heat the Grand Marnier or the rum in a saucepan with the extra sugar and pour over the soufflé just before you serve it.

## SEAKALE WITH ELIZA ACTON'S NORFOLK SAUCE (APRIL 11th, 1969)

Seakale is a not much known late-winter vegetable that, as Jean Robertson described so succinctly, looks like a cross between chicory and celery and has a flavour that puts it on a par with artichokes and asparagus. Like the latter two, it is at its best well-cleaned (the black roots get very dirty), tied into bundles of five or six, then boiled, or better still, steamed and served with a simple butter sauce. The winter must have been very late that year or the seakale would not have been around to have on the menu. It is particularly good with the Nineteenth Century cookery writer, Eliza Acton's Norfolk Sauce – an English version of the French *Sauce Beurre Blanc*.

Mrs Acton suggests that you simply put three tablespoons of water in a small saucepan, bring it to the boil and add 125g/4½oz/¾ cup of butter cut into pieces. Do not let the water boil again, but let the butter dissolve, take the saucepan from the heat, and shake it around till the butter and water have quite amalgamated and the sauce looks thick and smooth. Serve immediately.

## HANNAH GLASS' ALMOND CUSTARD (APRIL 11th, 1969)

I was obviously in old English mode for this dinner – Hannah Glass was another Victorian cook.

# RECIPES

**For four–six people you will need:**

*300ml/½ pt/1 cup double cream*

*2 large eggs separated*

*2 tbsp of castor sugar*

*4 tbsp skinned and pulverised almonds*

*A drop or two of pure almond essence*

Bring the cream to scalding point in a double saucepan then remove the top half of the pan from the hot water underneath and let it cool. While you are waiting for it to do so, beat the egg yolks with the sugar till the mixture is white and frothy and stir in the almonds so that they are well intregrated. Pour the mixture into the cooled cream and put the bain-marie back on the heat, stirring constantly till the custard coats the back of the (preferably) wooden spoon. Whip the egg whites till stiff and fold them into the custard. Add a drop or two of the almond essence. Preheat the oven to 170 °C/325 °F/gas mark 3.

Pour the custard into little glasses, set them in a pan of water, cover with foil and bake in the moderate oven for about 25–30 minutes or until set. Serve cold.


## INDIVIDUAL CHEESE SOUFFLÉS (MAY 9th, 1969)

These are delicious, very rich and very sinful little individual soufflés served with a tarragon cream sauce. These days I certainly would not serve them just before the veal escalopes with a cucumber cream sauce as I did then. For soufflés, they are quite tough, and have the rare virtue that they can be baked beforehand and then reheated up to 24 hours later in a bain marie 180 °C/350 °F/gas mark 4 preheated oven for six–eight minutes.They might not puff up quite as much as the first time round but the taste is excellent.

**For eight people you will need 16 little ramekin dishes or timbale moulds and:**

*2 tbsp butter, for greasing*

*3 level tbsp (self-raising) flour*

*300ml/½ pt/1 cup milk*

*Salt, freshly ground black pepper and nutmeg*

*4 egg yolks*

*5 egg whites*

*115g/4oz/½ cup grated Gruyèré or Emmenthal*

**For the Tarragon Sauce you will need:**

*450ml/16oz/1½ cups double cream*

*4–5 tbsp chopped fresh tarragon*

*Salt and freshly ground black pepper*

First heavily butter the little dishes and put them in the fridge to chill.

Pour the flour into an enamelled saucepan and very gradually add the milk, a little at a time, stirring with a whisk or wooden spoon or spatula to make a smooth paste. Pour in the rest of the milk and stir very well. Season with a little salt and a lot of freshly ground black pepper and nutmeg. The mixture must be highly seasoned.

Now set over a medium heat and stir for several minutes until the mixture is very smooth and thick, remove from the stove and set aside to cool a little. Preheat the oven to 190°C/375°F/gas mark 5.

Separate all five eggs. Drop four yolks, one by one, into the warm (but not hot) milk mixture, mixing one in thoroughly before adding the next. Beat the five whites with a little salt till stiff and peaked – but not dry. If, by then, the milk and egg mixture has got too cold you can put it back on the stove to warm it a little, but only a little. Now fold in the stiffly beaten egg whites, gradually sprinkling in the grated cheese at the same time.

Fill the ramekins or timbale dishes two-thirds full of the mixture, put them in a shallow baking pan and pour water into the pan: it should come just two-thirds of the way up the sides of the moulds. Bring the water to a simmer on top of the stove then, very carefully – so as not to slop the hot water – put the pan in the centre of the pre-heated oven for about 12–15 minutes. If the water shows any sign of boiling turn the temperature down a little. The soufflés are done when they have risen a good three quarters of an inch above the top of the moulds. If you intend to serve the soufflés right away, while they are baking, you should butter a flat ovenproof dish and also make the sauce by boiling the cream with four tablespoons of the tarragon, seasoning it well and letting it simmer slowly for several minutes until it takes on the taste of the tarragon.

When the soufflés are risen, take them out and do not worry if they sink a little. Leave the oven on. Unmould the soufflés upside down onto the buttered dish, pour the boiling sauce over and around them and return them to the oven for another 10–12 minutes or until they swell and absorb almost all of the tarragon cream. Serve right away in the same dish sprinkled, if you like, with a little more tarragon.

### CHICKEN AND GRAPE SALAD (MAY 20th, 1969)

This is always a good summer lunch dish and you can make it either with a poached chicken and a light mayonnaise (with or without some chopped chives), or with a cream and lemon sauce, as with the Chicken Veronique recipe below (or even a little curry powder if you want something a little more spicy).

### POULET VERONIQUE (MAY 25th, 1969)

This is another very nice cold chicken dish. 'Veronique' usually implies a dish garnished with grapes but not this old recipe, another variation of Elizabeth David's, which she said was far superior to the usual chicken salad with mayonnaise. In any case you could easily add some grapes to the dish if you wanted.

For four-six people poach a chicken as for the cold chicken recipe on page 235. Let it cool in the stock, then remove all the skin and bone and divide it into neat pieces.

**For the sauce you will need:**

*2 yolks of eggs*

*300ml/½ pt/1 cup double cream*

*75ml/2 fl oz/5 tbsp sherry*

*Salt and freshly ground black pepper*

*The finely chopped peel of one lemon*

Beat up the yolks with the cream, gradually adding the sherry then stir in a heavy pan over a low flame until it has thickened slightly. If you are worried about curdling you could stir the sauce in a double saucepan. When it is ready, season it well, pour it over the chicken and sprinkle it with the lemon peel. The sauce will thicken as it gets cold.

## VEAL ESCALOPES EN PAPILLOTTE (MAY 30th, 1969)

*En papillote* means in a paper case, although foil is just as good. You can season the veal escalopes, squeeze a little lemon juice over them and perhaps add some herbs like thyme or coriander plus a sprinkling of lemon zest. Or you can layer them with a little Duxelles of mushrooms or fennel or a mirepoix of vegetables. Either way, wrap them fairly loosely in foil, making sure the packages are sealed tight, and bake them in a pre-heated 180 °C/350 °F/gas mark 4 oven for 15–20 minutes. You can either serve them still in their *papilllottes* so that guests can unwrap them on their plates, or unwrap them, put them on a serving dish with some watercress or parsley and serve them immediately. The point of the *papillottes* is that they retain all the juices of the meat and that whatever garnish you use tastes its unalloyed best.

## NOISETTES D'AGNEAU WITH SAUCE CHEVREUIL
## (JUNE 5th, 1969)

Oh, what a debt we do owe to Elizabeth David and her various books. This was based on a recipe from *A Book of Mediteranean Food* which was first published by John Lehman as far back as 1950. I don't quite know why I thought to serve a venison sauce on lamb but it was good anyway, especially on indifferent lamb.

**You will need:**

*250ml/9 fl oz/¾ cup red wine (Mrs David said Burgundy if possible, but really, any reasonable red wine will do)*

*2 tbsp red wine vinegar*

*2 level tbsp caster sugar*

*½ lemon, peeled and cut into small dice*

*4 or 5 tbsp redcurrant jelly*

*1 tbsp butter*

*1 tbsp flour*

*200ml/7 fl oz/⅔ cup good stock*

*A good pinch of pepper*

# RECIPES

Put 200ml/7 fl oz/⅔ cup red wine into a saucepan with the vinegar, the sugar and the pieces of lemon. Mix in the jelly and boil until it is reduced by half. Meanwhile, in another saucepan, melt the butter, mix in the flour, stir well till smooth, add the stock and the rest of the wine and cook slowly for 20 minutes. Mix the contents of the two saucepans together, put though a sieve and reheat.

## STRAWBERRY SYLLABUB (JUNE 5th, 1969)

This is just a variation on one of the many recipes for the old English dish, syllabub. I simply added some finely chopped strawberries to the recipe given for syllabub (p. 222). A variation would be the addition of a couple of tablespoons of strawberry purée.

## CHICKEN WITH PRUNES (JULY 5th,1969)

This is a dish that became very popular in the 1980s as a party dish which could equally well be served hot or cold but was not so much known 20 years before. It has to be started at least the day before, in fact it can be started a couple of days before, which may improve the taste.

These are quantities for around 20 plus, which is what I was catering for that evening, but they can easily be lessened or expanded according to numbers. If you are short on time, or appropriately sharp knives, you can just buy chicken pieces rather than quartering chickens. (But that was not so easy then, except with a willing butcher. Now every supermarket offers chickens in every which way.)

**You will need:**

*8 medium chickens cut in quarters*
*(or the equivalent in breasts, thighs, wings and drumsticks)*
*1 whole head of garlic, peeled and crushed, and 4 extra cloves*
*4 tbsp dried oregano*
*Salt and freshly ground black pepper*
*300ml/½ pt/1 cup olive oil*
*300ml/½ pt/1 cup red wine vinegar*
*225gs/8oz/1 cup of capers, with a little of the juice from the bottle*
*8 bay leaves*

*450g/1lb/2 cups pitted prunes*

*225g/8oz/1 cup pitted Spanish green olives*

*450g/1lb/3 cups brown sugar*

*600ml/1 pt/2 cups white wine*

*A big bunch of fresh coriander, finely chopped*

Put the chicken quarters or pieces in a very large bowl (or two bowls) with the peeled and puréed garlic cloves, the oregano, seasonings, olive oil, vinegar, capers, bay leaves, prunes and olives. Cover and leave to marinate over night.

The next day, preheat the oven to 180 °C/350 °F/gas mark 4. Arrange the chicken in a single layer in two large shallow earthenware dishes or baking pans and pour the same amount of marinade over each. Scatter the chicken pieces with the brown sugar, pour the white wine around each dish and bake for 50 minutes to an hour, basting frequently with the pan juices. As usual, you can test if the chicken is really done by pricking the thickest part of the thigh to see if the juice runs out a clear yellow. When you are satisfied that it is quite cooked, transfer the chicken, prunes, olives and capers (using a slotted spoon) to a couple of large serving plates. Moisten with a few spoonfuls of the pan juices and sprinkle lavishly with the coriander. Pass the remaining pan juices separately.

You can also serve the dish cold by letting the chicken cool in its juices before ladling it onto the serving dishes. If you have covered and refrigerated it overnight, let it return to room temperature before serving. And again, spoon some of the reserved pan juices over the chicken pieces.

## SALMON MOUSSE WITH CUCUMBER SAUCE (JULY 23rd, 1969)

This is one of the most classic of summer dishes and especially practical if you have any salmon or salmon trout left over from the night before. You can follow the recipe for smoked salmon mousse (p. 257). You can either make the accompanying cucumber sauce by simply peeling, chopping up into small squares, salting and draining a cucumber and adding some chopped chives. Or you can peel and grate an ice cold cucumber into 150ml/5 fl oz/½ cup sour cream or crème fraîche, then season with salt, freshly ground black pepper and a teaspoon of tarragon vinegar. Stir thoroughly.

# RECIPES

## PUFFY POTATOES (AUGUST 17th, 1969)

I always thought that these puffy potatoes were a good accompaniment to any barbecued meat or chicken but I was never too pleased with what I'd achieved. However, the first time I visited Sydney, Australia I was much more impressed with the ones that Judy Lance had cooked. Her secret was to cut in half as many potatoes as were needed and to soak them in very salty water – at least four–six well dissolved tablespoons of salt – for at least an hour. Have ready a very hot oven (240 °C/475 °F/gas mark 9), and when you want to cook them just remove the potatoes from the water without drying them, place them – cut side up – in a roasting pan (or two, depending on quantities) and cook them until they are a puffy, golden brown – about 30 minutes. Serve some butter separately, as with baked potatoes.

## VEAL AND TOMATO CASSEROLE (AUGUST 30th, 1969)

This is really just another version of a veal fricassée. It can be made with so many variations and additions that it is worth making double the quantities so that you have the foundation ready for a different version. It can be made with fresh or tinned tomatoes.

**For six people you will need:**

3 tbsp olive oil

2 large sliced onions

1.3kg/3lb chopped stewing veal

Salt, freshly ground pepper, paprika and basil or thyme with some extra for garnishing

900g/2lb skinned and seeded tomatoes or 1 large tin

150ml/5 fl oz/½ cup sour cream or crème fraîche

Heat the oil, sauté the onions until golden, then add the pieces of veal and sauté them till golden on all sides. Sprinkle generously with paprika and stir very well before adding the tomatoes. Mix well together, season well, add your choice of herbs, cover and cook slowly for about two hours. Just before serving add the sour cream or crème fraîche. Stir well in, garnish with the the extra herbs and serve.

## SAUTÉD CHICKEN BREASTS WITH FINES HERBES
## (OCTOBER 16th, 1969)

This is a simple dish but very good. Buy as many fillets of chicken breast as there are people and have a few over for seconds. Flatten them a little, season and dust with flour.

Heat up a lump of butter (about 4 tablespoons) in a large, heavy sauté pan and put in the fillets. Let them cook quite fast for two or three minutes or until the undersides are nice and brown. Turn over, lower the heat and cover the pan. Let them cook slowly for another 15–20 minutes. Serve them in a hot dish, scattered with some finely chopped chives and parsley and maybe a little fresh thyme. Then pour over the hot buttery juices, together with the little brown scrapings from the sides and bottom of the pan. Serve immediately.

## CUMBERLAND SAUCE (NOVEMBER 16th, 1969)

This is such a traditional end of the year English sauce to serve with hot ham, gammon or game and it keeps very well in small jars in the fridge so it is worth making a good batch at a time. The quantities given are for a comparatively small amount but you can easily double or treble quantities.

**You will need:**

*2 oranges and ½ lemon*

*½ very finely chopped shallot*

*4 tbsp redcurrant jelly*

*A pinch each of ground ginger, allspice, ground coriander and cayenne pepper*

*½ tsp mustard powder*

*4 tbsp port*

Using a zester (it really makes this process so much better and quicker), remove the zest but not the pith from the oranges and the half lemon. Cut them into pin-sized slivers. Blanch both the zest and the shallot in boiling water for two–three minutes.

Use a bain Marie and melt the redcurrant jelly in the top half, when it is completely liquid add the spices and seasonings, the blanched zest and shallot and finally the port. Stir until all the ingredients are thoroughly mixed and leave to cook another 5 minutes. Take off the heat, cool a little, pour into small airtight jars and put in the fridge.

## FRICASSÉE OF VEAL (DECEMBER 13th, 1969)

You can follow the recipe for the veal and tomato casserole (p. 307) either leaving out the tomatoes or using them. To this basic recipe you can add 125g/4½oz/½ cup small mushrooms, or larger mushrooms sliced and if you like, some chopped ham and always two or three bits of lemon peel and the juice of half a lemon. If you don't use the tomatoes, you will need to add 300ml/½ pt/1 cup veal stock and four tablespoons of white wine. If you would like yet another variation, you can make a *Blanquette*. In this case, you definitely omit the tomatoes and use the veal stock and wine, but you can still use the mushrooms and a couple more tablespoons of sour cream or crème fraîche at the end.

## CULOTTE DE BOEUF AU FOUR (JANUARY 26th, 1970)

Here is another beef dish which practically cooks itself. All you have to do is cover 1kg/2lb 4oz piece of topside with thick pieces of fat bacon. Season with salt and freshly ground pepper and whatever chopped herbs, e.g. thyme, marjoram, or rosemary, that you care to use. Put it into a casserole, add 125ml/4½oz/⅓ cup white wine, seal the lid with a paste of flour and water and cook in a pre-heated oven 180°C/350°F/gas mark 4 for half an hour. Then turn down the heat to 170°C/325°F/gas mark 3 for another four to four and a half hours. Unseal and serve with the sauce.

## SCALOPPINI DI VITELLO (JUNE 2nd, 1970)

Veal is expensive and very rarely as good as in Italy so this is a useful dish to make the meat expand for a lot of people, as well as being an excellent way of dealing with less than perfect meat.

**These quantities are for four which can obviously be expanded to suit any number:**

*225g/8oz fillet or leg of veal*

*1 small onion*

*A minced clove of garlic*

*2 tbsp chopped parsley*

*2 eggs*

*Salt and freshly ground pepper*

*Flour, to dust*

*4 tbsp butter*

*2 tbsp Marsala*

*Parsley or coriander to garnish*

Mince the veal, the onion, the garlic and the parsley all together or whizz in a food processor. Beat in the eggs, season well and form the mixture into little round rissoles. Leave them for a couple of hours. Before you want to cook them, roll each rissole out flat into the shape of an escalope. Flour them lightly on each side and cook them gently in the butter. When they are browned on each side, add a little Marsala. Serve on a hot dish with a garnish of parsley or coriander.

## BOEUF À L'ITALIENNE (JUNE 8th, 1970)

This dish can be served hot or cold and can be cooked overnight if you prefer. In fact it really needs to be cooked the day before.

**For eight–ten people you will need:**

*2kg/4½ lb piece of beef*

*4 cloves of garlic, skinned and cut into slivers*

*Salt and freshly ground pepper*

*Some chopped thyme and rosemary*

*Strips of bacon fat*

*2 sliced onions*

# Recipes

*150ml/5 fl oz/½ cup tomato purée, thinned with a little water*

*4 whole carrots*

*2 whole turnips or 1 quartered celeriac*

*A large piece of orange peel*

*A piece of lemon peel*

*125ml/4½ fl oz/⅓ cup good red wine*

*Some mixed chopped parsley and lemon peel for garnish*

Pierce the piece of beef all over and lard with the slivers of garlic. Season with salt and pepper, rub with the thyme and rosemary, wrap with the pieces of bacon fat and tie with string.

Braise in its own fat in a deep braising pan or a large flameproof earthenware or Le Creuset casserole. Add the two sliced onions, the tomato purée, the whole carrots, turnips or quartered celeriac, the peel and the glass of wine. Cover the pan and simmer very slowly for eight hours or overnight in a pre-heated, very slow oven 140 °C/275 °F/ gas mark 1 overnight.

The sauce will be jam-like, the peel will have dissolved and the meat should be so soft that it will fall apart as soon as it is touched. To serve, cut the vegetables in big strips, sprinkle with fresh chopped parsley and chopped lemon peel and reheat slowly. If you want to serve it cold, let it get completely cold, skim off every bit of fat, reheat and then leave to cool again.

## PAUPIETTES DE VEAU CLEMENTINE (JULY 14th, 1970)

This easy recipe was another variation from Elizabeth David's *A Book of Mediterranean Food*, first published in 1950.

**For six people you will need:**

*6 veal escalopes*

*115g/4oz smoked bacon*

*Salt and freshly ground pepper*

*A little seasoned flour*

311

*125ml/4 fl oz/⅓ cup white wine*

*2 tbsp water*

*One finely chopped onion*

*The juice and peel of ½ lemon*

*1 tsp capers*

*A little chopped thyme for the paupiettes and a little more for garnishing*

*4 tbsp butter*

Pound the veal escalopes until they are very thin and cut into three or four bits. Cut the smoked bacon into small pieces, one for each paupiette. Squeeze some lemon juice over each little piece of veal and season them before laying a small slice of the bacon on each one. Roll and tie with some thread.

Roll the paupiettes in the seasoned flour, heat the butter in a large pan with a lid and put in the paupiettes along with the onion. Sauté until brown. Add the water, a small glass of white wine, the lemon peel, lemon juice, capers and chopped thyme. Cover and cook over a low heat for 45 minutes. Before serving, remove the thread from the paupiettes, strain the sauce, arrange the paupiettes on a hot dish, pour over the strained sauce and sprinkle with a little more chopped thyme.

## EGGS IN ASPIC WITH TARRAGON (JULY 14th, 1972)

There is really no point in doing this dish unless you use a natural meat jelly for a homemade aspic because you need the contrast of the fresh eggs and the meat, cream and herbs. It sounds a huge fiddle but it sounds much worse than it actually is and is one of those dishes you make on an occasion (if you like cooking, that is).

### For six people you will need:

*6 oeufs mollets (p. 227)*

*Some chopped fresh tarragon*

*2 tbsp or so of dry sherry*

*150ml/5 fl oz/½ cup cream*

*Some extra finely chopped tarragon to garnish*

# RECIPES

**For the aspic jelly you will need:**

*1kg/2lb 4oz veal bones*

*450g/1lb beef cut into squares*

*1 calf's foot cut in two lengthwise*

*2 onions, each stuck with a couple of cloves*

*2 carrots, sliced*

*900ml/1½ pt/3 cups water*

*6 peppercorns, salt*

Bring all the ingredients for the aspic jelly very slowly to the boil. Skim, cover and leave to simmer gently for three hours. Strain through a fine sieve and leave to cool before skimming every last bit of fat.

Measure out 150ml/5 fl oz/½ cup stock for each egg, add some chopped tarragon and simmer for a few moments. Add a dash of dry sherry (check by tasting – it is important not to overdo it). Leave the stock to cool.

Meanwhile, place an oeuf mollet in each little ramekin and pour the still liquid jelly through a sieve. Leave to set. Before serving, float a thin layer of cream over each surface and sprinkle with more chopped tarragon.

## BOMBE SURPRISE (DECEMBER 23rd, 2003)

I used the same recipe as for Mont Blanc en surprise (p. 224) but instead of the praline I used glacé fruits, chopped small and soaked overnight in rum.

# MAIN INDEX

# Main Index

# Main Index

# Main Index

# Main Index

Makerere University, 95

Makins, Sir Roger and Lady (see Lord and Lady Sherfield), 77

Makins, Virginia, 111, 74

Man Booker Prize, 186

Man Ray, 105

Margaret, Princess, Countess of Snowdon, 45, 71, 74–5, 78–9, 83, 100, 110, 112–3, 116, 127–8, 144–5, 157, 168, 181–2, 209–10, 214–5

Marion-Smith, Dr, 156

Mary, Princess, The Princess Royal, Countess of Harewood, 168

Maschler, Tom, 186

Mason, John and Ailsa (see also Ailsa Garland), 151–2

Master of the Queen's Household (Brigadier Sir Geoffrey Hardy-Roberts), 136

Matthews, Joy (see also Joy McWatters), 48, 188, 131, 197

Mattli, Jo and Claude, 101–2

Maudling, Mrs Reginald, 167–8, 175

Maudling, Rt. Hon Reginald, 118, 176

Maurois, André, 66

Mayfair Playboys, 172

Mboya, Tom, 49

McCarty, Billy, 123–4, 130, 138, 144, 165, 173, 180, 181, 184–5, 187, 190, 193–4

McCarthy Era, 93

McCarthy, Senator Joe, 1, 18, 26, 31, 43, 76, 93, 96

McCullers, Carson, 48

McDonald, Professor Ian, 140, 144, 177, 202

McGeorge, D'Arcy (see also D'Arcy Howell), 88

McKenna, Virginia, 102

McLeod, Rt. Hon., Ian, 48–9

McLeod, Professor Jim and Robin, 73

McLeod, Professor James, AO, 73

McNulty, Bettina, 61, 125

McNulty, Bettina and Henry, 62, 123–4

McNulty, Henry, 61

McWatters Family, 201

McWatters, Christopher, 201

McWatters, Dinah, 201

McWatters, George and Joy, 48, 87–8, 131, 197,

McWatters, George, 48, 88, 130, 201, 197

McWatters, Joy (see also Joy Matthews), 48, 87–8, 131, 197, 201, 204

McWatters, Micky, 201

McWatters, Sarah, 201

McWilliam, 'Mac' and Beth, 111, 118

Melly, George and Victoria, 176

Metcalfe, John and Sheelagh, 101–2, 111, 174

Meyer, Tom and Fleur Cowles Meyer, 144–5

Meyer, Tom Montague, 110, 112, 181

Middlesex Hospital, 135

*Migraine And Other Headaches* (James Lance), 156

Migraine Trust, UK, 157

Miller, Bea, 151, 154

Miller, Dr Jonathan and Mrs, 165

Miller, Dr Jonathan, 88, 134–5, 165

Miller-Jones, Mr and Mrs Kenneth, 187

Miller, Jonny, 88

Miller, Lee, 60–1, 104, 124, 126–7

Miller, Tim, 88

Milligan, Jane, 28, 70

Milligan, Paddy, 27, 69–70, 135, 173, 215

Milligan, Spike, 69, 70, 83, 125, 138, 158, 173, 213, 197, 214–5

Milligan, Spike and Paddy, 69, 84, 87, 92, 104, 107, 111, 118, 127, 133–4, 137–8, 181, 184, 197, 212–3, 214

Miro, Joan, 105

Mitchell-Beasley, 178–9

Mitchell, James, 178–9

Montagu Meyer, Tom, 110, 112, 181

Monty Python Show, 135

Moore, Dudley, 135

Moore, Henry, 105

Morris, James (Jan), 115

*Mrs Miniver* (Jan Struther), 123–4

321

# Main Index

# Main Index

Viking Books, 143, 174
Viking Penguin, 174
*Vogue*, UK, 151
*Vogue*, US, 143
Voltaire, Francois Marie, 171

Waddington Galleries, 106
Waddington, Leslie, 88, 90, 104–5, 105–6, 110, 191
Walmsley, Margot, 84–5, 86, 87, 108, 110, 115, 151, 155, 169, 176, 181, 202
Wain, John, 96
Waldorf Astoria Hotel, NY, 147
Walker, Susan (see also Lady Anstruther), 119–20
Walmsley, Alaric, 86
Watson, Sir Angus, 85
Waugh, Auberon, 91
Waugh, Harry, 88
Webb, Michael, 185
Weldon, Claire, 193–4
Wesker, Arnold, 96
White, Michael, 91, 105–6, 144–5
White, Paul William, 184, 191, 195, 201
Whitehorn, Katherine, 131–2
Wilkens, Jeanne, 109
Willard Hotel, Washington, DC, 144
William, Prince, 113
Williams, Tennessee, 145
Wilson, Angus, 159–60, 176–7, 184–5
Wilson, Peter, 198

Windsor, Duke of, 201,
Windsor, Duchess of, 145, 168
Winter, Ella Wheeler (see also Ella Ogden Stewart), 76, 94
Wolfers, David, 88,
Wolfers, David and Joy (see also Joy Matthews/McWatters), 43, 88–9
Women's Institute, 59, 161
Woolf, Virginia, 107
Woollands, 79
Worsthorne, Claudie, 60, 86, 129, 149, 176
Worsthorne, Perry and Claudie, 73, 82, 87, 157, 111, 181
Worsthorne, Sir Peregrine, 'Perry', 22, 30, 38, 43–4, 47, 60, 61, 68–9, 73, 82, 84, 86, 109, 111, 113, 121, 157, 176, 181
Woy Woy, NSW, Australia, 125
Wray, Professor Shirley, 116–7
Wreford, Joyce, 194
Writers' Guild of America, 91

Young, Liz (see also Lady Kennet), 69–70
Young, Wayland (see also Lord Kennet), 70
Young, Wayland and Liz, 111
Yeats, W.B., 91
Yeats, W.B., 91

Zuluetta de, Rev. Alphonse, 79

# RECIPE INDEX

# RECIPE INDEX

327